Confident Data Skills

Confident Data Skills

Master the fundamentals of working
with data and supercharge your career

Kirill Eremenko

KoganPage

First published in Great Britain and the United States in 2018 by Kogan Page Limited

2nd Floor, 45 Gee Street	c/o Martin P Hill Consulting	4737/23 Ansari Road
London	122 W 27th Street	Daryaganj
EC1V 3RS	New York, NY 10001	New Delhi 110002
United Kingdom	USA	India

© Kirill Eremenko 2018

The right of Kirill Eremenko to be identified as the author of this work has been asserted by him in accordance with the Copyright, Designs and Patents Act 1988.

ISBN 978 0 7494 8154 4
E-ISBN 978 0 7494 8155 1

British Library Cataloguing-in-Publication Data

A CIP record for this book is available from the British Library.

Typeset by Integra Software Services, Pondicherry
Print production managed by Jellyfish
Printed and bound in Great Britain by CPI Group (UK) Ltd, Croydon CR0 4YY

*To my parents, Alexander and Elena Eremenko,
who taught me the most important thing in life –
how to be a good person*

CONTENTS

PART THREE 'How can I present it?'
Communicating data 177

LIST OF FIGURES

BONUS FOR READERS

Thank you for picking this book. You've made a huge step in your journey into data science.

Please accept complimentary access to my Data Science A–Z course.

Just go to **www.superdatascience.com/bookbonus** and use the password datarockstar.

Happy analysing!

Introduction

'I guess you always wanted to be a data scientist – since you were little?'

I find it sweet that people ask me this. Yes, I love my job. I take great pleasure in teaching students the fundamentals of data science. And it's great that people seem to think that this enthusiasm for the subject can only have been something instilled in me at a young age. But this is absolutely not what happened. Let's be honest, no kid thinks about becoming a data scientist. Children want to be astronauts. Dancers. Doctors. Firefighters. And when you're busy dreaming about saving lives or shooting off into outer space, you can't be expected to have your feet on the ground.

When people ask me whether I had always wanted a career in data science, I'm taken back to my childhood, a little Russian boy growing up in Zimbabwe. The scent of smouldering embers, the brassy calls of African red toads, the unforgettable softness of a winter evening, fingertips rubbing page against page of a collection of children's stories – these fragments of memories are from so many wonderful evenings listening to Russian tales read by my mother.

My mother wanted me and my siblings to love Zimbabwe, but she was equally concerned to ensure that we knew about our cultural background. She had considered how to best transmit this information to us, and decided that the most powerful way to do it was through stories. These nuggets of information about Russia, woven into compelling tales, meant that when I eventually moved back to Moscow – to a country I barely remembered – I felt that I was going home.

That is the power of storytelling. And for all those many tales I heard, I wanted to break them down into their components. I needed to see the big picture – but I wanted to see it through the prism of all its little details. I was fascinated by all the nuts and bolts responsible for creating something so beautiful. I knew intuitively that, in order to tell a good story myself, I needed to first collect these little units of information. That, to me, is how I feel about data.

In today's Digital Age, data is used to shape the tales of who we are, how we present ourselves, what we enjoy and when we want things. To create a path of unique virtual footprints. As we shall discover in this book, machines now know more about us than we do ourselves because of all the data available to them. They read our personal data like it is a storybook about us. And the wonderful thing about data science is that every discipline these days records data, which means that, as data scientists, we can still 'be' the astronauts and dancers and doctors we had always dreamed of becoming.

Few people know that being a data scientist ultimately means being the storyteller of information. Just as there are structural components to stories, data science projects are also arranged logically. *Confident Data Skills* addresses this through five clear stages, which I call the Data Science Process. This is not the only approach we can take for data science projects, but it is the method for ensuring that our project keeps building on practice and moving towards a logical conclusion. It has that clear, satisfying structure I so adored as a child.

This is how I learned to tell the story of data.

But I'm a complete rookie

Data science is actually one of those areas that benefits from experience in a different field. It is my expectation that many readers will be professionals who are already relatively advanced in their career. That's fine. You haven't lost *anything* by coming to data science from another field. In fact, well done for getting a grounding in something else first. This is the kind of foundation you will need to become a good data scientist.

I am speaking from experience. When I started out at the multinational professional services firm Deloitte, I didn't know every single one of the algorithms that we will be looking at in this book. And it wasn't expected of me, either. There are very few people who will begin their careers in data science like that. As you read this book, you will find that a number of successful people in the industry did not even begin to think about the discipline until their career was well underway. So stash those fears of digital illiteracy away – by picking up this book, you have taken the first step on your data science journey.

Hey, where's the code?

If you're a book flipper like me, you may have noticed that there's not a single line of code in this book. 'But this is a book about data science,' I hear you say, 'so what's going on?' Data science is an extremely broad subject. *Confident Data* Skills will immerse you in it and inspire you to consider how the discipline can be incorporated into your current or future business practice. In these pages, you'll learn its *methods* – because its 'ingredients' (the code) are easy to source online. To take the cooking analogy further, this is less a simple book of recipes and more a study of the basic techniques used in data science. Learn these thoroughly and you'll start to intuitively understand *why* you need to use particular codes and methods, which I find a far more effective approach to learning than simply giving you lines of code to plug into your project.

How to use this book

I have purposely written this book to be delved into wherever you are: on the train, in the bath, waiting for the person of your dreams Read it in instalments, in one sitting, chapter by chapter, cherry-pick, attack sections with yellow highlighter, pepper it with Post-its, whatever does the job for you. At the beginning of each part, you'll find a short introduction so that you can quickly identify which chapter will be of most interest to you. Part one is broader in scope, explaining the journey of data science. Parts Two and Three focus on the Data Science Process, the intuition behind some of the most powerful analytics models to date and how to improve your chances of getting your foot in the door.

If you're a complete beginner, you will get the most out of the book by reading it cover to cover. If you know a little more about data science as a discipline and want to understand the brass tacks of how to apply the Data Science Process, feel free to turn to the chapter that will best help you.

PART ONE
'What is it?'
Key principles

With all the attention given to the apparently limitless potential of technology and the extensive opportunities for keen entrepreneurs, some may ask why they should bother with data science at all – why not simply learn the principles of technology? After all, technology powers the world, and it shows no signs of slowing down. Any reader with an eye to their career might think that learning how to develop new technologies would surely be the better way forward.

It is easy to regard technology as the force that changes the world – it has given us the personal computer, the internet, artificial organs, driverless cars, the Global Positioning System (GPS) – but few people think of data science as the propeller behind many of these inventions. That is why you should be reading *this* book over a book about technology; you need to understand the mechanics behind a system in order to make a change.

We should not consider data only as the boring-but-helpful parent, and technology as the stylish teenager. The importance of data science does not begin and end with the explanation that technology needs data as just one of many other functional elements. That would be denying the beauty of data, and the many exciting applications that it offers for work and play. In short, it is not possible to have one without the other. What this means is that if you have a grounding in data science, the door will be open to a wide range of other fields that need a data scientist, making it an unusual and propitious area of research and practice.

Part I introduces you to the ubiquity of data, and the developments and key principles of data science that are useful for entering the subject. The concepts in the three chapters will outline a clear picture of how data applies to you, and will get you thinking not only about how data can directly benefit you and your company but also how you can leverage data for the long term in your career and beyond.

Striding out

Chapter 1 will mark the beginning of our journey into data science. It will make clear the vast proliferation of data and how in this Computer Age we all contribute to its production, before moving on to show how people have collected it, worked with it and crucially how data can be used to bolster a great number of projects and methods within and outside the discipline.

We have established that part of the problem with data science is not its relative difficulty but rather that the discipline is still something of a grey area for so many. Only when we understand precisely how much data there is and how it is collected can we start to consider the various ways in which we can work with it. We have reached a point in our technological development where information can be efficiently collected and stored for making improvements across all manner of industries and disciplines – as evidenced in the quantity of publicly available databases and government-funded projects to aggregate data across cultural and political institutions – but there are comparatively few people who know how to access and analyse it. Without workers knowing why data is useful, these beautiful datasets will only gather dust. This chapter makes the case for why data science matters *right now*, why it is not just a trend that will soon go out of style, and why you should consider implementing its practices as a key component of your work tasks.

Lastly, this chapter details how the soaring trajectory of technology gives us no room for pause in the field of data science. Whatever fears we may have about the world towards which we are headed, we cannot put a stop to data being collected, prepared and used. Nevertheless, it is impossible to ignore the fact that data itself is not concerned with questions of morality, and this has left it open to exploitation and abuse. Those of you who are concerned *can* take charge of these developments and enter into discussion with global institutions that are dealing with issues surrounding data ethics, an area that I find so gripping that I gave it its own subsection in Chapter 3, The data science mindset.

The future is data

Everything, every process, every sensor, will soon be driven by data. This will dramatically change the way in which business is carried out. In 10 years from now, I predict that every employee of every organization in the world will be expected to have a level of data literacy and be able to work with data and derive some insights to add value to the business. Not such a wild thought if we consider how, at the time of this book's publication, many people are expected to know how to use the digital wallet service Apple Pay, which was only brought onto the market in 2014.

Chapter 2, How data fulfils our needs, makes clear that data is endemic to every aspect of our lives. It governs us, and it gathers power in numbers. While technology has only been important in recent human history, data has always played a seminal role in our existence. Our DNA provides the most elementary forms of data about us. We are governed by it: it is responsible for the way we look, for the shape of our limbs, for the way our brains are structured and their processing capabilities, and for the range of emotions we experience. We are vessels of this data, walking flash drives of biochemical information, passing it on to our children and 'coding' them with a mix of data from us and our partner. To be uninterested in data is to be uninterested in the most fundamental principles of existence.

This chapter explains how data is used across so many fields, and to illustrate this I use examples that directly respond to Abraham Maslow's hierarchy of needs, a theory that will be familiar to many students and practitioners in the field of business and management. If this hierarchy is news to you, don't worry – I will explain its structure and how it applies to us in Chapter 2.

Arresting developments

The final chapter in Part I will show how those new to data science can reshape their mindset to enter the subject, and reveal the areas that I believe show the most potential for immediate engagement with the discipline. Many of the developments made within the field have had knock-on effects on other subjects, and have raised questions about the future for data scientists as well as for scholars and practitioners beyond its disciplinary boundaries. If you are looking to develop your career in data science, this chapter could even fire up some ideas for niches within which you may already work.

To add further weight to the examples offered in Chapter 2 that show compelling arguments for data's supportive role across many walks of life, in Chapter 3 I also give you some critical approaches that you can use to get yourself started as a practitioner. We might think that its wide application will make data difficult to penetrate, but learning data science is much easier than becoming proficient in many other scientific disciplines. You do not need to be a life learner to master the principles of data science. What you *really* need is an ability to think about the various ways in which one or more questions – about business operations, about personal motivations – might be asked of data. Because data scientists are there to examine the *possibilities* of the information they have been given. You may be surprised to know that you already have some skills and experience that you can leverage in your journey to mastering the discipline.

Having said that, due caution is necessary for newcomers. Anyone who has used Excel, worked in an office environment or taken a subject comprising scientific components at university will probably have already come across data in their professional or academic lives. But some of the methods for using data that you may have picked up will be inefficient, and holding true to what you know may prevent you from learning the most effective ways of exploiting datasets: we will discuss this in detail in Parts Two and Three.

Despite the clear positive effects of data, it is also important not to be blinded by it. Thus, Chapter 3 also addresses the various security threats that data can pose to its users, and how data practitioners are working to address present and future issues that may arise. Data ethics is a particularly compelling area to make note of, as it holds the power to alter and direct future developments in data science. From what we understand of information collection, to the extent to which it can be used within machines and online, data ethics is setting the stage for how humans and technology communicate. When you read this chapter, consider how each of the areas might tie in with the way you work, and how beneficial further investment in the topic might be for your business.

Defining data 01

Think about the last film you saw at the cinema. How did you first hear about it? You might have clicked on the trailer when YouTube recommended it to you, or it may have appeared as an advertisement before YouTube showed you the video you actually wanted to see. You may have seen a friend sing its praises on your social network, or had an engaging clip from the film interrupt your newsfeed. If you're a keen moviegoer, it could have been picked out for you on an aggregate movie website as a film you might enjoy. Even outside the comfort of the internet, you may have found an advertisement for the film in your favourite magazine, or you could have taken an idle interest in the poster on your way to that coffeehouse with the best Wi-Fi.

None of these touchpoints was coincidental. The stars didn't just happen to align for you and the film at the right moment. Let's leave the idealistic serendipity to the onscreen encounters. What got you into the cinema was less a desire to see the film and more of a potent concoction of data-driven evidence that had marked you out as a likely audience member *before you even realized you wanted to see the film*.

When you interacted with each of these touchpoints, you left a little bit of data about yourself behind. We call this 'data exhaust'. It isn't confined to your online presence, nor is it only for the social media generation. Whether or not you use social media platforms, whether you *like* it or not, you're contributing data.

It has always been this way; we've just become better at recording and collecting it. Any number of your day-to-day interactions stand to contribute to this exhaust. On your way to the London Underground, CCTV cameras are recording you. Hop onto the Tube, and you're adding to Transport for London's statistical data about peak times and usage. When you bookmark or highlight the pages of a novel on your Kindle, you are helping distributors to understand what readers particularly enjoyed about it, what they could put in future marketing material and how far their readers tend to get into the novel before they stop.

When you finally decide to forgo the trials and punishments of public transport and instead drive your car to the supermarket, the speed you're going is helping GPS services to show their users in real time how much traffic there is in an area, and it also helps your car gauge how much more time you have left before you'll need to find a petrol station.

And today, when you emerge from these touchpoints, the data you leave behind is swept up and added to a blueprint about you that details your interests, actions and desires.

But this is only the beginning of the data story. This book will teach you about how absolutely pervasive data really is. You will learn the essential concepts you need to be on your way to mastering data science, as well as the key definitions, tools and techniques that will enable you to apply data skills to your own work. This book will broaden your horizons by showing you how data science can be applied to areas in ways that you may previously have never thought possible. I'll describe how data skills can give a boost to your career and transform the way you do business – whether that's through impressing top executives with your ideas or even starting up on your own.

Data *is* everywhere

Before we move any further, we should clarify what we mean by data. When people think of data, they think of it being actively collected, stashed away in databases on inscrutable corporate servers and funnelled into research. But this is an outdated view. Today, data is much more ubiquitous.[1]

Quite simply, data is any unit of information. It is the by-product of any and every action, pervading every part of our lives, not just within the sphere of the internet, but also in history, place and culture. A cave painting is data. A chord of music is data. The speed of a car is data. A ticket to a football match is data. A response to a survey question is data. A book is data, as is a chapter within that book, as is a word within that chapter, as is a letter within that word. It doesn't have to be *collected* for it to be considered data. It doesn't have to be stored in a vault of an organization for it to be considered data. Much of the world's data probably doesn't (yet) belong to any database at all.

Let's say that in this definition of data being a unit of information, data is the *tangible past*. This is quite profound when you think about it. Data is the past, and the past is data. The record of things to which data contributes is called a database. And data scientists can use it to better understand our present and future operations. They're applying the very same principle that historians have been telling us about for ages: we can learn from history. We can learn from our successes – and our mistakes – in order to improve the present and future.

The only aspect of data that has dramatically changed in recent years is our ability to collect, organize, analyse and visualize it in contexts that are only limited by our imagination. Wherever we go, whatever we buy, whatever interests we have, this data is all being collected and remodelled into trends that help advertisers and marketers push their products to the right people, that show the government people's political leanings according to their borough or age, and that help scientists create AI technologies that respond to complex emotions, ethics and ideologies, rather than simple queries.

All things considered, you might start to ask what the limits to the definition of data are. Does factual evidence about a plant's flowering cycle (quantitative data) count as data as much as the scientist's recording of the cultural stigma associated with giving a bunch to a dying relative in the native country (qualitative data)? The answer is yes. Data doesn't discriminate. It doesn't matter whether the unit of information collected is quantitative or qualitative. Qualitative data may have been less usable in the past when the technology wasn't sophisticated enough to process it, but thanks to advancements in the algorithms capable of dealing with such data, this is quickly becoming a thing of the past.

To define data by its limits, consider again that data is the past. You cannot get data from the future, unless you have managed to build a time machine. But while data can never be the future, it *can* make insights and predictions about it. And it is precisely data's ability to fill in the gaps in our knowledge that makes it so fascinating.

Big (data) is beautiful

Now that we have a handle on what data is, we need to shake up our understanding of where and how it actually gets stored. We have already shown our wide-reaching potential for emitting data (that's our data exhaust) and have explained that, in its being a unit of information, there is a very broad concept of what we understand as being data. So once it is out there, where does it all *go*?

By now, you're likely to have heard the term 'big data'. Put very simply, big data is the name given to datasets with columns and rows so considerable in number that they cannot be captured and processed by conventional hardware and software within a reasonable length of time. For that reason, the term is dynamic – what might once have been considered big data back in 2015 will no longer be thought of as such in 2020, because by that time technology will have been developed to tackle its magnitude with ease.

The 3 Vs

To give a dataset the label of big data, at least one of three requirements must be fulfilled:

- its volume – which refers to the size of the dataset (eg the number of its rows) – must be in the billions;
- its velocity – which considers how quickly the data is being gathered (such as online video streaming) – assumes that the speed of data being generated is too rapid for adequate processing with conventional methods; and
- its variety – this refers to either the *diversity* of the type of information contained in a dataset such as text, video, audio or image files (known as unstructured data) or a table that contains a significant number of columns which represent different data attributes.

Big data has been around for much longer than we'd care to imagine – it's just that the term for it didn't appear until the 1990s. We've been sitting on big data for years, for all manner of disciplines, and for far longer than you might expect. So I have to break it to you: big data is not big news. It's certainly not a new concept. Many if not all of the world's largest corporations have mammoth stores of data that have been collected over a long period of time on their customers, products and services. Governments store human data, from censuses to surveillance and habitation. Museums store cultural data, from artefacts and collector profiles to exhibition archives. Even our own bodies store big data, in the form of the genome (more on that later in Chapter 3, The data science mindset).

In short, if you just can't work with it, you can call it big data. When data scientists use the term, they don't use it loosely. It is used to draw attention to the fact that standard methods of analysing the dataset in question are not sufficient.

Why all the fuss about big data?

You might think it strange that we have only just started to realize how powerful data can be. But while we have been collecting data for centuries, what stopped us in the past from lassoing it all into something beneficial to us was the lack of technology. After all, it's not how big the data is that matters; it's what you do with it. Any data, 'big' or otherwise, is only useful to us if it can be mined for information, and before the technology was developed to help us analyse and scale this data, its usefulness could only be measured by the intellectual capability of the person wrangling the data.

But big data requires a faster and more powerful processor than the human brain to sort it. Before the technological developments of the 20th century, data was stored on paper, in archives, in libraries and in vaults. Now, almost all new data we capture is stored in a digital format (and even old data is being actively converted to digital, as evidenced by the sheer amount of resources being funnelled into such digital collection projects as the Europeana Collections and the Google Books project).

Storing and processing data

With the advent of the computer came the possibility of automating the process of data storage and processing. But large datasets bogged down the early machines; scientists working with electronic datasets in the 1950s would have had to wait for hours before a simple task was finally churned out. These scientists soon came to the conclusion that, in order to process large sets of data *properly* – to make connections between elements, and to use those connections to make accurate and meaningful predictions – they would need to build information carriers that could both manage the data and handle its storage. Sure enough, as the technology behind computing improved, so did computers' storage and processing capacities. And in the last 70 years, not only have we been able to store information in significantly more efficient ways, we have also been able to make that information portable. The same information that would in the 1970s have only fitted on 177,778 floppy disks could all fit on a *single flash drive* by the 2000s. Today, you can store all that and more in the cloud (a storage facility with a virtualized infrastructure that enables you to view your personal files from anywhere in the world).[2] Just bear in mind that the next time you access personal documents from your local library or place of work – or simply on your mobile device – you're effectively doing what would have required carrying over 100,000 floppy disks in the 1970s.

When these new technologies made the storing of data easier, researchers started to turn their attention to how this stored data could actually be used.

How did we start to create order from chaos? Let's return to our earlier example of the last film you watched at the cinema. You were probably cherry-picked to see that film not by an insightful marketer poring over the evidence but instead by a clever machine that looked at your data exhaust and matched it against the demographics that it found were the most likely to watch – and enjoy – that film. That might sound novel, but as we have already established, data and its (manual) processing have been around for a long time. Some of Hollywood's production houses were gathering data as early as the 1950s about what their audience wanted to see, from actor to director to genre, before slicing and dicing that information into respondent demographics that corresponded to age, location and gender. Even at that time, people were making potentially game-changing decisions through what the data told them.

RKO Pictures

Why did RKO Pictures, one of the Big Five Hollywood studios in the '50s, keep using Katharine Hepburn in their movies? Because the data showed them that she was a sure bet for getting people talking and, ultimately, filling up a cinema.

Of course, there's space for gut instinct. In her first test casting, director George Cukor found her odd, but he also conceded that '[t]here was an enormous feeling, a weight about the manner in which she picked up the glass. I thought she was very talented in that action' (Fowles, 1992). That's gut instinct for you.

With the important support of audience approval data, RKO was later able to take Cukor's inklings about Hepburn's talent and turn them into reliable predictions about how the studios might continue to make their millions.

This was all thanks to George Gallup, the first person to make Hollywood executives aware of the power in using data to inform decisions and make predictions, from casting lead actors to choosing which film genre would be the safest financial bet.[3]

To help RKO do this, Gallup collected, combined and analysed qualitative and quantitative data that covered the demographic information of RKO's audience members and their opinions of the film studio's output. In gathering this data, Gallup had created a model that for the first time segmented the movie-going audience into demographics that responded favourably to particular genres, a model that could and would be used for later data sampling and analysis.

Touted as a fortune teller for helping studios get rich, Gallup swiftly became the darling of many studio executives across the US film industry, checking the audience's pulse for personalities from Walt Disney to Orson Welles through the data gathered from surveys and interviews.[4]

Gallup had only data to thank for his success (perhaps he can be named the world's first high-paid data scientist). And the statistician's efforts resulted in a resource that continues to have value beyond its original design, in its potential to capture *unstructured* data: recorded interviews of audience members that reflect the cultural and social values of the time. Perhaps Gallup suspected that the potential of data-driven analyses could only grow.

Data can generate content

So, what if, after all the clever data-driven evidence, you ended up hating the film you last saw at the cinema? Well, data might not be able to predict everything, but it certainly got you in the seat. Data might sometimes get a C for achievement, but it always gets an A for effort. And the former is being worked on. Rather than attaching the right audience demographic to a new film or television series, production companies are now finding ways to respond by using audience data to make informed decisions about their entertainment output.

Affecting this movement requires more data. For that reason, data collection does not stop once you have watched the film that was picked for you to see; any follow-up responses that you make on social media, or through e-mail or through changing your viewing habits online, will generate a fresh set of data about you, 'the moviegoer', that will sharpen and tailor any future recommendations before finally subdividing the demographics of which you are a part. So, as you transition from that emo teen only interested in dystopian zombie flicks into the sophisticated surrealism buff who everyone avoids at cocktail parties, your data will move along with you and adapt to those fluctuating preferences.

As a nota bene: the even better news is that data will not deny you your interests. If you're only *playing* at being the connoisseur but still enjoy a trashy zombie movie once the curtains are drawn, your data will continue to keep that secret enthusiasm of yours fed.

Of course, the flip side of the coin here is that your data can spill the beans on those preferences. Be aware that data is a record of your actions – it will not lie on your behalf. Some people will even go to great lengths to hide their 'actual' data footprint on digital music service sites by vanity playing, that is, starting up an album of music that they consider to have social cachet and then leaving their desk while the album plays through, so that their historical data will show other users a skewed version of what they enjoy. In my view, these people have far too much time on their hands, but manipulating data is nevertheless an important topic, and one that we shall return to in due course.

CASE STUDY Netflix

Entertainment company Netflix's *House of Cards* first proved to the industry just how powerful data can be not only in reaching out to the right audience for specific types of content but also in driving the actual *production* of content. The 2013 political drama series was an early experiment in how data can be applied to produce hit shows. In the lead-up to *House of Cards'* production, Netflix had been gathering data from its users. This data included users' viewing habits, and those insights allowed Netflix to group its video content into diverse and surprising categories in accordance with the data. These categories were hidden from public view within its interface but were nevertheless exploited by the company to direct the right kind of film to the right kind of audience.

When the details of their subcategories were revealed online some years ago, the internet was abuzz. To give you a feel for just how specific Netflix became, among the subcategories were 'Exciting Horror Movies from the 1980s', 'Feel-good Education & Guidance starring Muppets', 'Showbiz Dramas', 'Goofy Independent Satires', 'Irreverent Movies Based on Real Life', 'Cerebral Foreign War Movies', 'Steamy Thrillers' and 'Critically Acclaimed Dark Movies Based on Books'. That's some specialist viewing habits. But Netflix had found a significant audience for each one of these categories, and for many more besides.

Eventually, Netflix's data scientists started to see overlap in their audience's viewing patterns. It appeared that there was a significant number of Netflix subscribers who enjoyed both Kevin Spacey's body of work *and* gritty political dramas. The rest – updating the original 1990s *House of Cards* and putting Kevin Spacey in the lead role – is history (or is it data?).

Riding the wave of success

Netflix were absolutely right to value their data: *House of Cards* became an award-winning and critically acclaimed series. So it came as no surprise when many of Netflix's competitors later sought to copy this winning model. Hadelin de

Ponteves, a data science entrepreneur and my business partner, worked for a competitor of Netflix to create a similar system that could work for them:

> We knew that Netflix already had a powerful recommendation system in place, and so the pressure on us as data scientists and systems developers was not to emulate the same system for our company but rather to find where we could bring about a difference. We realized that to develop a truly interesting system, we would need to do more than develop a tool to recommend movies that fit a known demographic. We also wanted to find an algorithm that could suggest movies that might initially take users out of their comfort zones but that they would nevertheless find enjoyable. We really wanted to get that element of surprise in there.
>
> (de Ponteves, 2017)

Hadelin knew that to achieve this, a complex system would be required to get into their user base's heads and understand their viewing interests better than they knew them themselves. He did this by extracting all the data that the company had related to their customers and applying the right combination of models to find connections between users' viewing habits. Remember that this approach is much the same as that of George Gallup all those years ago; thanks to the technology available to us and the imagination of the data scientist, we can now access the data in a much more sophisticated (and automated) way.

Using data

Some might complain that this approach to using data to drive creative content is actually killing off creativity. To that, I would answer that the data only follows what people want. This is desirable for any industry: to show the right audience at the right time and in the right place the relevant content to entice them to buy into their service. Data has in this way made industries more democratic. Because while the machines might start to drive our purchases, we still hold the most valuable information: human desire. The machines are not telling us what we want; they are making connections for us that we could not possibly have known.

Data is not telling people to go out and watch superhero movies and not to watch French surrealist films; it is listening to what people want and enjoy.[5] If you believe that there is a problem with creativity being stifled, it is not the fault of data – it is a fault in our society. I cannot emphasize enough that data *is* the past. It is merely a record of information. If you *do* want more French surrealist films, then make sure you go and see them – and make sure you are vocal about them afterwards.[6] It might seem as though you're just adding to the noise of the internet, but this noise is swiftly being rounded up and mined for use elsewhere. Thanks to data, this is an age where our voices can actually get heard and have real power – so why not make good use of it?

Besides which, the models for using data have not yet been perfected. In the case of the media industry, other corporations have since taken on the Netflix concept – and some may point out that they have had varying levels of success. But again, it's not the data that is at fault, it is the human, creative input. After all, *that* is where the current limit of our ability to use data in order to produce content lies. We might be able to assess the *likelihood* of the number of people interested in a concept, but there is also a great deal more at stake, as the ultimate success of any form of entertainment will rest on the talent involved in its creation. Let that be a warning to writers and directors hoping to get an easy ride by relying solely on the data: databases that show the varying success of film genres might be a useful guide to follow, but they can only remain a guide for as long as the work rests on human talent.

Why data matters now

Many are already aware of how technology is set to shake up jobs in the future. If you are feeling particularly brave, a quick Google search for 'technological impact on jobs' will show you there are myriad articles that speak to the likelihood of your job becoming automated.[7] While this information has been backed up by data, I would argue that there may have been a degree of subjectivity from the researchers when taking into account the tasks required of certain jobs. Nevertheless, I would certainly not recommend people train to be sports umpires for the very reason that their job rests on the *data* of a game – and machines will inevitably supply more accurate data to corroborate or flout any challenges made by competitors. The umpire might be a tradition that makes the experience more personable or entertaining *right now*, but in my opinion the nostalgia associated with the position doesn't mean that it will last forever.

Even after clarifying how all-consuming data is, some may still think that data science will not affect their business for some time to come. Things take time, after all, to develop. But thinking this way would be making a big mistake, because that would be denying the principle of Moore's law.

Moore's law

Moore's law is a law of predictions. Initially conceived by Intel co-founder Gordon Moore in 1965, Moore's law first referred to the expected increase in the number of transistors (devices used to control electrical power) per square inch on integrated circuits (eg computer chips, microprocessors, logic boards) over time. It was observed that the number of these transistors roughly doubled every two years, and the law stated that this phenomenon would only continue. To date, it has held true.

In layman's terms, this means that if you go to your local computer store today and buy a computer for £1,000, and after two years you purchase another for £1,000 at the same store, the second machine will be twice as powerful, even though it cost the same amount.

Many have applied this law to the mushrooming advancements made in the field of data science. Data science is one of the fastest-growing academic disciplines, and its practitioners are working on increasingly sophisticated ways to find novel means to capture the data, to construct cost-effective systems to store the data and to develop algorithms that turn all those chunks of big data into valuable insights. Ever feel as though technology is moving at so fast a pace you can't keep up? Then spare a thought for data scientists. They are playing a game of catch-up with technology that *hasn't even been invented*.

CASE STUDY   Siri

Take the developments made in voice recognition as a case example. The co-founders of Siri, Dag Kittlaus, Adam Cheyer and Tom Gruber, created the intelligent personal assistant well before the technology had advanced to the extent that it could actually produce their concepts and put them on the market. Siri's creators built algorithms and frameworks for the data they had available in order to support voice recognition technology that had not yet been invented. What they did know, however, was that while it was not possible to operate the software with the technology available at the time, it *would* ultimately be possible to run Siri once the technology had been given enough time to catch up. They were, in short, intercepting technological trends.

The concept that Siri's makers were applying to their prediction was Moore's law. And it's incredibly important for data science. The law has been applied to many technological processes, and is a necessary rule to consider when making business ventures and decisions; we will return to discuss it further in Chapter 3, The data science mindset.

Worrying achieves nothing

Hollywood and the entertainment industry in general have long held a dystopian idea of data and the dangers that future data abuse and exploitation can pose to humans. We only need to think of that ominous line from *2001: A Space Odyssey*, 'Open the pod bay doors, Hal', where Hal – the spaceship's AI technology – has become so sophisticated that it decides for itself to disobey human command in favour of its own (superior) reasoning. *Ex Machina*, *Her*, *Blade Runner*, *Ghost in the Shell* – all of these films imagine the problems that humans may face when that technology starts to develop consciousness and second-guess us.

But there is another area that is, to me, a far more likely, far more pressing and far more insidious way in which data could be exploited, and it has much more to do with *humans* abusing it than the robots themselves: privacy. Issues of privacy pervade many of our interactions online. People can choose to remain anonymous, but their information will always be collected – and used – somewhere. Even if that data is stripped of its characteristic indicators that can be traced back to an individual, some may ask: is it right that this data is being collected at all?

Your online footprint

Readers who were users of the internet in the 1990s will be familiar with the word 'avatar' as referring to the rather innocent images we chose to represent ourselves on online forums. The word avatar is today used to describe something much broader. It now means our intangible doppelgänger in the online world; a collection of data on us from the searches, choices and purchases we make online, and everything we post online, from text to images. This kind of data is a potential goldmine of information for credit agencies and companies that aggregate it. Companies can then use these insights to sell to others.

As data science has become a more prolific discipline, questions of ethics and security surrounding data's permeability, distortion and capture are being asked (and ethics is an area that we will cover in Chapter 5, Data preparation). We have very valid reasons to be concerned about the pathways that data science is opening up, and the fact that it does not discriminate in terms of who – or what – accesses this information. While moving from paper to digital has improved many practical methods in companies, data can still go missing, or deteriorate, and there is significant human influence on data (misplacing information, losing databases, and espionage) that can have devastating consequences.

CASE STUDY   The Heartbleed Bug

To my mind, the Heartbleed Bug represents the most radical violation of privacy in the world to date. This bug enabled hackers to exploit a vulnerability in a source code used on the internet, which allowed otherwise protected information sent through Secure Sockets Layer (SSL) connections to be stolen. This loophole exposed sensitive information on purchasing sites for years before we were made fully aware of its magnitude.

In 2014, Google's security team found this problem in the SSL source code during a regular review of their services. It was discovered that some 800,000 websites globally had this error in their source code, enabling access for information thieves and hackers who knew of the vulnerability. But during the two years leading up to its discovery, the bug went unnoticed, allowing potentially countless amounts of data to be stolen. Ironically as SSL-enabled websites (those starting with 'https'), they were supposed to be more secure than those with normal 'http' URLs.

Ignoring widespread speculation at the time about whether the bug had been allowed to continue by governmental or spurious organizations, the fact remains that the Heartbleed Bug represented a monumental violation of privacy.

Don't censor – educate

The inconvenient truth of data science, and indeed of any discipline where money is directly involved, is that as interest in the discipline grows, so will interest in the more nefarious means to tamper with its processes. Some might consider that to be enough of a reason to put a halt on data gathering and use. But I see it differently, and I would wager many other data scientists feel the same: rather than censoring and restricting, we need to educate people. We must take care to tell our children that their activities carried out online will form an avatar that may be used in their favour – or against them. We must ensure that people are generally better versed in how their data is being used, and why.

This is the world in which we live now. It will be much easier to remove yourself from this emotional attachment than to resist. After all, the youngest generation today has already let go, and these are the new consumers companies will approach through advertising. This is evidenced in the way that many businesses operate online, from Amazon to Outfittery.[8] Nowadays, consumers are willing to give their personal information in return for products and services that are better tailored to them. A quick glance at Instagram or Twitter will show you that relinquishing personal information online – to a variety of domains – may even feel like second nature to Millennials. Unless you are planning on living off-grid in the wilderness and speaking only to the birds, cybersecurity is simply another risk of living today. Fighting it will be futile; the Luddites may have violently protested against the use of machinery in the 19th century, but that changed little in the long run.

It is far less likely that we will shut down the services we all take for granted and have already integrated into our own lives, primarily because we now *need* these services. Where it was once a luxury, technology has swiftly become a basic need in the way we live and work. And in order for us to continue developing this technology, we need to exploit the data.

From social media's insistent barrage of information at all hours of the day to news sites constantly updating their pages as new information comes to them, the pace at which the world is moving, and the option for us to now watch it all happening in real time online, can feel overwhelming. This overload of data is coming at us from all sides, and there is no way of stopping it. You cannot put a cork in a volcano and expect it not to blow.

What we *can* do, however, is manage and analyse it. You may have heard of 'content curators' and 'aggregate websites' such as Feedly, through which you can collect and categorize news stories from blogs and websites that are of interest to you. These individuals and companies are working to organize the data relevant to them and to their followers or subscribers. These attempts to manage information should give us comfort, and they are among the many options that we have to process data. As the technology improves to help us manage and analyse our data, so will our acceptance of it as an integral part of our existence in the Computer Age. So set aside your doubts and let's focus instead on the possibilities of data, and how it can serve to improve your life.

References

Fowles, J (1992) *Starstruck: Celebrity performers and the American public*, Smithsonian Institution Press

Keynes, John Maynard (1963) Essays in Persuasion, Norton, pp. 358–73

Mishra, S and Sharma, M (2016) Bringing analytics into Indian film industry with back tracing algorithm, Analytics Vidhya [Online] www.analyticsvidhya.com/blog/2016/08/bringing-analytics-into-indian-film-industry-with-back-tracing-algorithm/ [accessed 20.06.2017]

Ohmer, S (2012) *George Gallup in Hollywood*, Columbia University Press

Notes

1 By now you're probably used to people nit-picking about the word 'data' as being a plural form of the word 'datum', and that it is in fact correct to say 'data are' rather than the more pervasive 'data is'. You can tell them that the 'data' was first recorded in 1645 as being used in the singular by Thomas Urquhart, and that it wasn't until almost 60 years later, in 1702, that it was used as a mass noun.

2 Cloud data is stored off-site, and largely travels through submarine cables that are laid at the bottom of the ocean. So the cloud is not in the air as we might think, but underwater. A map of these cables can be found at www.submarine-cablemap.com.

3 Gallup was a statistician who first came into the public eye when he developed a technique to accurately predict Franklin D Roosevelt's 1936 re-election.

4 For much more on George Gallup's pioneering work, see Ohmer (2012).

5 For an example of the challenges and potential of data analytics in the film industry, see Mishra and Sharma (2016), whose report analyses filmmaking and producing in India.

6 Naturally, there are obstacles to this approach. You're not going to beat the millions of superhero fans in China who have been largely responsible for the continuing number of films rolling out from Hollywood about men (and women) in tights, saving the world from evil. Questions of how data impinges on creativity are arguably outside the scope of this book, but I would estimate that there always has been and always will be space for creative expression, even in a data-driven world. We aren't dumbing down; we're just making industry more efficient.

7 Concerns for technological unemployment are not new – John Maynard Keynes was writing about it in the 1930s. 'We are being afflicted with a new disease of which some readers may not yet have heard the name, but of which they will hear a great deal in the years to come – namely, technological unemployment' (Keynes, 1963).

8 A Berlin-based men's outfitter that sells boxes containing products curated to the individual customer.

How data fulfils 02
our needs

There isn't a lot of mystery to data science – it is, after all, so endemic to modern life – and yet the misconception that data science is difficult and even inscrutable prevails. Unfortunately, many people today either willingly refuse to see its wide application or will outright dismiss it as something inaccessible to them or inapplicable to their line of work. Data science as a discipline *sounds* heavy. It seems like the sort of thing people do in small cubicles with no natural lighting, hunched over their desks crunching numbers.

That perspective is completely wrong.

In this chapter, we will learn precisely how ubiquitous data is, how broadly it is generated and collected, and why data science cannot ever be considered a fad.

The permeation of data

To illustrate just how essential data is in every aspect of our lives – a basic necessity rather than a luxury – I will use Maslow's hierarchy of needs, which I am sure many business practitioners will recognize. Though I only recently discovered it for myself, it appears a great deal in the literature on business psychology. I have found it to be a model that ties in surprisingly well with the pervasiveness and benefits of data.[1]

Maslow's hierarchy of needs was developed by Abraham Maslow in 1943 to portray the composite motivations that people will have in their lives. The hierarchy is illustrated in the shape of a pyramid, which in the order from bottom to top comprises the most to the least fundamental of needs. In brief, the hierarchy is organized in such a way that the needs outlined in the bottommost level of the pyramid must be met before the individual in question can feel motivated to meet the needs of the higher levels.[2]

2.1 Maslow's hierarchy of needs

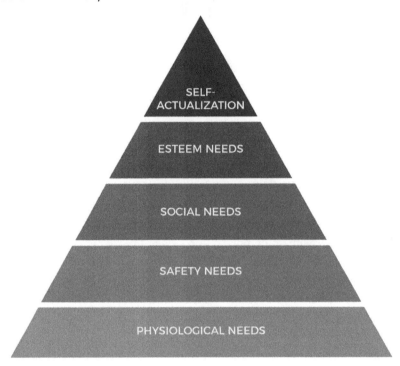

Data science and physiology

At the bottom of Maslow's hierarchy are physiological factors, the basic needs for humans to simply survive. How can data help with those most basic requirements? How can it improve upon them?

Let's take the air we breathe as an example. Air pollution has been a major global cause for concern ever since the Industrial Revolution of the late 18th and early 19th centuries. We might automatically imagine smog to be a phenomenon of the past, as in the case of London in the 1950s, when coal emissions regularly covered the city, but smog continues to affect a large number of places around the world, from China to Brazil.

Any technologies that are designed to reduce pollution in affected cities are reliant on data: to improve the condition of the air, it must first be monitored.

CASE STUDY Environmental data and Green Horizon

Green Horizon, launched by IBM in 2014, is responding to the severe state of China's air quality by 'transforming its national energy systems and support[ing] its needs for sustainable urbanization' (IBM, 2017a). Green Horizon assimilates data from 12 global research labs and applies cognitive models to the gathered data in order to inform the project's central initiative to reduce pollution. Here, data is essential for monitoring the fluctuations in air pollution in selected areas, and for scientists to analyse the various factors that directly and indirectly affect the air's quality, temperature and state in order to begin improving China's physical environment.

The great benefit of these projects is that environmental data is, more often than not, publicly available and on a global scale, meaning the technological developments to help combat the issue of air pollution can move swiftly. Having access to important datasets that improve our most basic need is essential for understanding how our technologies can perform better. That is why we now have special glass panes that can be installed in buildings to allow windows to 'breathe', cleaning the air inside the premises and thus protecting its inhabitants. That is also why we have filters that can be put into factories to reduce their emissions and protect local residents from poisoning.

Sustainable food

Food is another case example of how data can respond to the most basic of human needs (physiological factors on Maslow's hierarchy). It might be the stuff of science fiction for some, but food has been grown in laboratories for many years, and the phenomenon of 'cultured meat' is becoming increasingly imaginative. Silicon Valley start-up Memphis Meats is just one institution that has, since its establishment, developed a variety of cultured meat, from beef to poultry.

As it is still such a grey area for regulatory authorities, religions and science, cultured meat has drawn praise and ire from the world community to various degrees (Devitt, 2017). But whether we like it or not, cultured meat could soon be the future for what we eat. It will become the environmentally friendly solution to the severe strains that agriculture puts on the natural world, dramatically reducing water usage and carbon emissions. And the data we collect to produce such meat will eventually go beyond DNA capture. As food technology becomes more commonplace, additional consumer data will be exploited to address other factors such as how cultured meat might be best presented and flavoured for it to be the most palatable and – crucially for the companies producing it – saleable.

Data science and safety

Once physiological needs have been met, Maslow's hierarchy states that the need for safety (physical, financial, personal) will take precedence. Safety is the level, then, that largely includes personal health and wellbeing, and medicine is one of the most prominent disciplines on which data science is making its mark. In the medical industry, data science is used to revolutionize the medicine we need to diagnose and cure illnesses. All medical trials are analysed through participant data, and this gathered data can be used to inform diagnosis, recommend different practical approaches, and build new products. The diagnosis of complex and rare illnesses puts pressure on medical practitioners to stay informed about the many different manifestations and symptoms of disease, leaving a good deal of human error against finding the root of a problem and dealing with it efficiently. And as more complex problems come to require specialist doctors, illnesses could go unchecked for the weeks and months that it takes patients to get an appointment with the relevant specialist.

For data scientists, the pressure is on to develop advanced machine learning algorithms to get the most accurate data. This data can be built upon, enhanced and used to predict unusual situations. What's more, the data that is gathered is not reliant on the welfare of the data scientist (sorry). Once medical specialists retire, their specialist knowledge goes with them. Once data scientists do the same, the algorithms they have left behind or the data they have gathered can be used to build upon existing knowledge. Data science always builds upon what has been left behind, the information of our past.

It is this ability to crowdsource data that makes the application of data science in the discipline of medicine so powerful – for as long as the data remains, the gathered knowledge will not be dependent on individuals.

CASE STUDY   Diagnosing with SkinVision

There are a number of digital applications on the market that crowdsource data on a variety of things, from stars in the night sky to sunspots on your skin. SkinVision is an application for mobile devices that helps check users' moles for skin cancer. Using aggregated user data, SkinVision's algorithm can determine the likelihood of a user's mole showing malignant symptoms. It really is as simple as taking a photo of your skin with the app, which SkinVision will then record and analyse, before recommending the next steps for you to take with your doctor.

You might think that using technology like this for diagnosis on a mobile device is flippant, but that is entirely the wrong way to think about it. As more and more data is gathered on an illness, the databases on its causes and effects will grow, making the algorithm's ability to diagnose patients much more effective than even an experienced surgeon's. The more people who use a recognized digital application such as SkinVision to diagnose their condition, the more the technology will be able to distinguish the benign from the malignant – because it will have a large pool of data with which to cross-examine the user-submitted image. Think about it: would you rather be diagnosed by a human who might have looked at 1,000 individual cases, or by a machine that has an accumulated knowledge of 1,000,000 individual cases and counting?

Knowledge capacity

It is not only digital applications that are paving the way to data-driven medicine. IBM's Watson is, in their words, 'a cognitive technology that can think like a human' (IBM, 2017b). Watson entered the news when it became the first artificial intelligence to beat humans at jeopardy. But really that's just show for the papers.[3] What makes Watson so fascinating for us is how its technology can apply data to healthcare. Because its most significant asset is that it can be used as a support for doctors to *diagnose* patients.

Watson uses much the same principle as the SkinVision app – applying gathered data to inform practice – only it naturally requires more sophisticated algorithms for it to function. In one fascinating case, Watson was able to diagnose a rare type of leukaemia in just 10 minutes, in a woman whose condition had stumped human doctors for weeks (Otake, 2016).

Still feeling hesitant about the prospect of using AI in medicine?

Watson isn't the answer to all our problems, though. The machine's AI can still make mistakes. But the difference between machine doctors and human doctors is data, and as the technology to process growing quantities increases, so does the difference in ability between human and machine. After all, humans can absorb information from conferences, medical journals and articles, but we all have a finite capacity for storing knowledge. What's more, the knowledge that human doctors possess will largely be limited to their life experience. A machine doctor, on the other hand, can only get better the more data it is given. With instant access to data from other machines via the cloud, shared data can inform more accurate diagnoses and surgeries across the world. Thanks to exponential growth, these machines will have access to all manner of variations in the human body, leaving human knowledge flagging far behind.

Data science and belonging

After fulfilment of the second stage of Maslow's hierarchy (safety), the need for belonging within a social environment (family, friends, relationships) will follow. It states that humans need to be part of a community of people who share their interests and outlook on life. The perceived disconnect between technology and society has been a topic of much discussion in recent years. The internet is often criticized as contributing to an increasingly isolated existence where our every whim and need is catered for. As an outdoorsy person, I won't make any case in support of socializing in the digital over the physical world. However, I do believe that the relatively democratic accessibility that the internet affords to people all over the world at all hours of the day is to my mind a great asset to human existence and experience.

What's more, what makes social networks such as Facebook, Instagram and LinkedIn successful is not the usability of the platform – it's their *data*. A badly subscribed social network is unlikely to offer the same breadth of services as a well-subscribed network because social communication ultimately relies on relationships. If the data isn't there to connect us to the right information, whether that means human connections, images that appeal to us, or news stories on subjects in which we are interested, the social network will not be useful to us.

Data is helping to make our world much more interconnected, and it is not only aiding us in personal ventures like finding old school friends; it is also helping scholars and practitioners who are carrying out similar projects to find each other and partner up.

CASE STUDY Forging connections through LinkedIn

I love using LinkedIn – and I think that they have really applied their data to benefit both themselves and their users. A quick visit to the business network's 'People You May Know' tab will show you an inexhaustible list of recommendations for connections with LinkedIn's other users. Some of these might be people at your current workplace, but you may also notice people from your university, and even school friends, cropping up on the system as recommended connections. To do this, LinkedIn uses the data you post to your profile – background, experience, education, existing colleagues – and matches it with the profiles of others.

LinkedIn's technology has enabled thousands of people to rebuild connections with their past. And as these connections grow, so does the network's data, thereby generating yet more connections. Whenever you connect with another user, not only do you gain what they call a 'first-degree connection' but their linked colleagues become 'second-degree connections', thereby expanding your circle much further than may be apparent.

For LinkedIn, as with any other social media channels, all that is essential is input from its users. I have found numerous friends and ex-classmates on the site, many of whom have since gone into the same field as me and, thanks to data's ability to match us, this has opened up a new dialogue between old acquaintances. Knowing that I have access to friends and colleagues online builds a sense of community and maintains it long after we have moved on, whether that be from a city or a place of work, and I find this interconnectedness comforting.

By connecting with others who share our interests, courses of study and location, LinkedIn can also give us a good insight into jobs that are relevant to us. When I was in the market for a new job, I started posting status updates to LinkedIn – the platform's data algorithms identified my needs according to key words that I had used, and this is how recruiters started to find me. What was even better was that since I was writing about subjects that interested me, LinkedIn's algorithms matched me to jobs that specifically required those branches of knowledge. It was even how this book's commissioning editor found me. How's that for social media channels' abilities to improve happiness?

Community interference

As I have mentioned, while the benefits of having an online presence can be profound and can significantly contribute to our happiness and need for belonging in both the personal and professional spheres, we must also be aware of the problems it can cause us. One of the biggest concerns is how we can protect our data from being stolen. Cybersecurity has been a hot topic ever since the growth of online banking and since e-commerce became the modus operandi for the retail industry to reach new customers. In the past, we were told to frequently update our passwords, to only make purchases from reputable websites and, if our bank details were compromised, to contact our bank's fraud department as soon as possible. Considering that we are increasingly carrying out transactions online, it is reasonable for us to be concerned about how companies protect our information.

CASE STUDY Data breaches and ransomware

Your data exhaust will inevitably increase the more you use the internet, and the more connected you are to other users. The more data you produce, the more valuable you become to companies that sell user data. Data has superseded oil as the world's most valuable resource (*The Economist*, 2017).

But when things become valuable, they also become threatened by theft and abuse. And considering how well connected we are, concerns for our personal information today go far beyond our credit card numbers. A wealth of personal information is being put online, and whenever our personal computer is connected to the internet or an external server, we are at risk of having that information stolen. We only need to look back to the global WannaCry cyberattack in May 2017, a computer worm which infected Microsoft computers with ransomware in 150 countries, to see the potential magnitude of this risk. From FedEx in the United States to the Ministry of Foreign Affairs in Romania, the WannaCry worm locked user data from individuals and organizations on a global scale, with the worm's developers demanding payment in exchange for its restoration. Ultimately, those affected had no choice but to pay the team holding their data ransom in order to prevent it from being destroyed.

This is the power of data – its theft can bring an organization to its knees in seconds.

Another recent example of a major cybersecurity breach is the Equifax data breach. Aggregating data on over 800 million consumers and over 88 million businesses worldwide, Equifax is considered to be one of the big three credit businesses. On 7 September 2017, Equifax announced that it had fallen victim to a cybercrime identity theft that potentially affected 143 million consumers in the US. Stolen information included first and last names, birth dates, social security numbers, addresses and more (Haselton, 2017). Considering that the population of the US at the time was 324 million, almost every second person in the country was affected.

The rise of cybersecurity

Cyberattacks on consumers and institutions alike are growing in both number and scale. At the same time, cybercriminals are also getting better at covering their footsteps, which makes even finding their location difficult. The rise of Bitcoin, a digital payment system that enables anonymized transfers, adds a further layer to the already complicated issue of finding and bringing these hackers to justice. As information can be breached from anywhere in the world, this makes it difficult for law enforcement to deter criminals.

Today, it is no surprise that cybersecurity specialists are in real demand. What cybersecurity does is prevent fraudsters and hackers in real time, and it also carries out forensic analyses once attacks have occurred. Our interactions online have changed, and as the digital systems develop and change, so does the way people commit fraud online and, by proxy, the means at our disposal to combat it. Cybersecurity experts must constantly play a game of cat and mouse if they want to remain ahead of the threats.

My tip if you want to get involved with cybersecurity? Get to know how to work with unstructured data, that is, non-numerical information. Typically, 80 per cent of a company's data is unstructured (SuperDataScience, 2016). We will look in further detail at the developments in working with unstructured data in the following chapter.

How can we protect ourselves from cyberattacks?

If we use computers that are connected to the internet or to external servers, and especially if we use social channels for sharing information, we cannot completely protect ourselves from data theft. However, we can become more careful about storing and managing our data, to ensure that any issues can be efficiently dealt with. Here are a few guidelines that I use for protecting my data:

1 Keep copies of all the files that you cannot afford to lose on an external hard drive or data stick.

2 Clone your hard drive to a reliable external hard drive on a regular basis.

3 Keep tabs on your online accounts, and close any accounts that you no longer use.

4 Archive data that you no longer use, and disconnect it from the internet. Make sure that these files are only stored locally, and keep your archives in a cool, secure environment.

5 Keep all sensitive information away from sharing servers like the cloud.

6 Run regular checks on your hardware to detect data breaches before they occur. Ransomware bugs and worms can spend months within a user's system before being activated, probing and infecting every last corner of the database, even corrupting backup files, before they finally encrypt the data.

Data science and esteem

Acquiring esteem is the fourth most important need, as Maslow suggests in his hierarchy. There is a very clear link to creating esteem through data. Due to the rise in people working online, many digital work platforms are helping clients, agencies and freelancers to find the best person for the task by using recommendation and starring systems. Once a project is complete, online freelancing platforms give those involved the opportunity to publicly rate each other, based on factors that range from availability to quality of work. Each platform's rating system is slightly different, but what this ratings data ultimately does is both help match clients with the best freelancer for them *and* contribute to the freelancer's overall work score, intended to encourage those who receive a good score to continue working in that way, and to motivate those who receive a negative review to improve their performance. Some may be resistant to the idea of being subject to such scrutiny, but consistent performance data allows people to identify where they excel, and where they may need further training.

Keeping data in high esteem

What is to be done about managing data relative to esteem? The next step for companies will be to encourage users to include relevant demographic data about themselves (such as age and location), and to develop a more comprehensive system beyond the simple starring method and to carry out unstructured analytics on these reviews, which should give a more valuable and accurate example of how a user feels. This data might then be visualized in word clouds (popular visual representations of text, which we will discover more about in the following chapter) or accessed through filters applicable to user demographics.

Data science and self-actualization

Here is where the fun (literally) starts. With 'self-actualization', Maslow refers to a person's need to fulfil his or her potential in life. Unlike the earlier levels in the hierarchy that largely reflected needs innate to all people, need here can manifest itself in very different ways – tangibly or intangibly – depending on a person's interests. One person's need for self-actualization may be alleviated through mastering watercolour painting, while another's might be to become a compelling public speaker, and so on.

CASE STUDY Experience gaming

Ultimately, self-actualization represents the human need for joy. And we have already seen something of the importance this has in/for the entertainment industries. The billion-dollar video game industry has obvious connections with data science in their dependency on technology. Virtual reality (VR) is one of the most exciting areas in which data has specifically been used to further develop and improve the gaming experience. Where VR had once been considered a fad, it is now a major strand in the industry – and that is largely thanks to technology's improved capabilities in processing data, for instance in the frame rates and detail necessary for creating a realistic VR world. Before the developments made in the 1990s, computer-aided design (CAD) data had been limited by the lack of technology capable of processing it. Now, data can be used to build a life-size, 3D virtual environment, and algorithms are used to dynamically track where you 'are' in this environment, enabling the players' screens to match their gaze through active shutter glasses and multi-surface projection units.

That is how data improves the engineering behind the video game. But data can also be used to enhance a gamer's experience through its capture of how a game is being played. And data can be gathered from users in many more ways than is possible for other entertainment industries such as film. The data exhaust that users leave spans across their interactions, playing time, expenditure on additional game components and their gaming chats, among other things, thereby not only improving recommendation systems and advertising but also the game's mechanics to make it more enjoyable, and even utilizing the big data produced by software distribution platforms to predict their peak times and so attend to their servers accordingly.

Some final thoughts

It is clear that the developments in data science have directly benefited a vast number of areas in our lives. And data is continuing to drive a permeable layer between the physical and digital landscapes, redefining the way we engage with both environments. This might bring with it some conflicting thoughts, but as we can see from how responsively data can be attributed to Maslow's hierarchy of needs, data-driven developments will fundamentally facilitate human existence.

Naturally, a great deal of these developments and how we adapt to them depend on the data scientist, which is why I will use the next chapter to describe how we can think like one and ensure that our first foray into the discipline is well guided and utilizes the experiences we already have at hand.

References

Conley, C (2007) *Peak: How great companies get their mojo from Maslow*, John Wiley

Devitt, E (2017) Artificial chicken grown from cells gets a taste test—but who will regulate it? *Science*, 15 March [Online] www.sciencemag.org/news/2016/08/lab-grown-meat-inches-closer-us-market-industry-wonders-who-will-regulate [accessed 20.05.2017]

The Economist (2017) The world's most valuable resource is no longer oil, but data, 6 May [Online] www.economist.com/news/leaders/21721656-data-economy-demands-new-approach-antitrust-rules-worlds-most-valuable-resource [accessed 01.06.2017]

Haselton, T (2017) Credit reporting firm Equifax says data breach could potentially affect 143 million US consumers. CNBC, 7 September. Available from: www.cnbc.com/2017/09/07/credit-reporting-firm-equifax-says-cybersecurity-incident-could-potentially-affect-143-million-us-consumers.html [Last accessed 29.09.2017]

IBM (2017a) Green Horizon: driving sustainable development [Online] www.research.ibm.com/labs/china/greenhorizon.html [accessed 12.06.2017]

IBM (2017b) Watson [Online] www.ibm.com/watson/ [accessed 15.02.2017]

Mateos-Garcia, J and Gardiner, J (2016) From detecting to engaging: an analysis of emerging tech topics using Meetup data. *Nesta*, 1 August [Online] www.nesta.org.uk/blog/find-emerging-tech-topics-with-meetup-data [accessed 12.06.2017]

Otake, T (2016) IBM big data used for rapid diagnosis of rare leukemia case in Japan, *Japan Times*, 11 August [Online] www.japantimes.co.jp/news/2016/08/11/national/science-health/ibm-big-data-used-for-rapid-diagnosis-of-rare-leukemia-case-in-japan/#.WWXyS4pLeqB [accessed 01.02.2017]

SuperDataScience (2016) SDS 005: Computer forensics, fraud analytics and knowing when to take a break with Dmitry Korneev [Podcast] 29 March [Online] www.superdatascience.com/5 [accessed 05.06.17]

Notes

1 This will not provide us with a comprehensive overview of how and where data science is used in our lives, as Maslow's hierarchy discounts non-basic human needs. Areas such as military defence and space exploration, for example, would not be included here as they are not basic human needs.

2 I am using Maslow's hierarchy of needs as a means to an end here in describing the comprehensive power of data, but if you want to learn more about how the hierarchy can be implemented in business, see Conley (2007).

3 Which, by the way, is yet another example of how data is changing the way we consume information. The most read or clicked online news articles will get pushed to the top of the pile, making it a war for the sexiest title, rather than the most compelling content.

The data science 03 mindset

I'm not here to tell you that if you'll read this book you'll be an expert in data science, but there are certainly ways in which you can start changing your mindset to gain an advantage on others looking to enter the discipline. That is the purpose of this chapter. Everyone knows that, when taking up a musical instrument, years of practice are necessary before it will ever be possible to play it to a professional standard. Scales and arpeggios have to be mastered, your fingers should glide down the keys like butter, and your neighbours will probably take out an injunction against the noisemaking before you can even hope to tackle Rachmaninov. In short, learning to play an instrument *well* will require a significant investment of your time and money.

Data science sidesteps this cumbersome process. Even if you only learn its most basic scales – the first few algorithms given in Chapter 6, Data analysis (Part I), for example – you will still be well on your way to working with very complex material. And as anyone who has access to a computer will also be able to acquire a lot of free-to-use online data analysis and presentation software (as well as data science courses), you can get started on your technique very early on, letting the software do much of the legwork for you, while you focus on the creative thrust of your project.

While I would always encourage those who plan to be data scientists to read around and learn as much as they can about the subject in order to get to the top of their profession, I must also emphasize that the first entry into the subject need not be overwhelming. While there are some prerequisites for being a data scientist – which we will cover in more detail in Chapter 10 – for now, and to get you started right away, I've picked out five key attributes to get you into the right mindset to master the discipline.

1 Pick the right place to start

Data scientists do not need to know the ins and outs of every piece of software and every algorithm to make a difference in the field. The available programs are innumerable, and the algorithms range from the most basic options that classify our data to the most complex that help drive artificial intelligence. When you are first starting out, the trick is to take the time to acknowledge where your interests lie, whether that is visualization or machine learning, before pursuing a specific area. Hold off from taking a knee-jerk response to this – that will not only limit you in your early exploration of data science but may also leave you uninspired if you choose to invest in the wrong area. To many, visualization may sound more interesting than analysis at a superficial level, but you should take the time to understand what is required of each before making a rash judgment. The good news is that by the time you have finished reading this book, you will be much clearer about which area interests you the most.

Let's also be explicit here about what we mean by targeting a specific area; there is a big difference between choosing a niche from which you can springboard your career and specializing in it. The latter is a dangerous move, and is one that I would never advise. After all, data science is a dynamic subject that requires its practitioners to be equally dynamic in their exploration of how to tackle new problems in the field. Algorithms change, software alters and specializing in something that will only become defunct in the future is not a constructive way to practise the discipline. As we discussed in Chapter 1, data scientists must be acutely aware of growth and change. This is especially true considering how the rate of technological development directly affects their work, as identified by our old friend Moore's law.

Moore's law 2.0

To recap what we learned in Chapter 1, Moore's law is a projection of exponential growth, and is based on the initial observation that the number of transistors in an integrated circuit will double every two years. It has since been used to account for the rate of development (and inversely proportionate costs) in technology, and to forecast how soon future advancements might be completed. The fact that every year we have a new iPhone with a processor approximately 50 per cent faster than the previous model's is one such example of Moore's law in action.

In contrast to 30 years ago – when the only people with access to data-processing facilities were from the intelligence and security branches of government – even pre-school children can now access a wide variety of data from handheld devices that fit in their back pocket. Moore's law enables us to access, explore and exploit the potential of data through this explosion of technological advancement.

One of my favourite examples of Moore's law in practice is the Human Genome Project, which was launched in 1990.[1] The project's researchers set out to determine the sequence of the nucleotide base pairs that comprise human DNA. The slow pace at which the project moved in its initial years was a cause for concern for those watching its development from the outside. Once the first seven years had passed, forecasters took stock of how much of the genome had been sequenced so far, and they predicted that the rest of it would take another 300 years to complete. In these predictions, however, they failed to account for Moore's law. Sure enough, the next seven years of the project saw the full and successful sequencing of the genome – some 294 years ahead of schedule if we were to take linear progression into account.

2 Flex your creative muscles

As we have learned, the dataset is only going to be as useful as the data scientist. Thus, for any project, a good degree of creativity is required to get the most out of the data. Data scientists must get into the mindset of asking the right questions of their data, and I want to emphasize here that you should absolutely embrace blue-sky thinking: considering the wider implications of a project through its sets of data. After all, data can give us surprising results to the questions asked of it, and it can highlight problems, issues and gaps that we may not have known about had we not explored the data thoroughly. That can be said for all disciplines and industries that use data to drive practice: the creativity that its data scientists bring to the table on how to best solve a given problem will significantly affect the task.

There is of course a spectrum in the required level of creativity: some challenges may only need a rudimentary approach, while others might warrant some extreme out-of-the-box thinking. And if you ask me what lies to the far end of this spectrum, what is at the cutting edge of data science and technology, without a shadow of doubt I will answer: artificial intelligence.

Artificial intelligence

Whoever it is I talk to, mention of artificial intelligence (AI) will always get them sitting forward in their seats. It is a fascinating area of development, and one that is guaranteed to make headlines. AI is, however, entirely dependent on the availability of data, and the computer's ability to process it.

The first thing that many will think of when discussing AI is Hollywood's treatment of it in movies forewarning that improvements in this area will eventually lead to our undoing. In *Blade Runner*, adapted from Philip K Dick's science fiction novel *Do Androids Dream of Electric Sheep*, robots ('replicants') are so lifelike in their design and responses that they eventually become a threat to human existence. For that reason, they are banished to off-world colonies, where they can be kept separate from Earth's citizens. Some of these replicants, however, find their way back to Earth, and become hostile towards our species. As it is impossible to distinguish these robots from humans by simply looking at them, the Voigt-Kampff machine is developed. This polygraph-like machine poses a series of questions to its test subjects, specifically designed to scrutinize emotional response. It is reasoned that these questions will perplex the robot subjects – where emotion is deemed to be absent – and therefore reveal their true 'identity'.

This test has its roots in reality, as the Turing test. Proposed by codebreaker Alan Turing in the 1950s to assess the ability of humans to distinguish a machine from another human being, the Turing test would evaluate responses given during an interrogation. Unlike the Voigt-Kampff, there would be two subjects in the Turing test – one a robot, the other a human being – and both are hidden from the examiner's view. The examiner, whose job is to discern which of the subjects is a robot, will ask both subjects a series of text-only questions and will evaluate how closely their answers resemble the responses a human being might give.

To date, no robot has passed the Turing test.

We may still be a little while away from the highly sentient robots of *Blade Runner*, but there have been many examples of situations where robots have quite literally beaten humans at their own game.

CASE STUDY Deep Blue and AlphaGo

In a 2016 competition of Go – an abstract, two-player, strategy board game that is hugely popular in East Asia – the machine known as AlphaGo which was created by Google's subsidiary DeepMind managed to beat 18-time world champion Lee Sedol in four out of five games.

You may not consider this any great feat, remembering the famous game of chess played between Russian grandmaster Garry Kasparov and Deep Blue, a computer developed for the purpose by IBM. Deep Blue won, and that was back in 1997. But even though the robot's success came almost 20 years before that of AlphaGo, the accomplishment of the latter machine should be of special interest to us. The game of chess is entirely based on logic. The goal for Deep Blue, then, was to flawlessly observe this logic and wait until its opponent made an error. Humans make errors, machines do not.

Unlike chess, the game of Go is based on intuition. Intuition is a much more complicated concept than logic for a computer to handle, as it requires the machine to develop intrinsic knowledge about the game that cannot be simply pre-programmed into it.[2]

In Go, players use black and white stones on a 19×19 grid board. The object of Go is to cordon off more areas of the board than your opponent. AlphaGo was initially given a large database of around 30 million (human player) moves, which were analysed through a combination of machine algorithms and tree search techniques, before it was used as a Go player. Once a significant number of games had been played against human contestants and enough knowledge of its opponents' behaviours had been gathered, AlphaGo was made to play against itself millions of times to further improve its performance. (This is a type of reinforcement learning, which I will discuss in more detail in Chapter 6.) Only after this training period had passed did the machine's creators pit it against the world's top players. From chess to Go, artificial intelligence has come a considerable way, learning through doing and observing, rather than applying mathematical logic.[3]

At this point you might be thinking: 'AI winning in chess and Go is exciting, but how is this all relevant to adding value to businesses?'

The application of artificial intelligence isn't limited to beating humans at Go. The same company, DeepMind, developed an AI to help Google better manage cooling in its vast data centres. The system was able to consistently achieve an astonishing 40% reduction in the amount of energy used for cooling. Not only does this create a huge potential for savings for the company, but it also means improved energy efficiency, reduced emissions and, ultimately, a contribution towards addressing climate change (DeepMind, 2016). Now if that is not a creative approach to a *business* problem, then I don't know what is.

3 Make use of your background

As I have said under Point 1, the real beauty of data science is that unlike many other disciplines it will not take years of practice to master. Readers who may be just getting started in data science, then, should not feel at a disadvantage when comparing themselves to their peers who may have worked with and studied data all their lives. Again, all you need is a slight shift in mindset – to focus on what you *do* know, rather than what you don't. Leverage your background, both in terms of your in-depth knowledge of another subject, and any of the soft skills that you will probably have picked up from your professional and/or educational experience.

In-depth knowledge

Not only is data science simple to pick up, it is also *beneficial* to have come to work in the discipline after having a grounding in another. Here's where the creative hinges of data science can be highlighted once again. Let us take writing professionals as an example. If a writer has spent all of his or her education and professional development in only studying and producing writing, and no time at all learning about other disciplines, or understanding the way people work, or reading extensively, or experiencing the world at large, then that writer is going to have a limited spectrum of knowledge and experiences about which they can write. It's a similar concept with data science: those who have studied data science all their lives and have limited professional or personal experience elsewhere will approach a project somewhat underdeveloped.

So, let's say that somebody with a background in linguistics has decided to transition into data science. They will have a significant advantage over other data scientists for projects within that subject area. The example isn't facetious; name a profession and I'll tell you how data science can be applied to it. Someone with such a background, for example, might be better able to access material from the International Dialects of English Archive, which records the voices of thousands of participants from across the globe and uses those sound files to populate a map of the world. A 'raw' data scientist may be able to play with the material, but a data scientist *with the right background* will be able to ask the right questions of the project in order to produce truly interesting results. A geographical pocket of the West Indies, for example, known by the linguist for its unusual use of slang, could be taken as an initial case study from which we might glean further insights, such as development of expressions between generations, between ethnic backgrounds and between genders.

Undertaking a career in data science, then, does not mean performing a U-turn on everything you have learned from previous disciplines. Quite the opposite is true. Sometimes, the most interesting projects for you will naturally be close to home. Consider the problems that you face in your workplace: could there be a way to resolve them through data?

Soft skills

While undoubtedly helpful, you do not necessarily have to be an expert in a field to get a head start in data science. Even soft, transferable skills such as teamwork and public speaking can afford you significant leverage in the discipline. This may be more useful than in-depth knowledge for those who have just left school or university, for example, or those who may not have the same level of life experience or education as others. Consider your skills: are you a good communicator? Can you adapt established solutions? Do you have an eye for aesthetic appeal? Are you an out-of-the-box thinker?

I entered the discipline of data science with considerable knowledge in finance, but while that was undeniably helpful in my time at multinational consulting firm Deloitte, I think what ultimately helped me were the soft skills that I had picked up much earlier on, even during my formative school years. I also came to data science with a good understanding of creating graphics to visualize the results of a project in an aesthetically appealing way. During my childhood, I lived in Zimbabwe where I studied art twice a week. I came away from this school with only a basic ability to paint and mould funny-looking pottery, but while the course may not have set me up for success as the next Joan Miró, it did train me to think more constructively about colours and aesthetics and the positive psychological effects that they can have on my final report.

Once I returned to Russia some years later, my schooling took a very different turn, largely comprising the hard sciences at three different senior schools simultaneously. That type of schooling drilled into me the academic rigour that I needed for my coming years at university, but it also left me somewhat lacking in social skills. As an almost incurable intro-vert, I took to teaching myself some of the confidence and communication skills that I knew I would need. I found a self-help book that told me all I needed to know about how to get out of my shell. Its exercises were a little unorthodox (lying down in the middle of a busy coffee shop, drumming up conversation with people on public transport) but it worked for me. This effort may have been initially motivated by juvenile thoughts of engaging in university socials and sports teams, but it later helped me in establishing myself as an approachable and communicative figure who was attractive to my place of work, which needed their data scientists to deliver their reports to a wide range of stakeholders across the company.

This is another crucial factor for data scientists: if you want to be able to run a data science project, you will need to be able to speak to the right people. That will often mean asking *around*, outside your team and poten-tial comfort zone. The data won't tell you anything unless you ask the right questions, so it is your job to get out there and find answers from the people who have contributed towards your data.

In both points we discussed here – whether you are leveraging your in-depth knowledge to locate information or using your soft skills to gain answers from people – you will probably come across data that is non-numerical and that therefore depends on a level of context and subjectivity of analysis to get right. This kind of information – which we call unstruc-tured data – can be a written response, a recorded (video/audio) interview or an image. Since it cannot be quantified, it is the reason why companies often favour subject matter specialists to analyse it.

Unstructured analytics

Unstructured analytics work with – you guessed it – unstructured data, which comprises the majority of information in the world. In defining unstructured data, it may be easier to say it is everything that structured data (numerical information) is not. It can be text, audio, video or an image. The reason for the name is that this kind of data cannot be forced into a dataset – it must first be prepared, and as unstructured data is oftentimes not automatically quantifiable, a certain degree of subjectivity or bias becomes unavoidable to analyse it. This makes unstructured analytics an essential area for any data scientist.

A classic example of unstructured analytics is working with qualitative surveys, which give data in a textual or other non-numerical format. In the past this data had to be converted into numerical form before it could be understood by an analytics tool. This meant any survey questions that were not multiple choice or single answer – and thus could not easily be transposed to a numerical format – required a further manual effort from the data scientist to numerically categorize each answer.

For example, a question about what a visitor to Yellowstone National Park enjoyed about their stay could result in a range of responses including 'the wildflowers', 'picnicking', 'painting', 'bird watching', 'kayaking', 'great bed and breakfast' and so on. The data scientist would have to read all these results and then manually group them into categories that they felt were significant, such as 'nature', 'activities', 'sightseeing' and 'relaxation'. It is not always so easy to group a response into a category, leaving them open to human subjectivity.

You can imagine that transposing those responses into numbers left the resulting dataset a little skewed, at best.

Today, methods of ordering results by context have dramatically changed the way we carry out research, and new algorithms in this area are helping us to accurately work with images as well. Data scientists saw the problematic methodology behind organizing qualitative data and made a concerted effort to deal with values that could not easily be converted into numbers. The resulting algorithms tackle media to make far more accurate predictions than had previously been possible. Now, we can treat words in a similar way to numerical data, for example, by teaching analytics tools to identify the support verbs as well as idiomatic phrases that are of peripheral interest to the actual key word. This enables a machine to explore textual data in a far more qualitative way. The trend in the digital humanities to analyse literary works may spring to mind here, but that's only scratching the surface of what the machine algorithms in this area can do. Unstructured analytics has applications that extend well beyond the academic realm and into the commercial world. Even in forensics, machines can now trawl through suspects' written communication to make behavioural connections that a detective might not have been able to see.

You may think that humans will always be better than machines at trawling through media, because most of us still feel that we will always better understand this wider contextual environment. How can a computer recognize a period of art, or a flock of gulls, or emotion, better than a human? In reality, machines have long been able to make stunningly accurate predictions about non-numerical data. As early as 2011, a study carried out between the Institute for Neuroinformatics at the Ruhr-Universität, Bochum and the Department of Computer Science at the University of Copenhagen found that machines could outperform humans, even in complex tasks like identifying traffic signs (Stallkamp et al, 2012). For this study, the team presented their machine and human test subjects with a photograph that had been divided into squares. The task was to assert which (if any) of the squares contained all or part of a traffic sign. You may have seen these tests online – they are currently used as an additional security check before a user logs on to a site, and they are specifically designed to confound robots from accessing secure data. The results of this study suggest that we are already failing to create sufficient safeguards if there were to be an AI takeover.

Word clouds

I see word clouds used a lot in public presentations, and I suspect the reason for that is because they artfully *and* meaningfully combine image with text. Word clouds (or tag clouds) are popular ways of visualizing textual information, and if you aren't yet using them in your presentations, you may want to once you've learned how they work. A word cloud creator will take a set of the most commonly used words from a targeted piece of text and group them in a single image, identifying their order of importance by font size and sometimes also by colour.

Word clouds can naturally be used to highlight those terms that appear most frequently in a text, whether this text is a press release or a work of literature. They can also be run on survey data, which makes them a very simple but effective way of showing users the key concepts or feelings associated with a given question. Their effectiveness is therefore demonstrated in their versatility and in identifying key or significant

3.1

words from anything that contains text: metadata, novels, reports, questionnaires, essays or historical accounts. There are plenty of simple word cloud generators that are available to use online, where you can play around with fonts, layouts and colour schemes. (The wordcloud above, for example, was generated from the introduction of this book using www. wordclouds.com.) They are much more appealing to the eye than ordered lists. Try it out for your next presentation; you might be surprised how you can generate a discussion around them (for more on how to create visual analytics, see Chapter 6).

Data science has significantly improved the techniques for companies accessing and analysing media. Most business owners and marketers will be familiar with SurveyMonkey, an online, free-to-use questionnaire provider that runs your surveys through its data analytics tools. Users acquire access to their consumer data in real time, and responses from their questionnaire's participants are visualized in simple graphics and a front-end dashboard. At the time of writing, the provider's data analytics offer includes real-time results, custom reporting through charts and graphs, filtering your data to uncover trends by demographic – and text analysis, where users will receive the most relevant text data from their survey in a word cloud.

4 Practice makes perfect

One great aspect of data science is that there are so many free and open-source materials that make it easy to keep practising. When people are new to a discipline, there is a tendency to spend month after month learning its theories – instead of doing this, get into the mindset of always applying what you learn in a practical environment. As an exercise, just type 'free datasets' into a search engine and you will find a huge number of sites that allow you to download their .csv files (files for storing tabular data) directly to your computer, ready for analysis. Considering the sheer amount and range of data, from NASA space exploration to Reddit comments or even sports data (basketball, football, baseball – take your pick), I am positive that you will find something of value and interest.[4]

While the best analysis tools out there are not currently free to use, an increasing amount of software is either open source or freely available online. If you were a painter, this would be like having an endless supply of easels, paints and canvases to work with, with no worry about using your materials up.

I urge you to make use of these publicly available datasets to test your skills and run your own analyses. There is no shortcut to the practice. Much of what you do, especially in the initial stages, will be trial and error. The best way to train yourself to think laterally about solving problems through data is to increase your exposure to different scenarios – in other words, different datasets.

Where to begin? The best place may be right under your nose. I expect that many readers will be business owners or individuals working in a company that expects to use data in the near future. Those of you who have been working with a company in any shape or form will have at one point come across business intelligence.

Business intelligence vs data science

If you have already used business intelligence (BI) in your place of work, you will have a degree of practice under your belt. With business intelligence, you are required to identify the business question, find the relevant data and both visualize and present it in a compelling way to investors and stakeholders. Those are already four of the five stages of the Data Science Process, to which we will return in Parts II and III. The main exception is that BI does not carry out detailed, investigative analyses on the data. It simply *describes* what has happened, in a process that we call 'descriptive analytics'.

Data science, then, gives us the edge needed to answer further questions that may arise from a company's datasets, as well as make predictions and reliable suggestions for improvement. Technology research firm Gartner have a model to divide business analytics into four types, and while business intelligence responds to the first type of analysis, data science can help us tick the boxes for the final three.

3.2   Analytic value escalator

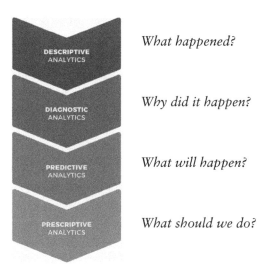

What happened?

Why did it happen?

What will happen?

What should we do?

That's the good news, but practising business intelligence outside the principles of data science can end up as harmful to your progress. It is true that you will be using data the first time that you generate a business report. But business owners will often need reports on a regular basis. When this happens it is common for attention to the data to fall to the wayside in favour of the end results.

This is one of the problems with BI, that data often comes second to an updated report. But data *needs* to be at the heart of any results and insights we make in a business – for every report we make, we must carry out analyses of our data beforehand because otherwise we will only be scrutinizing our data according to the limitations of our previous investigation.

It may be tempting to cling to BI because you or your company has operated in this way for years, but data science simply offers a far more impressive toolset – figuratively and literally – for analytics. Data science opens the door to a variety of analytical software and a thriving online community of data scientists working on open-source codes to improve and share their processes. An ability to use these tools eliminates the human burden of looking for insights manually, enabling you to focus on isolating bottlenecks, uncovering sales opportunities and evaluating the health of a business division. Unfortunately, BI's traditional dependence on Excel can teach you bad habits.

Everything you think you know is wrong

All readers will have worked with Excel. It has become one of the most important programs for corporations, and most spreadsheets will be shared in the .xlsx format. However, Excel can have the effect of over simplifying things and so people may have a skewed perception of data. If the only data you know is Excel, you have to be open to changing your perception of analytics.

We will cover the difficulties with Excel in detail in Chapter 5, Data preparation, but to give an overview: there are arguably no data types in the software. We are certainly not dealing with them directly, and that means that in an untrained person's spreadsheet strings, formulae and visuals will quite happily be mixed up. Even though Excel might look like a table, we can insert numbers, words, links and fractions into the same column, thereby mixing up all data types indiscriminately. No data science tool will allow you to mix data with logic, a problem that you will come to appreciate in Chapter 5. In any database management system, data and logic must be considered separately.

Be prepared to use a program that is not Excel. In my view, some of the best programs for analysing datasets are R and Python.

---

5 Keep ethics in mind

On a crisp February morning, and long before any reasonable person would be awake, I got a phone call from the Queensland police. Still bleary of eye and furry of tongue, I could barely get my words out: yes, I was Kirill

Eremenko; yes, I was at my home in Brisbane; yes, I owned the number plate that they read out to me. So what was the problem? They asked me whether anyone apart from me used the motorbike I owned and whether I knew where the vehicle was. The question launched me into consciousness and had me leaping down the stairs to my garage.

With relief, I saw that my pride and joy was still there. But the question remained: if everything they were asking me about (including me) was safely locked away, what were the police doing with all of my details?

They told me that they had spotted a motorcycle with my number plate evading the police in Gold Coast, a beach city not far from Brisbane. They said that considering my motorbike was at my home, my number plate must have been forged – and they later found it was.

Imagine for a moment that my bike had indeed been stolen. How could I have proved that it wasn't me who had been evading the law enforcement officers? That night I had been alone, and I had no alibi to speak of. As far as the police were concerned, it could certainly have been me, particularly considering how difficult it is to forge a number plate in so heavily regulated a country as Australia.

Even though at the start of the conversation I didn't know if my motorbike had been stolen, I realized that I hadn't been at all worried about an alibi during this phone interrogation, not even for a second, because I knew that I had done nothing wrong. I knew that technology would act as my witness. I carry my phone with me much of the time, I charge it near my bed and any actions I perform with it are registered. This brought to mind my time at Deloitte when I worked with the forensics division. We worked on countless situations where people professed that they were doing something or that they were in one place, but the tracking recorded on their phones told quite a different story. These records were used as evidence, because from mobile devices to CCTV cameras, recorded data doesn't lie.

The point here is that data *can* heal. It can act as your alibi. It can act as proof in criminal cases. Many people have a mindset that data can only harm – you won't get very far in the discipline if you only think of yourself as the villain. A little change in how you consider data science and its functions will encourage you to look for new ways that practices can be improved and enhanced through data, rather than feeling that you need to justify your work to colleagues.

The ethical cost of data

We know that data can do harm, as evidenced by the boom in conferences and institutions that serve to investigate the implications of technological development on human ethics and codes of practice. Who has access to our data? Should they have access to it at all?[5] As we have seen, data opens up new ways of working, of living, of investigating, of waging war – and it is doing so at an incredible rate.

Take 3D printing as one such example. As the cost to develop these printers decreases, the number of people with access to this technology will increase. While commercial 3D printers might at the moment be producing toys and games, they also have the potential to print any number of items, items that could prove dangerous – all they need is a data blueprint. This alone is surely enough to provoke concern, considering the disproportionate rate of technological development against our ability to legislate and protect. Can we ever hope to keep up with this rapid rate of change?

Data abuse and misuse

As data scientists, one of the most pressing matters in the debate surrounding technology and ethics is the amount of access that machines have to information (Mulgan, 2016). As the processing capabilities of robots increase, machines will soon be capable of handling information in a way that wildly surpasses human limits.

Information of all kinds is becoming digitized. Keeping information in a digital rather than physical format is becoming the norm. Historical artefacts are digitally curated, books and journals are made available online and personal photographs are uploaded to social clouds. After all, information is much safer when it's kept electronically: it is less subject to wear and tear, multiple copies can be made, content can be shared and connections between related items can be established. Of course, digital data is not completely protected from damage. It can deteriorate or get lost – but it is ultimately less susceptible to spoiling than data that is only kept in physical form.

The fact that there is so much information on the web – both in breadth and depth – increases the possibilities for machines that have access to this data and widens the divide between human and computer capabilities.

Computers have not reached their processing limits – but we have. The machines are only waiting for three things: access to data, access to faster hardware and access to more advanced algorithms.

When these three needs are met, the use and misuse of machines that can handle the amount of available data will only be a matter of time. And that is already making for a powerful weapon, whether through analysing online behaviour or masquerading as a human on social media sites for the purposes of propaganda. If we are to believe futurist Raymond Kurzweil's prediction that, by 2029, a computer will pass the Turing test, then giving machines unfettered access to the internet could make data access a most powerful tool for manipulation.

Why don't we just stop time?

Returning home after a night out in Brisbane's city centre, I found myself unwittingly pulled into a heated conversation with my taxi driver. Learning that I was a data scientist seemed to have an adverse effect on him. He started to accuse me of the apparently negative consequences that my work would have on the future. Fearing the worst, the taxi driver gestured to the night sky and asked either me or the heavens above, 'Why not just – stop where we are, right now?'

That simply isn't possible. It is in our nature to explore the world, and to continue expanding our horizons. It was natural for my agitated taxi driver to have hesitations about how data – and the algorithms to process them – will be used in the future. But anxiety about what may or may not happen will only hold us back; a disastrous move considering that while we're busy panicking, technology will continue to develop.

We must also understand that the concerns of one generation will not necessarily be the concerns of another. What bothers us today about how information about us is gathered, stored and used will probably not be the case for younger generations who have grown up with technology. This evolution of what we consider 'the norm' is reflected in the way we approach the gathering and processing of data. Consider the case of internet cookie storage. Many websites choose to capture data from their users. This data is called a cookie. It is recorded in a file that is stored on the user's computer to be accessed the next time they log on to the site, and it can range from user names to webpages accessed, even advertising for third-party sites, and helps a website to tailor its services to its visitors.

CASE STUDY Internet cookies

You may find the following statement familiar: 'To make this site work properly, we sometimes place small data files called cookies on your device. Most big websites do this too.' This is a notice from the European Commission (EC), which has passed legislation demanding that every EUROPA website using cookies must state, in the form of a popup or otherwise, that it records viewer data. Those who wish to continue to use the website can either agree to the conditions or find out more before agreeing to comply.[6] This legislation was passed at a time when people were concerned that their privacy was being invaded by companies who were using cookies to track pages viewed, interactions made and more.

Since then, those ethical concerns about cookies have slowly but surely been laid to rest. No one really cares about cookies any more, certainly not the Millennials, and that's largely because we have become accustomed to them as a part of our online lives. In other words, the concern surrounding internet cookies has eased off, and so the requirement for a company's website to clearly state that it is collecting data on its users will be phased out at the beginning of 2018.

Cookies are one example of how data collection is becoming an accepted part of our society. The way that most Millennials use social media – for example, freely expressing their opinion, chatting publicly, uploading their personal photos, tagging friends – must feel worlds apart for the Baby Boomers and how they (generally) behave online. I do not consider the ethical implications that factor into the discussion to be merely awkward obstructions that a data scientist might prefer to ignore. But I put the question to the reader: should we really suppress the development of technology based on our present concerns? Or should we rather seek to strike a balance between the rate of technological growth and the rate that we can develop suitable ethical guidelines for them?[7]

Prepare for Part Two

Hopefully, you will by now have found something in your personal and/or professional experience that you can utilize in your own work with data. Keep a note of the skills that you can leverage, write them on a dummy CV – employers are looking for data scientists who can apply themselves, and evidence of just why you are switched on to the mindset needed for data scientists will get you far.

References

British Academy (2017) Do we need robot law? [Video] [Online] www.britac.ac.uk/video/do-we-need-robot-law [accessed 03.04.2017]

British Academy and The Royal Society (2017) Data management and use: governance in the 21st century' [Online] www.britac.ac.uk/sites/default/files/Data%20management%20and%20use%20-%20Governance%20in%20the%2021st%20century.pdf [accessed 07.07.2017]

DeepMind (2016) 'DeepMind AI Reduces Google Data Centre Cooling Bill by 40%' [Online] www.deepmind.com/blog/deepmind-ai-reduces-google-data-centre-cooling-bill-40 [accessed 29.09.2017]

DeepMind (2017) 'AlphaGo Zero: Learning from scratch' [Online] www.deepmind.com/blog/alphago-zero-learning-scratch [accessed 19.11.2017]

Mulgan, G (2016) A machine intelligence commission for the UK: how to grow informed public trust and maximise the positive impact of smart machines, *Nesta* [Online] www.nesta.org.uk/sites/default/files/a_machine_intelligence_commission_for_the_uk_-_geoff_mulgan.pdf [accessed 25.05.17]

Service, R (2017) DNA could store all of the world's data in one room, *Science*, 2 March [Online] www.sciencemag.org/news/2017/03/dna-could-store-all-worlds-data-one-room [accessed 27.03.17]

Stallkamp, J et al (2012) Man vs computer: benchmark learning algorithms for traffic sign recognition [Online] http://image.diku.dk/igel/paper/MvCBMLAfTSR.pdf [accessed 22.09.17]

UK Cabinet Office (2016) Data science ethical framework [Online] www.gov.uk/government/publications/data-science-ethical-framework [accessed 07.07.2017]

Notes

1 The data from this project is freely available to use online at www.internationalgenome.org.

2 Google DeepMind's CEO Demis Hassabis defines intuition as implicit knowledge that's acquired through experience and that is not consciously expressible or even accessible, so we can't access that knowledge consciously ourselves and certainly not in a way that we can express to others.

3 In October 2017 Google DeepMind announced their latest creation, AlphaGo Zero. The beauty of it is that it doesn't use any human data whatsoever, but rather learns entirely from self-play (DeepMind, 2017). This new version is so powerful that it beat the original AlphaGo 100 games to zero. How's that for exponential advancements in data science?

4 We also offer plenty of free datasets for our students at
   www.superdatascience.com.

5 For more on data governance, see the report conducted by The British Academy
   and The Royal Society (2017), as well as the enlightening series of talks given
   at the British Academy as part of its season on Robotics, AI and Society (British
   Academy, 2017, recording available online).

6 Exemptions apply. An information providers' guide on how to prepare user
   consent on websites is available on the EC's website: http://ec.europa.eu.

7 If you have ethical concerns about your data science project, I would suggest
   finding or developing an ethical framework to which your company can adhere.
   One of the most useful is the UK Government's Data Science Ethical Framework
   (UK Cabinet Office, 2016), which is available online.

PART TWO
'When and where can I get it?' Data gathering and analysis

As with almost anything in life, it is often the truly challenging things that excite us the most. And data-driven projects will frequently offer just that sort of challenge. With these types of projects, you need to ask something *new* of the data, as data scientists are always expected to solve a *problem*. When I commence a new project, I like to think that I am having a conversation with the data; I am communicating with it to ensure that I represent it in the most honest and fruitful way for my client or the project's stakeholders. In my own experience and those of my colleagues, the final results are often eye-opening, leading to significant changes across institutions, from work practice to organizational structure. Some of these results can be directly related to the business question you were asked to solve, and others can illuminate aspects of business activity to which the organization had no prior access.

In data, then, there lies potential. That is what makes it so exciting. It will always tell us *something*, whether that information is new or not. And with data, you have the opportunity to continue exploring possibilities and thereby acquiring different results by asking different questions of it, by transforming it through different techniques, and by applying different algorithms to it.

The data science process

IDENTIFY THE QUESTION

What is the goal of your analysis? What questions do you want to answer? Identify the scope of the project.

PREPARE THE DATA

Source, clean and prepare the data for analysis. Check for completeness, resolve anomalies and perform quality assurance verifications.

ANALYZE THE DATA

Build models, perform data mining, run text analytics – the list goes on. This is the most exciting part where you get to be a creator.

VISUALIZE THE DATA

Translate complex insights into easy-to-digest visuals and animations. Here you are playing the role of an artist – unleash your imagination!

PRESENT YOUR FINDINGS

Insights need to be understood to be acted upon. Translate your findings into a language your audience will comprehend. In short – Make The Complex Simple™.

Because of the immense potential of data, accessing it afresh can be daunting, particularly if it is a large dataset, if it comprises various kinds of data or if the company for which you are working simply does not know what data they have collected. That is precisely where the Data Science Process comes in. This process offers a robust and reliable workflow for any kind of data project, irrespective of the amount and kind of data available, to help you structure your project from concept to delivery. First devised by Joe Blitzstein and Hanspeter Pfister,[2] the Data Science Process leads us through every stage of our project, from the moment we first consider how to approach the data, to presenting our findings in a clear and actionable way.

The process has five stages, which are:

1 Identify the question.

2 Prepare the data.

3 Analyse the data.

4 Visualize the insights.

5 Present the insights.

Each of these stages adds what I like to call a 'layer of interest' to your dataset. Although some of these stages can be returned to in the course of the process, following the stages in a linear fashion will reduce the chance of error at a later stage in the project, and will help you to retrace your steps, should you make a mistake.

As this process is so integral to every data science project, and as each stage requires a different skill set, we will be splitting it across Parts Two and Three. In Part Two, we will explore the first three stages. These initial three steps will enable us to 1) formulate a sound question or series of questions to ask of our data, 2) assemble the dataset in such a way that it responds to the questions posed to it and 3) get a response from the dataset by way of insights or predictions. To my mind, these stages will require the most input from you. If you put in the legwork here, then visualizing and presenting the data will be simple because you will have already achieved your project's goals.

Data scientist, private investigator

Today, we have an incredible amount of data at our fingertips. Think of the number of combinations we can get from a deck of 52 playing cards. Just shuffle a deck – it's extremely unlikely that anyone else, in the course of human history, will have had the same order of cards. Beginning to work with data is like being handed a pack of playing cards – sometimes there are more you can work with, and sometimes there are fewer, but the opportunities for variations are significant. Once you've established some ground rules (for cards, this means a game, for data science, this means a hypothesis and algorithm), you can truly get started. Identifying the question helps us to construct and plan our approach to the data, to ensure that we will get the most relevant results.

As Sherlock Holmes tells Dr Watson in *A Scandal in Bohemia*:

> It is a capital mistake to theorize before one has data. Insensibly one begins to twist facts to suit theories, instead of theories to suit facts.

Holmes warns Watson against making assumptions about a mystery in the absence of evidence to prove them. But what Conan Doyle has also struck upon here is the need for data scientists to take a step back before they dive in and make any claims or responses to a problem. With data, we have the advantage of deriving our insights from actual evidence, and so taking the time to consider what we want to ask of the data will help us to funnel it into telling us precisely what we need to know, without the outside biases of our own suppositions or those of others.

This is the first stage of the Data Science Process. Data scientists are required to exhibit some creativity at this point. We are not changing the information to suit our ideas, we are formulating ideas in order to derive insights that will be beneficial to us. In Chapter 4, Identify the question, we will explore the various methods that we can apply to ensure that the questions we end up asking of our data will ultimately suit our project's goals and cover us against gaps and 'scope creep' – the uncontrolled growth of a project beyond its original conditions.

The right ingredients

We are well into the Computer Age, and most institutions across the public and private sectors will already be sitting on a vast quantity of their own data. But data was being collected long before we knew what we could do with it, and information is oftentimes gathered by workers who are not aware of the methods necessary to standardize and analyse information so that it is actually useful. This knowledge gap will result in an organized chaos at best, with datasets often comprising garbled and dirty data, which we will learn more about in Chapter 5, Data preparation.

To clean up this data, to make it legible, we need to take our time. For an illustrative example of just how important it is to prepare our data before we do anything else with it, consider optimal character recognition (OCR) scans. OCR software will scan a physical page of written or printed text and will translate that text into a digital format. But OCR scans are not always 100 per cent correct – their accuracy depends both on the capabilities of the software and the quality of the printed page. Handwritten documents from the 17th century will give the software more difficulty and will return more errors that must then be manually cleaned up at a later date. Those who don't know how to record data properly or those who are using outdated or non-optimal rules as set by their institution will generate datasets that must similarly be 'cleaned up'.

The game's afoot

Actual data analysis does not need the same level of care essential for the previous two stages. If you have taken the time to postulate the right question and to prepare your data for answering what is required of it, you can afford to experiment with your analyses. The beauty of working with datasets is that you can duplicate them, so running one type of algorithm on a dataset will not make it unusable by another. That is the charm of digital information – it can be used, recaptured, restructured, and excerpted, yet you can still return to an earlier version once you have finished and start again.

This is the stage where you can afford to play around. You have spent time building the scaffolding for your project and ensuring that it won't collapse under the weight of the questions you ask of it, so now it's time to explore. Chapters 6 and 7 give solutions to the types of analyses that you can run, and they also provide a shortlist of their benefits and limitations, to increase your confidence in choosing the right algorithm for your project's purpose.

Getting started

While this part is largely theoretical, it has practical applications, and so I would strongly recommend that you consider applying each of the five stages outlined above to a project of your own in tandem with your reading. It will help to have some of the tools you need to hand before you get started with this part.

Datasets

If you do not yet have a dataset of your own that you can work with, don't worry. There are a good number of datasets that are publicly available and free for you to use in your own experiments. The great benefit of this is that you will be able to get immediately stuck in with using *real* datasets rather than those that have been specifically created for training. In my experience, real datasets will give you a sense of achievement from deriving insights from actual information, and will add weight to the claim that data science is essential for future development in a significant number of disciplines.

There is a wide variety of truly exciting datasets available online for you to download and use however you so choose. Here are just a handful to get you started:

- **World Bank Data**: a valuable resource of global development data.
- **European Union Open Data Portal**: governmental data from EU member states.
- **Million Song Dataset**: a compilation of metadata and audio features for popular music.
- **The CIA World Factbook**: datasets from 267 countries on subjects from history to infrastructure.
- **National Climatic Data Center**: data on the US environment.

Software

What is necessary for someone new to data science to understand is that data does not have a 'language' of its own, and that it can only 'speak' to us through a machine or piece of software. By data's 'language', I here mean the way in which a machine communicates data to the data scientist. From the speed of a car and the flowering cycle of a plant, to outside temperature and the number of residents in a city, data simply *is*. It is a series of components, but the relations that we make between them must be established by a human or a computer. If we were to take the language analogy further, I would say that data can be compared to individual letters which are waiting for someone to put them in the relevant lexical and grammatical order to form words and sentences. So it is up to us (through the tools we apply) to make our data work.

Having access to software is not a requirement for this book, because it focuses on practical application rather than coding. Even so, if you'd like to try out some of the examples provided in this book, then I would recommend getting your hands on either R or Python, both of which are data analytics programming tools and are available as free downloads for Windows, Linux/UNIX and Mac OS X. These two programs are currently the most commonly used open-source software packages in the industry.

Identify
the question

04

A grievance that I will often hear from other data scientists is that there is simply *too much* data out there – and that the very idea of grappling with that amount of information to answer a business question is overwhelming. Given our near constant data exhaust, how can we hope to manage the information that has been collected, in a way that will be conducive to examination? We cannot just dump all the information we have into an algorithm and cross our fingers that we will get the results we need.

Before we can prepare and analyse our data, then, we must know what kind of data we need. And for that, a little fine tuning of our project's question is necessary.

Business managers will often throw a question at a data scientist and expect them to dive straight into the database armed only with that. But that question first has to be understood, deconstructed, analysed. We have to know what is being asked of us; if we are not properly answering the question, our project's outcomes will be useless. Consider the process of school essay writing: going headfirst into answering a question as soon as it has been given to you will only (unless you are very lucky) result in an unwieldy, unstructured mess of information. It is only if you take the time to step back and think about the big picture – to consider its multiple components and the context in which the question sits – that you can hope to make a persuasive and logical argument.

Fully understanding the question also helps us to keep course and reduces the chances of our project diverging from the path. Let's say that our history teacher wanted us to write about the American War of Independence. Anecdotes from George Washington's biography may be interesting, but they do not answer the question that has been asked of us. Essays that are filled with such irrelevant information are the product of students going into a subject without having considered how to tackle the root of the question, instead taking everything that they can gather and not caring to trim the unnecessary data.

That is why, *first and foremost*, we need to identify the question.

In this chapter, I will show you the most suitable/fruitful way for tackling this stage of the Data Science Process. As identifying the question can feel overwhelming, I have given you a tried-and-tested approach that will guide you through this stage and ensure that you have considered all pathways to the question, as well as protect you from bosses who want to slip in additional work after the project has begun.

Look, Ma, no data!

Even though it is so crucial, identifying the problem tends to be the most commonly neglected part in projects that use data. I have been guilty of it myself; for a long time, I started projects by preparing the data. But that was not because I wanted to skip ahead; I had simply thought that identifying the problem was a given. After all, data scientists are often called in to work on *problems*, and in my first job at Deloitte all my projects began with an engagement letter that specified the task and where help was needed. It is no surprise that such a firm has standardized and streamlined this process, but that only got me into bad habits – jumping ahead of myself before I took note of the big picture.

Another reason for the neglect in identifying the question is that this stage does not use much, if any, data, leaving many data scientists feeling a little self-indulgent about carrying out this step. But it is important to note that those who proposed the question are probably not data scientists, and they do not know the preparations needed for cleaning up and analysing the data. Few companies to date educate their employees about the importance of storing and accessing information, and this knowledge gap means that many data scientists are still being asked, 'We have a lot of data, so can you find some insights for us?' This type of question is commonplace, and yet it is obscure, vague, and will go nowhere in helping to solve a company's problems.[1]

So, even if a question has been formulated beforehand and your boss is querying why you're not getting on with handling the data, don't feel as though you're being extravagant in undertaking this step. Make your case for this stage if you feel it necessary. Simply, it is not good enough for a question to be proposed – that question must be recalibrated in terms that the data will be able to understand or the project will not move ahead.

How do you solve a problem like...

Problems that come from organizational boards or investors are frequently postulated as open-ended pathways to a question rather than a real question in their own right: 'We are under-delivering on product units' or 'Our customers are leaving us at a rate higher than expected' or 'There is a defect in our product'. None of these are questions – they are issues. I urge readers to take the following step-by-step approach to identifying and solving the problem through data. That will both make this stage more efficient and reduce the risk of you focusing on the wrong problem.

1 Understand the problem

Anyone who plans to participate in data-driven projects must first be aware of the trap that they can be unwittingly led into before the project even begins: that if they follow the lead of a colleague who has given them a question to solve, they may in fact be solving the incorrect problem. A colleague might have good intentions and try to be more helpful by presenting you with their own devised questions, but their questions will not necessarily be suitable for asking the data. It may be tempting, upon being given a handful of apparently well-formulated queries, to not bother with identifying the question ourselves. But doing so can lead to disaster later on in the process; it falls to *you* to identify all the parameters of the business problem because you have been *trained* to do so. Blindly taking a non-data scientist's set of questions and applying them to your project could end up solving the wrong problem, or could simply return no results, because you don't have the data for it.

Before we jump into our project, then, we must *speak* with the person who presented us with the problem in the first place. Understanding not only what the problem *is* but also why it must be resolved *now*, who its key stakeholders are, and what it will *mean for the institution* when it is resolved, will help you to start refining your investigation. Without this step, the outcome can be dangerous for a data scientist, since later on in the project we undoubtedly end up interpreting the question differently to our stakeholders. Once we have expanded upon the central problem, we can move on to the second step.

> ## Stop to smell the roses
>
> Although a good data scientist should begin with a problem and have a clear idea of its various facets, don't worry at this stage about taking some unexpected detours. We are actively looking into a company's archive of information – much of which may not ever have been processed – and we are also carrying out a good deal of groundwork during this stage of the process to understand the company's issue, so it stands to reason that we will be faced with surprises along the way. Don't write these detours off as being ancillary to your project, make note of them as you go. This journey is what data science is all about, and additional insights are a big part of it. These may at times be irrelevant to the problem, but they can add further value to the business. At times, I have found these insights can drive even more value than the solution to the problem that I have been asked to solve.

2 Develop your industry knowledge

If you have previous knowledge of the sector within which you are asked to work, you're off to a great start. You can apply your existing experience to the problem. You may already know, for example, the particular problems that companies operating in this sector typically run into; or the departments that have, in your experience, typically contributed to those problems, for better or worse; or you may be aware of competing companies that have identified and resolved precisely the problems that have been asked of you.

If you do not have knowledge of the industry, all is not lost. Spend some time researching it in more detail. What are the common pitfalls in the industry? Have your company's competitors run into the same problems, or are there significant differences? How have they resolved similar problems? Are the mission and goals for this company reflected across the industry? How is the company different in terms of output, organizational structure and operations?

Google may be your best friend for answering many of these questions, but also remember that, as a data scientist, you are not working in a vacuum. Having a solid knowledge of the environment within which you are operating, as well as its individual characteristics and its limitations, will help you to devise an approach that is meaningful to the project's stakeholders. Don't be a hermit. If you find yourself with gaps in information, make use of the best resource you have available: your colleagues. And even if you have all the information you need, still get out and talk about what you have learned with the relevant people. The people who have instigated your project will always be a good starting point in helping you to ensure you are speaking to the right people. They will not only help you with filling any gaps in your information but will also direct you to the custodians of the process – those who are responsible for the areas of the organization in which the problem has arisen.

Be a people person

Data-driven projects will often affect more than one area of a company. You will find that, in order to truly nail the question, you must work across multiple divisions – and with people who don't often have reason to speak with each other. Be prepared to work in this way, and to be social. I count this as one of the many joys of being a data scientist. After all, having access to information across the organization puts you in a unique position to gather as much information as possible about how an organization operates, and how the business question you have been called in to answer will affect operations across the company. That's quite exciting.

In one role where I analysed customer experiences for an organization, I was technically based in the marketing department's customer experience and insights team. But half of my time was actually spent working in the IT department: naturally, I needed access to their databases, servers, tools and software. Before I came along, there had been no data scientist at the company and these two departments were separate entities that rarely had reason to communicate.

When you start out on a project, you will find that you may act as a bridge between departments, helping to synchronize their efforts on behalf of data. This can help immensely in learning about how a company functions and how your project can help improve their services and methods of working. By the end of my time with that organization, I was working with the marketing, IT *and* operations departments, and my reports frequently brought them all round the table to discuss their plans for the upcoming weeks.

Every time that you speak to a new department, make sure to maintain your connections so that the team knows about the work you are doing, thus keeping the channel of communication open if you need information from them further down the line.

3 Think like a consultant

Most will agree that data science requires a bottom-up approach: we use the company's bedrock of data to make analyses, and we incrementally build upon our results as we get to better understand the problems within the company. That potential to go exploring can be what makes this first step so exciting. But in order to identify the question, we need to pay more heed to business consulting methods.

In consulting, we outline the possible strategic approaches for our business. Consultants tend to be people who have worked in the business or the industry for several years, and they will have accrued a lot of knowledge about the sector. These people are often concerned with improving the large-scale strategic and organizational aspects of a company, which demands a top-down approach – and this methodology to analyse the big picture requires certain assumptions about a given problem to be made.

It may seem counterproductive for us to use consulting methods; as data scientists, we are told to try and limit assumptions as much as we can in favour of factual evidence. But taking a leaf out of the consultants' book can be extremely beneficial, particularly during this stage of the process. So, put your technical knowledge to the side for a moment and look instead at the organization, the stakeholders, and the company's strategy before even considering the data. Identifying the question, after all, is all about filtering our options, and this third step will start to refine our questions so that they are specific to the needs of our company.

Jot down a list of the key stakeholders for the project, and make special note of who the final decision makers will be. Spend some time with them and don't move on to the fourth step until you are able to answer the following questions:

- What do each of the project's stakeholders think of the problem?
- What are the facets of this problem?
- Which departments need to be given priority in my investigation?
- What might be the root causes of the problem?
- Do the stakeholders think I should be talking to anyone else? Have I spoken to them?
- Where is the data located, and who is in charge of it?
- What would success look like for this project?

Top-down or bottom-up?

Deloitte, PricewaterhouseCoopers, KPMG, Ernst & Young – these are the renowned 'big four' companies that all swear by a top-down consulting approach to all their projects. But what is a top-down method, how does it differ from a bottom-up approach, and is one really better than the other?

Let's take these questions one by one. A top-down approach is one that considers the project's big picture first, and then drills down into its details. Consultants who are brought onto a new project will begin their investigations at the top of a company's hierarchy, reading the relevant executive reports and then working their way from CEOs to executives to managers until they reach the people at the very 'bottom' – *if* they ever get there. However thorough their research may be, consultants that use a top-down approach will ultimately frame their project by their initial findings, such as those given in the company's end-of-year financial reports. The top-down approach remains the typical method used by consultancy firms.

For a bottom-up approach, exactly the opposite path is taken. This method places the *numbers first*. It initially examines a company's data before moving up the hierarchy, from project managers to heads of divisions, snowballing information before finally reaching the top floor of executives. This approach relies on facts and figures to tell the investigator about the day-to-day workings of the company. Readers will be unsurprised to know that the bottom-up approach is almost always used by data scientists.

Considering this is a book about data science, we might automatically reach for the bottom-up approach, thinking that a method that focuses on databases is surely preferable to one that begins with filtered data. This, however, would be jumping the gun. Yes, as a bottom-up approach has its basis in facts, it is possible to reach a conclusion much faster than if we use a top-down approach. *However*, any project investigator using a bottom-up approach will tell you that it is near impossible to drive change with this method. Companies don't just run on data – they run on people and relationships. We cannot crunch numbers and then rush into the director's office, proclaiming that we know how to solve a problem and waving a piece of paper with the data to prove it. The numbers are, as you will find out in this book, just one piece of the puzzle. We also have to understand a company's culture, its mission and its people.

So if we want to reach reliable conclusions, a little more detective work is necessary. For that, a top-down approach is perfect. To illustrate this necessary caution when using a bottom-up approach, Richard Hopkins, my mentor and director at PricewaterhouseCoopers, says that if you only go by the numbers:

> the company's not really going to listen to you because you haven't collaborated, you haven't talked. Let's say you find from the numbers that their sale of a certain product is losing them money, and draw the conclusion that they should stop production of those items. But they might be selling those products for a specific reason – perhaps to sell another product, or perhaps it's already being phased out. Yes, a bottom-up approach will get you to an outcome quickly, from which you can make a decision. But without understanding the big picture, that decision may not be the best one to make.
>
> (SuperDataScience, 2016)

With a top-down approach, we get stakeholder buy-in. We draw our conclusions from our colleagues' input. With that level of engagement, we can make changes in the company much more quickly.

So, rather than using the bottom-up method, should we emulate the people at KPMG and use a top-down approach? Not necessarily. Getting the big picture takes a lot of time. We have to work with stakeholders, organize workshops, and when we are given so much information at such an early stage we are forced to make crucial decisions about what information is useful and what should be omitted. That's a great deal of responsibility. What's more, the results from a top-down approach may not end up matching the data.

What to do? Richard introduced me to the distinct advantages of applying both these methods to a single project:

> Quite often, there is a disconnect between the numbers that you get from the databases and those you get from the final reports. I've found that I get the best results when I do both analyses and then link them together. This allows me to work out what happens with the final reports, and what levers in the operation are causing those financial results. So, using both a top-down *and* a bottom-up approach links the data to operations and gives us the full picture.
>
> (SuperDataScience, 2016)

The best approach then, whenever possible, is to combine the two. This will not only ensure that you can reach an answer quickly and with the data on your side, but will also give you the much-needed support from the project's stakeholders to actually implement your best ideas.

4 Understand the limitations

We are at step four and are still not yet working with data, but we will eventually need to gather and prepare our information. That is going to be difficult if, after all the work we have done here, we find that the data we have identified as necessary for our investigation is not there. So what is to be done?

The most efficient approach is to understand – at a top level – what data we actually have, and whether more data gathering is necessary before the project can go ahead. Again, this means speaking with the right people: those in charge of the company's existing data. Investigating them further will help us to begin considering where in the data we might find problems, and where we might need further information in order to ensure that any sampling we carry out will be statistically relevant. This step is ever so slightly chicken-and-egg, in that we must know the questions to ask of the data *before* we look at our datasets, but we should also ensure that we have the right data available early on so that we lose as little time as necessary before proceeding with the next stage of the Data Science Process.

The best way to learn this step is through practice. Remember your thoughts on what types of data will be useful for answering your questions. List them next to your questions as you carry out this stage, and make a note to take stock of what you need at each checkpoint. It may seem like plate spinning in your first project, but it will become much easier with experience.

CASE STUDY Filling the gaps

Ruben Kogel is Head of Data at VSCO, a California-based art and technology company that helps artists to create digital user experience tools through online subscriptions. At the time of his appointment, he was the only data scientist at his company, and VSCO did not have a standardized practice for creating data-driven reports. But Kogel saw an opportunity in their data to answer key questions that the company wanted to answer: who are the people that buy VSCO subscriptions, and does their purchase make them 'behave differently' afterwards?

Ruben knew that the problem required looking at the free account users who then upgraded to their paid-for subscription services. But that was only the tip of the iceberg – it was necessary for Ruben to start drilling down and specifying:

I needed to know more before I could get started. I wanted to know, among other things, what indicated changes in behaviour, and why it was important to 'know' our customers. At the time, I didn't know how VSCO's users were targeted for subscriptions, so that was a knowledge gap I needed to fill before I could consider answering the question.

(SuperDataScience, 2017)

Deconstructing the question in this way helped Ruben to focus his analysis. It became clear, through discussing its parameters with colleagues, that the question was really to do with marketing. The question, then, was reformulated to specifically target marketing needs: 'VSCO has millions of users who are all potential buyers, but they are not uniformly as likely to purchase a VSCO subscription. To that end, (1) how are our users segmented in terms of their preferences, behaviours and demographics, and (2) which of these customer segments represent the most likely purchasers?'

Once that had been clarified, the rest was straightforward for Ruben. From speaking with the marketing department he knew the behaviours that predicted whether a customer would be likely to purchase a subscription. What Ruben had effectively done was take a rather unstructured question at the beginning and formulate it into something that not only responded to precisely what the investor wanted to know, but also identified where the company could be gathering more data in order to improve its marketing practices.

If you are working within an established company that has accumulated a lot of data over time, identifying the problem first and foremost becomes all the more important. I have often found that, while colleagues might be open to the idea of using data-driven techniques to solve a problem, unless they are also working as data scientists they are less open to the idea of having to work for it. This can even be true for the people who manage the databases. And it is where many companies start out on the back foot – in an ironic twist, due to the unmanageable amount of data they have, they lose sense of its purpose and therefore devalue it. It is up to us to help them understand data's importance, and that journey begins here.

Get people on board

Your data science *will* shake things up. As the key game-changer, you may find yourself up against resistance. If you find yourself deliberately stonewalled by a colleague, do something about it. If you are missing information as the result of intentional stalling by a co-worker, do not hesitate to escalate the matter. The bottom line for any data science project is to add value to the company, and if your stakeholders know this, they should also know that it must take priority. You won't win everyone over to this idea, but my personal philosophy is to never take this kind of opposition lying down: be prepared to go over their heads to get the job done.

---

5 Mine the data (optional)

Data mining might be my favourite part of the process in any project. Preventing a data scientist from mining the data is a little like disallowing museum curators from researching the materials for which they are responsible. This step is where you can afford to be explorative. To me, data mining is a process where you carry out tests to scrutinize the data at a top level and find areas that could yield interesting insights for further investigation.

At this experimental stage, I like to put the data into Tableau,[2] which will read the data and help you create some initial descriptive visualizations such as easy-to-read tables, charts and graphs. This generates a wonderful top layer – which you can use as a lens to formulate your project's questions.

Ultimately, when carried out at this stage of the process, mining data is a basic way to better understand the problem and to guide your eventual analytics process. It is a test drive for your data, where you trial it raw to see whether any trends might emerge even at this early stage. Data mining can save you a lot of effort later on. At the same time, don't be disheartened if this process does not result in anything. The data may or may not suggest steps or solutions to us, depending on several factors: the company, the quality of the data, and the complexity of the problem. So, take this step with a pinch of salt. And if you do find something of interest, make a note of it and ensure that you are aware of your findings when you continue to step six...

6 Refine the problem

Now that we have understood the scope of the problem and the amount of data at our disposal, we can start to dig a little deeper. Here is where we begin to match up the project's scope with the data, to distinguish the variables and data that will be useful from those which will not, and to truly deconstruct the question.

While all data has the potential to be useful, we cannot deploy all the information we have for every problem – which can only be a good thing: if all data was always useful, the amount of information returned to us would simply be too unwieldy to manage. For this reason, we can be choosy about the data we select. This means making sure that we consider the *parameters* and *context* of the problem that we want to solve before moving forward. Ultimately, refining the problem saves us time by eliminating data that is irrelevant to our question.

Subdividing our data

Let's take the example of a company suffering from low profits. Their top-level problem is low profitability. We may initially want to ask: what are the contributing factors here? Perhaps the company's overall *revenues* are too low. Or the company's *expenses* could be too high. These are already two possibilities. Using these two categories (revenues and expenses), we may be able to further dissect the issue. What kind of expenses does the company incur? What are the different products and services that the company offers? Asking these additional questions might take us back to our stakeholders with specific requests: to look at the finances of the company, to see how the product/service offer is segmented, to define what the company's profit goals have been over time, and so on.

If stakeholders know their data, they might be able to give a direct answer to some of your questions. It is likely, for example, that they would know whether or not expenses have significantly changed over a period of time. Merely by asking this question, we can discount the potential problem of expenses. And that enables us to potentially[3] whittle down the problem to one of revenue.

7 Gather additional data

At this stage, you will already have identified the data that you need and gathered a reasonable list of questions to solve the problem. Now is the time to evaluate the efficacy of your sub-questions. After all, it is simply not worth answering questions that you know the company will have no interest in or will not act upon. Ask yourself now: what are the expected outcomes for these sub-questions? Do they help to solve the problem, or is there anything still missing?

This is where you will thank yourself for having worked through the previous six steps before reaching this point; isolating the key areas from which you need additional data will hone and therefore accelerate the data-gathering process. Draw up your plan and then put it aside; hold off from doing any data gathering at all until you have finished step eight.

Quantitative and qualitative methods

If we have identified that we need more data (and this is very likely; I have never been involved in a single project that did not require additional data), it is at this point that we must consider what *kind* of data would result in the best outcomes. The most significant questions for data gathering are 'Where *are* our sources?' and 'Do we want to use quantitative or qualitative research methods to interrogate them?'

What *are* quantitative and qualitative methods? Simply put, quantitative methods gather numerical information, while qualitative methods gather non-numerical information. But there are a few additional differences that we should take note of before we decide which method to use in our additional data gathering.

Quantitative methods

Quantitative methods should be used when we want to gather statistical information. As we will discover in the next chapter, they are *much* simpler to gather into a dataset than qualitative methods, but our final decision as to what kind of data we collect must not rest on simplicity for simplicity's sake. Both methods will answer different questions. We cannot, for example, decide to use a qualitative approach to collecting something like age, because it is a fact, not an opinion (whatever you may want to tell yourself). We would use quantitative methods if we needed to count items, or to measure salary development, or to find out more about consumer demographics. Be careful to note here that quantitative data isn't just numerical data – rather, it is data that can be counted. Questions that ask about respondents' favourite brands or political affiliation are still quantitative, because the answers can technically be counted into categories.

Qualitative methods

Qualitative methods use the open-ended questions that can result in an infinite number of answers. They are exploratory in nature, and they help to isolate – but not quantify – trends in opinions, thoughts and feelings. We might want to use this approach when we need more context to understand a problem, or when a problem is too complex to be answered in a quantitative way. Qualitative methods, then, are preferable for gathering data on a consumer's emotional investment in a product, or when we want to build a broader picture of the way respondents might feel about a political party.

8 Inform your stakeholders[4]

Once we have taken into account all of the previous seven steps, it is absolutely necessary that we, our team, and *every one of the project's stakeholders* are on the same page. Making clear the problem that you will be solving – as identified through the parameters we have devised – will ensure that we have clarified precisely what your approach will be, and this will reduce the chances of others changing the goalposts as the project gets underway.

The stakeholder who has requested that the project be carried out *must agree* to our problem outline, which ideally should sketch out not only the content of the project but also its timeframe. I would highly recommend that you divide the project up into milestones, which will allow your stakeholders to stay informed of your progress and safeguard you against any backlash at the end of the project, had you kept your cards too close to your chest.

It is also necessary that we highlight to our stakeholders that this is *not* a regular business project. Data science projects will not always fit the PRINCE2 models that are so familiar and favoured in businesses. This will help protect us against stakeholders coming to the project with any preconceptions, and will give us an opportunity to explain to them precisely what steps we *will* be taking towards completing our tasks.

The one thing that I insist on at the outset of any data science project is to make sure that you *get stakeholder buy-in in writing*. You may be the best of mates in your personal life, but in my experience, stakeholders have a tendency to change their concept of what they want as the project develops, no matter who they are. It's understandable for undefined projects, but this contributes to scope creep, which can either overwork you beyond the original parameters of the project or it can kill the project completely. So before you move on to preparing your data, get that confirmation in writing.

The truth is not always pretty

How do you deal with not alienating stakeholders when your results aren't giving them what they were hoping for? How can you avoid this minefield? Unfortunately, there's no positive spin that you can put on what the data is telling you, if the truth is a negative result. The truth is not always pretty. In data science, you are looking at hard facts – overlooking or prettying up results for the sake of sparing a stakeholder's feelings is not conducive to anything.

If I can give any advice here, it would be this: prepare your audience for the possibility that the results may not be what they want. Make it clear upfront you do not know what the outcomes will be. They may not like their insights. Put it in their head right away that you are mining for facts, not flattery, and with luck they won't shoot the messenger if the report is less than favourable.

Timekeeping

This stage of the Data Science Process should only take up a small amount of time in the project's cycle. Sometimes, those who are new to the process can find themselves spending too long on it because they want to ensure that they have developed a robust methodology. Remember: you can never refine a problem to the extent where you will know exactly what you want. If you do a good job at this stage, then you are likely to save time, but you must also learn to let go, and that comes with experience.

If you follow the steps outlined above, you can both cover yourself in the event of difficulties further down the line and gain the confidence for moving on to preparing data in a timely fashion. Ultimately, unless the problem that you have been given is particularly fiendish or is one that requires speaking to multiple, disparate stakeholders, identifying and refining the problem should take you a week at the most. But any deadlines you enforce here should, if possible, not be shared with others – that would only add undue pressure for you. If it takes you a few more days to be happy and comfortable with the progress you have made, then so much the better.

My recommendation? Give yourself ample time to meet the deadline. It is far better to under-promise and over-deliver than to do the opposite. A good rule of thumb is to work out how many days you think the project will take as a whole and then add 20 per cent to that number. More often than not in data science, you barely meet your deadline. And if you come up against any obstacles and you think that you may not meet the date on which you had initially agreed, make sure to tell the person who needs to know as early as possible. Keeping people informed will build trust between you and your stakeholders, and keep them on your side.

The art of saying no

As you get better within your organization and you start to add value and make people's roles more efficient, people will flock to you for help on their project. Unfortunately, you will not have the time to assist all of them – and for that reason, you will have to learn how to say no.

The first question to ask yourself when you're asked to help with a problem is: is this a project that I want to work on? Some may be interesting, and others may be run by friends, but ultimately your decision should be based on the business value that you derive.[5] You can then compare your options and select the one that will be the most fruitful for your company. Always remember that the essential job of a data scientist is to derive value for the company. This defining criterion for success will also serve as an aid for you when you tell people why you are not taking on their project.

How *do* you say no? First, refrain from responding to a project idea immediately. Tell the person with whom you are speaking that you will think about it and that you will get back to them within a certain timeframe (I give myself two working days to mull a request over).

If you want to take a more diplomatic pathway, one trick is to make sure that you are not considered 'the data guy' or 'the data girl' – a number cruncher. If you position yourself instead as an *adviser*, even if you cannot assist them on the project itself, you can give them help with how they can use data. I believe this to be far better than giving an outright 'no', and it also gives colleagues something to work with. Take just half an hour to research what they need – perhaps you will find a tool that will guide them in the right direction.

From there, they will perceive you as a consultant rather than the data holder; someone who will give valuable feedback and help them *towards* their goal, rather than giving them the answers. This will also benefit you, as you will gain exposure to different parts of the business.

Onward!

By following the eight steps outlined in this chapter, you will not only have protected yourself against the most common snags in data science projects but you will also already have begun to establish yourself within the company. Enjoy this explorative and communicative stage of the process – in the next stage, you will be almost entirely confined to your desk.

References

SuperDataScience (2016) SDS 016: Data-driven operations, consulting approaches and mentoring with Richard Hopkins [Podcast] 22 December [Online] www.superdatascience.com/16 [accessed 01.08.17]

SuperDataScience (2017) SDS 039: Key data science and statistical skills to get hired at VSCO [Podcast] 29 March [Online] www.superdatascience.com/39 [accessed 05.06.17]

Notes

1 Many executives are under the impression that data should be used to identify the problem – but this approach seldom works. We cannot force data to speak of its own accord – we must first consider what it is that we want it to say.

2 Tableau is a visualization software that I will discuss in further detail in Chapter 8, Data Visualization.

3 I say potentially here, because it is important not to completely discount your other options too early in the process. Keep tabs on the decisions that you make, and make a note of how and why you have reduced the importance of a set of data. Doing so will enable you to quickly return to the drawing board if you need to reformulate your question later on.

4 This might not be a method to establish your parameters for identifying the question, but it is nonetheless crucial that you carry out this step.

5 This doesn't have to be measured in monetary terms. Value may also be calculated by the number of customer subscriptions, by increased business efficiency and so on. The key here is to establish how your company derives value and to base your response on that.

Data preparation

05

Most of us have at some time been abroad in countries where we don't speak the language. With this basic method of communication closed off to us, it can be very difficult to get our meaning across. Even if we do have some knowledge of the language, the gaps in our vocabulary and grammar will often cause us (and the listener) some frustration.

Language, then, is a fundamental necessity if we want to understand and communicate with another individual. And preparing data is all about establishing a common language between human and machine.

In this chapter, we will learn why data should never be analysed without first having been prepared, the step-by-step process in which data can be prepared and the best methods that I have learned for managing problems in datasets.

Encouraging data to talk

As practitioners, unless we are very lucky, data will often come to us 'dirty'. It is often collected by people who do not standardize their records, managed by people who might tamper with their datasets' column and row names to suit their own projects, and stored in non-optimal locations that can cause damage to the data. With so many different people working on a single dataset and using different methods for adding data, the resulting datasets in many organizations are unsurprisingly riddled with errors and gaps. And we cannot expect a machine to know where the errors lie or how to fix inconsistencies in information.

So it is our job to prepare the data in such a way that it can be comprehended – and correctly analysed – by a machine.

With great power comes great responsibility

Data preparation (also known as 'data wrangling') is a complex component of the entire process and, as it comprises a number of tasks that can only be completed manually, this stage normally takes the most amount of time.[1] The reason behind this close attention to data preparation is that, if the raw data is not first structured properly in the dataset, then the later stages of the process will either not work at all or, even worse, will give us inaccurate predictions and/or incorrect results. This can spell disaster for you and your company, and at the very worst end of the scale, neglect of this stage can result in firings and, in the case of freelance work, even lawsuits.

It is not my intention to scare you – I simply mean to show you how essential it is to prepare our data. Surprisingly, despite its importance, this is where I have found a serious gap in the educational materials on data science, which largely focus on the later stages of the process: analysing and visualizing. These books and courses use datasets that have already been prepared. But while this approach may be fine if you're just getting to grips with the discipline, paying no attention to preparation means that you are effectively only learning the cosmetic ways to work with data.

Working only with datasets from educational courses will merely show you data that has been cleaned up to fit the case example. But in the real world, data is often dirty, messy and corrupt, and without knowing the causes and symptoms of dirty data, we cannot adequately complete our project. If you do not prepare your data, when you get out into the real world on your first project, and your algorithm inevitably returns 'missing data' errors, or 'text qualifier' errors, or 'division by zero', your project will grind to a halt.

How do we know, then, that our data has been sufficiently prepared? Quite simply, once we have ensured that it is suitable for our data analysis stage. It must:

- be in the right format;
- be free from errors; and
- have all gaps and anomalies accounted for.

A common phrase that data scientists use is 'garbage in, garbage out', which means if you put unclean data into an algorithm, you will only get nonsensical results, making your analyses useless. It is true that a number of practitioners struggle with this step, but that is only because they don't have a framework to follow. This usually leads to an unstructured, undocumented approach and means they have to reinvent the wheel every time they prepare their data; an ineffective and time-consuming approach in the long run.

So, let's get started with the process of preparation.

CASE STUDY Ubisoft – making the case for data preparation

Ulf Morys is Finance Director at the German branch of Ubisoft, a game design, development and distribution company that has created popular game franchises from *Assassin's Creed* to *Far Cry*. Ulf oversees a distribution subsidiary, which distributes Ubisoft's video games in the area of Germany, Switzerland and Austria (GSA) and is also responsible for the financial components of the company's operations in central Europe.

Ubisoft had historically had its data used solely by the production team for in-game analytics and monetization. Until Ulf changed matters, finance did not number among its strategic areas for data science.[2] But ignoring the improvements that data science makes can be a costly oversight, and having prior experience of leveraging data to make important business decisions (in his previous job, Ulf saved his company $40 million in a merger thanks to his attention to the data) meant that he knew that a deliberate strategy for using company data was essential.

He says, crucially:

Preparing data doesn't add more data, it just improves the way you look at it. It's like that scene in the film *The Wizard of Oz* when Dorothy opens the door of her house to the kingdom of Oz and the black and white world of Kansas is replaced with Technicolor. There's nothing fundamentally different to the way the story functions on a technical level, and yet everything has changed. It has been cleaned up.

(SuperDataScience, 2016)

To better understand how Ubisoft in particular benefited from data preparation, Ulf turned to Ubisoft's production team, who had been collecting data from its thousands of online gamers for years, from the length of time the game was played and the length of time that it took to complete individual levels, to what the player did in the game and where they failed on the game map. Ulf found that they were using this past data to assess the likelihood that customers would purchase in-game products through a 'freemium model'.[3] Having the data to hand not only helped Ubisoft to find out the purchasing patterns of its core customers but also to identify the behaviours that could be applied to future players.

Talking to his team about the grand steps the production team were making thanks to data science turned their heads to the idea. During a financial strategy meeting, Ulf's team mapped out the sources of all Ubisoft's available data and what was missing from the picture, which offered something tangible from which colleagues could bounce off their ideas. 'Very simply,' says Ulf, 'if you don't know something is there, you can't ask questions of it' (SuperDataScience, 2016).

The gaps showed what key data they needed to gather from their customers (store dimensions, space provided for selling video games, attitudes of typical buyers to video games and consumer feelings about Ubisoft's output) before they could make meaningful analyses. Ulf says:

> It was evident why we weren't taking a more systematic approach to our customers: *we didn't have the data*. When I went to our sales department, I was told which of our customers were good based on their own insider knowledge. But that knowledge hadn't been collected systematically. Getting the data – the hard facts – was absolutely necessary.
>
> (SuperDataScience, 2016)

Gathering that information for 2,000 stores enabled Ulf to prepare statistically relevant data that would finally be suitable for analysis. This helped Ubisoft to better target its customers in a way that had not been possible before.

Preparing your data for a journey

In order to get our raw data (information that has not been prepared) to respond to analysis, we first have to prepare it. The method for doing so comprises just three stages:

1 **Extract** the data from its sources;

2 **Transform** the data into a comprehensible language for access in a relational database;

3 **Load** the data into the end source.

This process is known as ETL, and it will help us to gather our data into a suitable format in our end source – known as the 'warehouse' – which can be accessed and analysed in the later stages of the Data Science Process. A data warehouse stores otherwise disparate data in a single system. Oftentimes, it will comprise relational databases.

What is a relational database?

Relational databases allow us to examine relational data across them. In this type of database, the relationships *between* the units of information across datasets matter.

The datasets in a relational database are linked by columns that share the same name. For example, if multiple datasets contained columns with the header 'Country', the data from those columns could be compared across them in a relational database. The benefit of having this type of database is that they facilitate the methods of analysis and visualization that are required to derive insights, where data can be examined across multiple sets without the need for individual extraction.

Perhaps the best way to illustrate how advantageous a relational database can be is to compare it to Excel, which is frequently used by people unaccustomed to working with databases:

1 **It maintains integrity.** Every cell in Excel is individual; there are no limitations to the types of values that you can place into them. You can add dates or text, for example, underneath phone numbers or monetary values, and Excel will be perfectly happy. A relational database will rap you over the wrist for such negligence. In a database, columns have predefined types, which means that a column that has been set up to accept dates will not accept any value that does not fit the date format. Databases, then, will keep an eye on the process for you, querying any values that do not match those predefined by the column.

2 **It combines datasets.** Combining datasets within a relational database is easy; it is much harder to do in Excel. Relational databases have been designed for that purpose, and that makes it easy to create new datasets from combining common values across the relational database. All that is required of you is the ability to execute a simple command. As combining tables is not a primary function of Excel,[4] an advanced knowledge of programming is required to shoehorn your data into a single table.

3 **It is scalable.** Relational databases have been especially designed for scalability; as they combine datasets, it is expected that they must be able to cope with a large number of informational units. That means – regardless of whether you have five or five billion rows – your relational database is unlikely to crash at a crucial moment. Excel is far more limited in this capacity, and as your dataset grows, the software's performance will deteriorate as it struggles to cope with the overload.

The data cleanse

We know that in the real world, data is more likely to come to us dirty, but there is some disagreement among practitioners as to how and when data should be cleaned. Some people clean before they transform, and others only once they have loaded it into the new database. My preference is to clean the data at *each stage* of the ETL process – it might seem an inefficient use of your time but I have found this to be the best way to protect yourself against obstacles further on. Unfortunately, data preparation is always going to be time-consuming, but the more due diligence you take in this stage, the more you will speed up the Data Science Process as a whole.

1 Extract your data

We need to extract data in the first instance 1) to ensure that we are not altering the original source in any way, and 2) because the data that we want to analyse is often stored across a number of different locations. Some examples of possible locations are:

- a database;
- an Excel spreadsheet;
- a website;
- Twitter;
- a .csv file;
- paper reports.

If we are using data from multiple sources, then we will have to extract it into a single database or warehouse in order for our analyses to work. But it is not always easy to extract from locations that use formatting particular to that system – Excel is one such culprit, to which we will return later on in this chapter.

.csv files

You will get to know these types of files quite intimately as a data scientist. They are the simplest type of raw files of data – completely stripped of any formatting – which makes them accessible to any number of programs into which we may want to import them. In .csv files, rows are placed on new lines, and columns are separated by commas in each line. Hence the abbreviation, which stands for 'comma separated values'.

The beauty of working with raw files is that you will never lose or corrupt information when you load your dataset into a program. This is why they are the standard for most practitioners.

Why it's important to extract data even if it is only in one location

Technically, you *could* analyse the data directly within its storage facility (the original database, an Excel spreadsheet and so on). While it is not recommended, this method is acceptable for making quick calculations, such as computing the sum of a column of values in Excel. However, for serious data science projects, carrying out data tasks within its original storage facility is a huge red flag. In doing so, you might accidentally modify the raw data, thereby jeopardizing your work.

And this is the *best-case* scenario, as it only affects you and your individual project. Working within the storage facility rather than extracting the original data to a test database leaves it vulnerable to user damage, and your work may even end up crashing the internal systems of your institution. That should give any data scientist pause when they start working with an organization's data. They are entrusting us with important if not essential company information, so we must ensure that we leave the data just as it was when we started on the project.

Software for extracting data

There are a couple of exceptional free-to-use programs for extracting and reading data that are sure to wean you off any bad habits as have often been formed by Excel users. These programs work well with data that is in a raw .csv file format.[5]

Although it can take time, data can in most cases be stripped down to a raw .csv file. And if you're working for a large organization where you have to request data extracts, then good news: the data will most likely be given to you in a .csv format anyway.

Notepad++ This is my go-to tool when I want to look at the data I have extracted. Among other features it is a powerful editor for viewing .csv files, and it is much more user-friendly than the notepad software that comes as standard with Windows. Notepad++ also has a few other significant advantages:

- row numbering, enabling you to navigate through your files and keep tabs on where potential errors might be found;

- a search and replace feature, which enables you to quickly find values or text that you don't want in the dataset and amend them;

- it has been designed for purpose, which means that you can be confident it will not inadvertently modify your data as will other spreadsheet software;

- while the Notepad software that comes with Windows generally has trouble dealing with large files, Notepad++ can open files up to 2 GB.

EditPad Lite   EditPad Lite is a program that is free for personal use. It offers similar features to Notepad++, with one major benefit: although both work well with files that are under 2 GB, I have noticed that Notepad++ can sometimes struggle with datasets at the top end of this file size. As a result, I have found EditPad Lite to perform much better with my larger files. If you find that you are overworking Notepad++ with your files, consider EditPad Lite.

2 Transform your data

You cannot simply dump your data from its original source directly into a data warehouse. Not unless you *want* to work with a messy dataset. By transforming your data, you can reformat the information you plan to use into a language that will suit your objectives.

In a broad sense, the transformation step includes alterations such as joining, splitting and aggregating data. These are functions that allow us to create derived tables to better suit the problem at hand. But the most important function of transformation is data cleaning – and that's what we will focus on.

In this step, we must identify and manage any errors in our original database, which in the real world will often run the gamut from formatting inconsistencies, through outliers, to significant gaps in information. But to do so, we first have to understand what we are looking for. So, how can we identify dirty data?

Dirty data

Dirty data is information that is either incorrect, corrupt or missing. These three qualifiers are due to the following factors.

Incorrect data In these instances, information has been (partially or completely) incorrectly added to the database (eg inputting a currency value into a date cell). Sometimes, we will know that data is incorrect. It may be evident when there is a mismatch between columns.

For example, if we had a single row, where the country cell was 'France' and the city cell was 'Rome', we would know that one was incorrect. We may also be able to identify incorrect data by simply using our common sense – we would know that an entry in a date of birth column that has been given as '12/41/2001' simply cannot be correct.

Corrupt data Corrupt data refers to information that may originally have been correct in the dataset but is now mangled. Information can become corrupted in different ways. Contributing factors can include if the database to which it belongs has been physically damaged, if it has been altered by another software or if it has been previously extracted in unadvisable ways. Sometimes, data can simply become corrupted due to transfer to a database that does not support the format it had in the previous storage.

Missing data Missing data either occurs when no information is available for a given cell, or when the person responsible for inserting the data has neglected to add it into the cell. Missing data is a common topic in data science, and it is most likely to occur because of human error.

What can happen when we don't deal with missing data

We should always be aware of any gaps in our information. Below, you'll see a real-life example of data that we have extracted from an Excel spreadsheet into a .csv file that shows dividend pay-outs, organized by year.

5.1

```
487  19-May-15,533.98,540.66,533.04,537.36,537.36,1966900
488  18-May-15,532.01,534.82,528.85,532.3,532.3,2003400
489  15-May-15,539.18,539.27,530.38,533.85,533.85,1971300
490  14-May-15,533.77,539,532.41,538.4,538.4,1403900
491  13-May-15,530.56,534.32,528.66,529.62,529.62,1252300
492  12-May-15,531.6,533.21,525.26,529.04,529.04,1634200
493  11-May-15,538.37,541.98,535.4,535.7,535.7,905300
494  08-May-15,536.65,541.15,525,538.22,538.22,1527600
495  07-May-15,523.99,533.46,521.75,530.7,530.7,1546300
496  06-May-15,531.24,532.38,521.09,524.22,524.22,1567000
497  05-May-15,538.21,539.74,530.39,530.8,530.8,1383100
498  04-May-15,538.53,544.07,535.06,540.78,540.78,1308000
499  01-May-15,538.43,539.54,532.1,537.9,537.9,1768200
500  30-Apr-15,547.87,548.59,535.05,537.34,537.34,2082200
501  29-Apr-15,550.47,553.68,546.91,549.08,549.08,1698800
502  28-Apr-15,554.64,556.02,550.37,553.68,553.68,1491000
503  27-Apr-15,563.39,565.95,553.2,555.37,555.37,2398000
504  26-Apr-15,10000000/10000000 Stock Split,,,,
505  24-Apr-15,564.55,569.58,555.72,563.51,563.51,4932500
506  23-Apr-15,539.52,549.45,538.75,545.5,545.5,4184800
507  22-Apr-15,532.94,539.6,530.29,537.89,537.89,1593500
508  21-Apr-15,536.04,537.91,532.21,532.51,532.51,1844700
509  20-Apr-15,524.16,534.62,523.06,533.91,533.91,1679200
510  17-Apr-15,527.21,528.39,519.58,522.62,522.62,2151800
511  16-Apr-15,528.45,534.12,528.16,532.34,532.34,1299800
512  15-Apr-15,527.25,533.27,521.79,531.07,531.07,2318800
513  14-Apr-15,534.78,536.1,526.65,528.94,528.94,2604100
```

As you can see from the commas enclosing no information, five of the columns at the highlighted row **504 (26-Apr-15)** have missing fields of data.

We have been lucky in this instance that the missing columns have survived the extraction – oftentimes, the missing data values are not defined by commas. What this would mean is that when we plug the dataset into an algorithm, it would recalibrate our data incorrectly, pushing the data in the row below up to fit the number of columns required in the dataset. In the above example, this would mean that the date 24-Apr-15 would be brought up to the column directly to the right of the '10000000/10000000 Stock Split' value.

Missing data in this way can cause us significant trouble in the analysis stage if we don't catch the problem beforehand. I have known some newbie data scientists who will check the top 100 rows of their dataset, but this is a rookie mistake – if there are errors in the data, you are much more likely to see them at the end of the dataset because the errors will shift information.

Fixing corrupt data

To fix corrupt data so that it can be read by a machine, we can first try the following:

- re-extract it from its original file to see if something has corrupted the file during the first extraction;

- talk to the person in charge of the data to see if they can cast light on what the actual data should be; or

- exclude the rows that contain corrupt data from your analysis.[6]

Approaching people

If you find yourself in a situation where you are missing data and need to retrace your steps to obtain additional input before the project can progress, here are three ways in which you can facilitate the process:

- Always be courteous to the people who are giving you data. Some people may find data collection frustrating and will let that show in their communication, but try to stay neutral. Remember that they are not data scientists, and may not take the same joy in the process of gathering data as you! Explain to them that every data-driven project will have different outcomes, and that each project requires different types of data. You may need to approach the team responsible for your datasets multiple times, so be friendly and get them on your side.

- Make sure that anyone you speak to fully understands the problem that you are trying to solve, as well as their role in combating it. Seeing the bigger picture will help your colleagues be more patient with your requests.

- Keep a list of the company's data assets with you at all times. Having this to hand means that when you're off on the hunt for new data, you will be able to cross-check what the organization already has and reduce the likelihood of you collecting duplicates. When you list the data assets, I recommend recording the names of the data sources as well as the databases' columns and their descriptors.

Fixing missing data

If we cannot resolve our problem by using any one of these methods, then we must consider our data as missing. There are various methods for resolving the problem of missing fields in spreadsheets:

- **Predict the missing data with 100 per cent accuracy.** We can do this for information that we can derive from other data. For example, say we have a spreadsheet with customer location data that contains column values for both 'State' and 'City'; the entry for State is missing but the

City entry is 'Salt Lake City'. Then we can be certain that the state is 'Utah'.[7] It is also possible to derive a missing value based on more than one value, for example, to derive a profit value from both revenue and expenses values. Bear in mind that when we are inputting information in both examples, we are doing so on the assumption that there were no errors in the collection of the data.

- **Leave the record as it is.** In this scenario, you would simply leave the cell with no data empty. This is most useful when specific fields have no bearing on our analysis and therefore can be left out of our testing, but it can also be used if we are planning to use a method that isn't significantly affected by missing data (ie methods that can use averaged values) or if we use a software package that can deal appropriately with this lack of information. In cases where you leave the record as it is, I would recommend keeping notes of where your data contains gaps, so that any later anomalies can be accounted for.

- **Remove the record entirely.** Sometimes, the data that is missing would have been critical to our analysis. In these instances, our only option is to remove the entire row of data from our analysis, as the missing information makes them unable to contribute. Obviously, the major drawback in this case is that our results will become less significant as the sample has decreased. So this approach is likely to work best with large datasets, where the omission of a single row will not greatly affect the dataset's statistical significance.

- **Replace the missing data with the mean/median value.** This is a popular approach for columns that contain numerical information, as it allows us to arbitrarily fill any gaps without tampering too significantly with our dataset. To calculate the mean, we add all of the values together and divide that total by the number of values. To calculate the median, we find the sequential middle value in our data range (if there are an uneven number of values, just add the two middle numbers and divide that total by two). Calculating the median rather than the mean is usually preferable, because the former is less affected by outliers, which means that extreme values either side of the median range will not skew our results.

- **Fill in by exploring correlations and similarities.** This approach is again dependent on your missing data value being numerical, and it requires the use of models to predict what the missing values might have been. For instance, we could use a predictive algorithm (such as K-nearest neighbours, which we will discuss in Chapter 6) to forecast the missing data based on existing similarities among records in your dataset.

- **Introduce a dummy variable for missing data.** This requires adding a column to our dataset: wherever we find missing values in the dataset, we allocate a 'yes' value to it – and when it is not missing we give it a 'no' value. We can then explore how the variable correlates with other values in our analysis, and so retrospectively consider the implications of why this data might be missing.

Dealing with outliers

Let's say that we are working for a company selling phone accessories and we want to find the average number of units that we have sold of one of our phone cases to each of our distributors. We have been in business for years, and so our datasets are large. The person responsible for inputting these values into our database was having a bad day, and instead of inputting the number of product units into the product column, they put the distributor's telephone number. That error would abnormally raise our average in this column (and would mean that a single distributor has purchased at least 100 million units!).

If we were to analyse that record on its own, we would probably notice the error. But if we simply calculated the average without looking at the data, our report would be skewed by that outlier – and that would make the report unusable.

Nevertheless, it's important to distinguish between outliers that can be attributed to erroneous information and outliers that are correct but that fall outside the normal range of values. The value for a distributor that *did* purchase 100 million units of your product will still be an outlier, as the value is higher than the normative number of units purchased.

Many datasets will have outliers – our job is to understand where they are and to ensure that they do not unfairly skew our reports. This will largely depend on the type of analysis that we want to carry out. For example, if we wanted to work out for a publishing house the average number of units sold to book stores around the world, and we know that the outlier was an exceptional purchase order, we might choose to remove the record even though it's valid.

It is possible to find outliers in your dataset without searching for them manually, by generating a distribution curve (also known as a bell curve for normal distributions) from your column values. Distribution curves graphically depict the most probable value or event from your data by way of their apex, and it is simple enough to create them directly, even in Excel.[8] Once you have created your distribution curve, you can identify the values that fall outside the normal range.

CASE STUDY Applied approaches to dealing with dirty data

We have been given a dataset from an imaginary venture capital fund that is looking at the overall growth of start-ups in the United States. As the data gatherer was not affiliated with the start-ups, some information was missing, as it was either not publicly available or the start-ups were unwilling to provide that level of information.

5.2

ID	Name	Industry	Inception	Employees	State	City	Revenue	Expenses	Profit	Growth
1	Over-Hex	Software	2006	25	TN	Franklin	$9,684,527	1,130,700 Dollars	8553827	19%
2	Unimattax	IT Services	2009	38		Kirill:	$14,016,543	804,035 Dollars	13212508	20%
3	Greenfax	Retail	2012			Proxy with Industry Median	$9,746,272	1,044,375 Dollars	8701897	16%
4	Blacklane	IT Services	2011	66			$15,359,369	4,631,808 Dollars	10727561	19%
5	Yearflex	Software	2013	45			$8,567,910	4,374,841 Dollars	4193069	19%
6	Indigoplanet	IT Services	2013	60			$12,805,452	4,626,275 Dollars	8179177	22%
7	Treslam	Financial Services	2009	116	MO	Clayton	$5,387,489	2,127,984 Dollars	3259485	17%
8	Rednimdox	Construction	2013	73	NY	Woodside				
9	Lamtone	IT Services	2009	55	CA	San Ramon	$11,757,018	6,482,465 Dollars	5274553	30%
10	Stripfind	Financial Services	2010	25	FL	Boca Raton	$12,329,371	916,455 Dollars	11412916	20%
11	Canecorporation	Health	2012	6		New York	$10,597,009	7,591,189 Dollars	3005820	7%
12	Mattouch	IT Services	2013	6	WA	Bellevue	$14,026,934	7,429,377 Dollars	6597557	26%
13	Techdrill	Health	2009	9	MS	Flowood	$10,573,990	7,435,363 Dollars	3138627	8%
14	Techline		2006	65	CA	San Ramon	$13,898,119	5,470,303 Dollars	8427816	23%
15	Cityace		2010	25	CO	Louisville	$9,254,614	6,249,498 Dollars	3005116	6%
16	Kayelectronics	Health	2009	687	NC	Clayton	$9,451,943	3,878,113 Dollars	5573830	4%
17	Ganzlax	IT Services	2011	75	NJ	Iselin	$14,001,180		11901180	18%
18	Trantraxalax	Government Services	2011	35	VA	Suffolk	$11,088,336	5,635,276 Dollars	5453060	7%
19	E-Zim	Retail	2008	320	OH	Monroe	$10,746,451	4,762,319 Dollars	5984132	13%
20	Dalfase	Software	2011	78	NC	Durham	$10,410,628	6,196,409 Dollars	4214219	17%
21	Hotlane	Government Services	2012	87	AL	Huntsville	$7,976,332	5,666,574 Dollars	2291758	2%
22	Lathotline	Health		103	VA	McLean	$9,418,303	7,567,233 Dollars	1851070	2%
23	Lambam	IT Services	2012	210	SC	Columbia	$11,950,148	4,365,512 Dollars	7584636	20%
24	Quozap	Software	2004	21	NJ	Collingswood	$8,304,480	7,019,973 Dollars	1284507	20%
25	Tampware	Construction	2011	13	TX	Houston	$9,785,982	2,910,756 Dollars	6875226	11%
26	Dalthow	Health	2000	20	GA	Dacula	$10,800,718	7,731,820 Dollars	3068898	7%
27	Ranktech	Government Services	2010	607	FL	Tampa	$10,515,557	7,439,384 Dollars	3076173	8%
28	Unadex	Software	2013	280	NC	Cary	$5,231,275	2,388,521 Dollars	2842754	19%

As you can see, various types of information are missing across our columns, and sometimes multiple values are empty in a single row. Let's put the methods for fixing missing data into practice. Return to the methods given above and consider how you might resolve the problem of missing data yourself before reading the answers below.

Employees

Replace the missing data with the mean/median value. This is a numerical value, and so we can proxy any of the missing employee values with the overall or industry median for that column. (The industry median is preferable as it will provide a like-for-like figure.)

Industry

Leave the record as it is *or* **predict the missing data with 100 per cent accuracy** *or* **remove the record entirely**. It should be relatively easy to find out to which industry the company belongs by simply investigating what it does and taking your cues from there. But our choice depends on how important industry is to our analysis. If industry is important, and we cannot research it, we must remove the record from the analysis.

Inception

Leave the record as it is *or* predict the missing data with 100 per cent accuracy *or* remove the record entirely. Even though inception is a number, it is not a numerical value (you cannot perform arithmetic operations with it). For that reason, we cannot proxy it with an average, and so if we cannot find out when the company was established, then we must accept it as missing.

State

Leave the record as it is *or* predict the missing data with 100 per cent accuracy *or* remove the record entirely. In the example given above, we can predict the missing data with 100 per cent certainty. But we must be careful that we are being accurate: for values where a city name can belong to more than one state, we will not be able to predict the data with 100 per cent accuracy and so must decide how important the data is to our analysis.

Expenses

Predict the missing data with 100 per cent accuracy. This is an easy one; we can calculate expenses by simply subtracting profit from revenue.

Revenue, expenses and profit, growth

Replace the missing data with the mean/median value. Calculating this block of missing values requires taking more than one step. We need to first proxy our growth revenue and expenses by using the industries' medians, and then we can calculate the profit as the difference between revenue and expenses.

Transforming data from MS Excel

Excel tries to make things easier by automatically reformatting certain values. This can lead to various hiccups during the ETL process, and as this program is so frequently used to store data, I will give special attention to it here. One common complaint I have heard from Excel users is the program's insistence on converting long numerical values (such as phone and credit card numbers) into a scientific formula.[9] And that's not the worst of it. Excel can also convert dates and monetary amounts into a single format that accords to your computer's regional settings. While this may be convenient for single spreadsheets which are often used for business intelligence, those kinds of automations will only end up doing you a disfavour in data science, as Excel's formatting does not translate well into a database. And if we are dealing with a lot of data, unpicking all of the instances that Excel has altered can be time-consuming.

If we do not transform the data from Excel into a .csv file, then we will only be presented with problems further down the line. While it may be possible to restore dates that have been altered, it is near impossible to restore credit card numbers if they have been changed to scientific formulae. Just imagine the consequences for an organization that loses its customers' credit card numbers, especially if you had been working on the only copy of the file.

Some of the most common issues are to do with dates and currency, as these values are not international and are therefore susceptible to our machines' regional settings.

Date formats The formatting of dates will differ depending on our geographic region, and Excel has been programmed to display the date that accords to our computer's regional settings. Most countries use a little-endian date format that begins with the day, followed by the month and the year (dd/mm/yyyy). In the United States, however, the date format begins with the month, followed by the day and year (mm/dd/yyyy). We need to ensure that we are working with a consistent date format in our database.

How to fix them The best method to prevent Excel from making changes to our records is to change all of our date formats to yyyy-mm-dd, as this is the unambiguous international standard that is also not subject to regional rules. In Excel, select the column that you want to fix, right-click, and select 'Format Cells'. In the Category window, select 'Date'. In the 'Type' window you should see the yyyy-mm-dd format. Select that and then click 'OK'. Your dates will have been reformatted.

Currency formats Currency will also depend on our computer's regional settings. In these cases, it is not only necessary to consider the symbol of currency but also the decimal marks that are being used. Symbols of currency should be completely stripped from your data as they will otherwise be read as text. Countries use different decimal marks for their currency – indicated either by a point (eg £30.00 in the UK) or a comma (eg €30,00 in Germany).

Take note that this affects both the decimal place *and* the thousands separator. The sum of £30,000 would be read as thirty thousand pounds in countries such as Australia that use the comma to indicate thousands, but it may be read as thirty pounds in countries such as Sweden that use the comma to indicate decimal places. Databases function with the decimal point system, and any commas, including thousands separators, must be stripped from your data.

How to fix them We want to strip our numbers of symbols and commas. If your country uses a decimal comma system, you must first change the regional settings of your computer to make sure the comma is changed to a dot. Select the column, right-click it and select 'Format Cells'. In the 'Category' window, select 'Currency'. Uncheck the 'Use 1000 separator' box to ensure that no commas will be used, choose 'None' from the 'Symbol' dropdown box and select '2' as the number of decimal places. That will remove the commas and symbols from our data.

3 Load your data

Once we have transformed our data into the format we need, we can load our data into our end target: the warehouse. Once this process is complete, we should manually look through our data one last time before we run it through a machine algorithm, to be absolutely certain that we are not working with underprepared data.

Quality assurance after the load

Loading the data into a warehouse can sometimes cause problems. You may have missed cleaning up some of the dirty data in the previous stage, or some of the data may have simply been loaded incorrectly. For that reason, you must learn to double-check your data within the warehouse.

The following are the quality assurance (QA) checks that you should always make at this stage:

- **Count the number of rows** that you have in your final dataset and compare it to the initial dataset. If it is different, return to the initial dataset to find out what happened. Unfortunately, sometimes the quickest way to check is just by looking at it, and this will mean scrolling through the data line by line. The quickest way to do this is to go from the bottom up rather than the top down, because any errors in data are likely to carry downwards.

- **Check the columns for skewness.** To completely safeguard yourself against problems in the analysis stage, check both the top 100 and the bottom 100 rows.

- **Check the columns that are susceptible to corruption.** This usually refers to dates and balances, as we have earlier established that they are the most prone to error.

- **Check text values.** If we have free-form text values from surveys where respondents have typed up answers to an open-ended question, then uploading this kind of text to a database can be tricky. Usually, databases will limit the maximum number of letters in a column. That might result in cutting off an answer, which leaves our data as missing or can even sometimes affect the rest of the dataset. Free-form text can also contain symbols that databases either cannot recognize or misuse because they are qualifier symbols such as quotation marks.

Think (again) like a consultant

Quality assurance is the most important part of data preparation and, as it comes right at the end of the process, be careful not to lose steam at this stage. I was lucky to enter into the field of data science through the world of consulting, which pays great diligence to QA. With quality assurance, work is peer reviewed. The numbers need to add up, and results have to make sense. Don't be afraid of this stage – it's not designed to trip you up, it is there to help protect you from making errors later on in the process.

Those companies that have worked with data for a while have set up rigorous, predetermined procedures that data scientists must follow to the letter before any analysis can be carried out. Some companies will even have consultants to check your process, and expect them to take a lot of time with this step. Delivering an incorrect result will at the very least cost money and, in the worst case, may severely affect business operations. That is why it is so important to ensure that QA is carried out before you move on to the next step.

Now that you have a beautiful warehouse of squeaky-clean data, and you know the question or series of questions that you want to pose to it, you can finally move on to my favourite part: the analysis.

Reference

SuperDataScience (2016) SDS 008: data science in computer games, learning to learn and a 40m euro case study with Ulf Morys [Podcast] 28 October [Online] www.superdatascience.com/8 [accessed 05.06.17]

Notes

1 Opinions differ among data scientists, but most will attribute 60–80 per cent of project time to the data preparation stage.

2 Many large organizations that have been collecting data for years suffer from an institutional blindness to data science – without knowing that data must be prepared before it can be analysed, their information is unusable.

3 A game that is downloaded for free but that sells in-game items for players who want to advance more quickly in the game.

4 Tabs are used for different tables, but it can be tricky to combine values across them.

5 As you progress in your career as a data scientist you will learn to work with various data storage facilities. We are talking about .csv files here because they are the most common and versatile and are a good place to get started.

6 Your decision will ultimately depend on whether or not you need the data, and that can easily be answered if you have taken the time to identify the question in Stage 1 of the Data Science Process.

7 Be careful with fields like this. There is only one Salt Lake City in the United States, but sometimes you will find more than one city with the same name.

8 MS Office versions vary. Typing 'distribution curve' into Excel's Help menu will return the results you need to generate a curve.

9 For example, 4556919574658621 would be shown as 4.55692E+15.

Data analysis   06
Part 1

When explaining the five principles of data science to those new to the concept, the analytics stage is where practitioners tend to lose their audience. But this has more to do with psychology than anything else: an irrational fear of the word 'analytics' will automatically make many feel that they are starting out on the back foot.

What I want to do in the next two chapters, rather than simply explain how individual algorithms work, is to also highlight the *context* in which data scientists use them. In contrast to handbooks that detail the theoretical intricacies of an algorithm, I have found a contextual approach to be far more suitable for all types of learners, regardless of their current ability.

In the previous two chapters, we looked at 1) how we might approach a task concerning data and 2) how to prepare this data for analysis. Now we are finally ready to proceed to analysing the data. This stage really *is* plug and play – the hardest part of the Data Science Process is to understand the complexity of the problem and take into account its variables. Once we have understood the task and the questions we need to pose to it, applying the algorithm to answer those questions should be a piece of cake.

Don't skip this step

Even if you think that you do not have the necessary tools or mathematical ability, do not let yourself be tempted to skip the next two chapters, thinking you can simply hire someone to do the analysis legwork for you. A grounding in mathematics or another science subject may be beneficial at this point but it is not compulsory. And even though you can find success simply by knowing how to present, prepare and gather data, we still need at least to understand every stage of the process in order to become professional data scientists.

The most basic algorithms used in data analytics that we will discuss in Chapters 6 and 7 broadly fall into three groups:[1]

- classification;
- clustering;
- reinforcement learning.

By using these algorithms, we can look into how we might begin to drill down into the data, developing insights that may not have been readily apparent through our visual analysis. The algorithms that we will use in this chapter fall under the first two categories: classification and clustering. While it is important to note that these are only two branches of analytics, classification and clustering comprise relatively simple and commonly used algorithms that will get you working with data quickly.

Information vs mathematics in data science

Most of the algorithms we discuss in this book are driven by complex mathematics and statistics. Having said that, you will notice a lack of mathematical formulae to accompany them. This may cause alarm – can we truly understand an algorithm if we don't delve into its nuts and bolts?

My analogy for answering this question is to imagine driving a car. Have you ever taken a car apart? Can you tell your camshafts from your crankshafts? How does a vehicle's cruise control actually function? Most of us don't know all about the technical operation of the cars we drive. And yet almost all of us do drive them. Frequently. This is the difference between mathematics and intuition.

Mathematics pulls an algorithm apart to understand exactly how it works and why. There's nothing wrong with that, and there will be situations when you need this level of detail. But for the most part, when working as a data scientist, this will not be necessary. Just as a basic understanding of a car's pedals and steering will get you from A to B, so will knowledge of the intuition behind analytics models in data science enable you to bring value to your given task.

If this gives you some relief, then I've done my job. All too often, I find that data science is overcomplicated. My aim is to prove to you that, just as anyone can drive a car, anyone can be a data scientist.

Classification and clustering

Let us first distinguish between these two categories. Put simply, we use classification when we already know the groups into which we want an analysis to place our data, and we use clustering when we *do not* know what the groups will be, in terms of either number or name. For example, if we wanted to run an analysis on survey responses to a yes/no question, then we would use a classification algorithm because we know what the resulting two groups will be: Yes and No. Alternatively, if we wanted to assess respondents of the same survey based on their age and distance from our company's closest store, we would use clustering, because the resulting groups that will be useful to us cannot be precisely defined in advance (unless we have already conducted this analysis previously).

Let's say an airline company calls upon us to learn whether their customers will or will not stop using their services (known as 'customer churn'). As the company has collected data on customer responses and movements (flying frequency, travel destination, transport class, use of inflight services, baggage requests), we can use these variables to identify behaviours which would be the most telling of a customer's intent to leave the airline. In this case, we would try to use these factors to split the customers into two groups: Group 1 comprises customers who are likely to stop using the airline, while Group 2 contains customers who are likely to continue using the airline. For this reason, we would use classification because we are *classifying* customers into one of two groups.

And classification is where we will begin.

Classification

Knowing the groups into which our data will fall *before* we carry out our analysis makes classification rather easier than clustering techniques. The customers in the example given above can be observed through data recorded about them – this might include their usual flight routes, spending capacity, membership tier in the airline frequent flyer programme and even seating preference. These descriptive features may seem expansive, but they are just tools. The central aim of the task is to classify customers into *only one of two* groups – the company is not interested in finding out anything else at this point.

With this kind of data analysis, it is essential that we also have prior data through which we can observe the characteristics in which we are interested. This is the only way in which we can create a classification algorithm – through our case history.

The following classification algorithms have been organized in order of difficulty. We will begin with decision trees, as many readers will already be familiar with flowcharts – they both use the same principle of splitting information into individual steps before presenting the participant with a final response. Random forest regression is simply an expansion of the decision trees algorithm, for it uses multiple decision trees for individual components of a dataset in order to provide more accurate results. Both the K-nearest neighbours and Naive Bayes algorithms classify data points into groups according to their relative distance from each other, as measured by each record's variables. The difference between the two will become apparent in their individual sections. We end our foray into classification with logistic regression, which is *the* algorithm to use when we want to examine the likelihood of an event occurring.

When you read through these algorithms, bear in mind my initial advice to learn *through intuition*: focus on understanding the *objective* of each algorithm and try to see the *purpose* behind the underlying steps. Take the time to digest each of them – slow and steady really does win the race here.

Decision trees

A decision tree functions similarly to a flowchart. It runs tests on individual attributes in your dataset in order to determine the possible outcomes and continues to add results as further tests are run, only stopping when all outcomes have been exhausted.

The leaves of our decision trees give us all the possible answers to all the questions that we can pose to our data. We have all at some point taken a magazine quiz that asks you to answer a series of 'yes or no' questions, before disclosing what personality type you are, or whether you're a Leonard or a Sheldon, or how you really feel about yoghurt – in these cases, the questions are our branches and the outcomes are our leaves.

In the world of business, decision trees can be used to classify, say, groups of customers. Think back to the Ubisoft case study in Chapter 5: if the games company's production team had gathered information about a potential new subscriber, then they could use a decision tree to test whether or not they would be likely to become a member based on the company's dataset of current subscribers. A decision tree algorithm would split the data from the games company into leaves that showed clear differences between values such as time spent playing and age, and classify the new data into one of the outcomes we have defined – in this case, 'beneficial' or 'not beneficial' to the company.

How decision trees work

Let's test this problem here. As we have information about our gamers' average time played and their age, we can use a decision tree classification to make an informed decision about them. This means we first need to have the following data on our games company's current subscribers: total time spent playing our games in the past month and age.[2]

We have created a scatter plot with lots of data points based on age (X1) and time spent gaming in hours (X2).

6.1

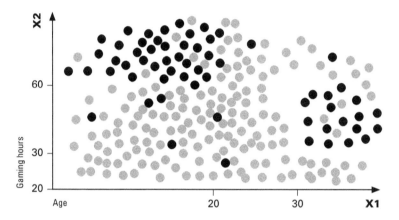

They grey points represent users who didn't become members; the black points represent those who did. If we were to run a decision tree classification algorithm, the scatter plot would be split into leaves, as determined by the algorithm.

6.2

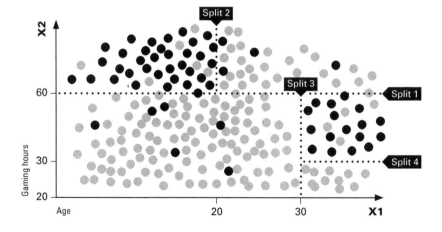

As we can see, Split 1 has divided the data at X2 = 60, Split 2 has divided the data at X1 = 20 and so on. The algorithm has now grouped our data points into leaves that add value to our classification, and it stops once the optimal number of leaves has been created. This optimal number is reached when splitting the data any further would make the leaves' outcome statistically insignificant.

Steps to the decision tree classification algorithm

In Figure 6.2, we can follow the train of thought that the decision tree algorithm has taken:

1 Split 1 divides our data points into those that fall above and below 60 (hours) on the X2 axis.

2 For those points that fall above 60 (hours) on the X2 axis, Split 2 makes a *further* division for our data points into those that fall above and below 20 (years old) on the X1 axis. This means that Split 2 *only* divides the data above 60 (hours) on the X2 axis.

3 Split 3 addresses the data points that Split 2 has ignored, dividing those that fall *below* 60 (hours) on the X2 axis. This time, the split divides data points that fall above and below 30 (years old) on the X1 axis.

4 Split 4 divides the data points under 60 (hours) on the X2 axis (as divided by Split 1) *and* those over 30 (years old) on the X1 axis (as divided by Split 3). This time, the split divides data points that fall above and below 20 (hours) on the X2 axis.

We can translate this process into this flowchart.[3]

 6.3

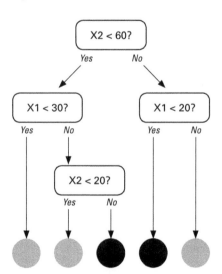

How is this algorithm helpful to us? Let's say that our new customer is 19 years old and has racked up 65 hours of gaming time in their first month (X1 = 19 and X2 = 65). On the scatter plot which has been divided by our splits into leaves, we can see where this data point would fit. Our algorithm has already uncovered that a statistically significant number of people under 20 who play for over 60 hours will become members, which means we can target this customer with adverts that will entice him or her to subscribe to our company.

Random forest

Random forest classification builds upon the principles of decision trees through ensemble learning. Instead of there being only one tree, a random forest will use many different trees to make the same prediction, taking the average of the individual trees' results.

While some of the trees might not be ideal in their effectiveness depending on our business question, we can apply the power of the crowd; when the decision trees are taken in sum, they can make much more informed predictions. Think of this like the process of voting – every decision tree will cast its vote (make a prediction) and then the random forest algorithm will take the most voted for option as its result. A democracy of trees!

This makes the original algorithm a great deal more powerful. Instead of drawing up a single decision tree for our entire dataset, random forest builds a number of decision trees. To make the decision trees unique, they are created from varying subsets of the dataset.

Ensemble methods intuition

Here's my favourite example of an ensemble method, which should make the concept feel more intuitive. Have you ever been to an event where you've needed to guess the number of sweets inside a glass jar? The one who guesses the closest number wins a prize.[4]

This is my strategy for how to make the best guess, based on the ensemble method. Rather than simply choosing a number yourself, look at what the game's other participants have guessed (most games will have a sheet or chalkboard of guessed numbers). Calculate the average, round the result up to the nearest whole number, *et voila!* There is your guess.

The more guesses that are available to you, the closer your average will be to the actual number of sweets in the jar. This happens because some people would have guessed higher and some lower, but overall (unless there is some trickery in the jar itself) the guesses will be normally distributed around the actual number of sweets. Picture the experiment and it should feel intuitive. And if it doesn't – you can always try it out for yourself.

If you replace the 'sweets in a jar' game with a data science problem, and each of the participants' guesses with a decision tree, then you have an ensemble method. That's precisely its principle: the opinion of the crowd (the ensemble) will always be more reliable – and oftentimes more accurate – than the opinion of a single respondent (a tree).

Let's explore random forest a little further, with a case example.

CASE STUDY BCG – finding the best locations for new bank branches

Random forest algorithms are perfect for tasks that require a more complex assessment of our data than that which could be analysed through the decision tree algorithm. For example, if we wanted to assess the potential for a bank opening a branch in an individual district based on a pattern of variables, then we would use the random forest algorithm.

I am based in Australia, and when I want to register with a new bank in the country my main priority is convenience. I want to have a branch near my home, near my place of work and near where I shop. If a bank also has a good number of branches near the beach, even better. There is nothing worse than having to commute to the other end of town just to speak to an advisor or cash a cheque.

While banks know this to be a major influencing factor in a prospective customer's decision making, they also want to ensure that their newly opened branches are going to be cost-effective for them. Artem Vladimirov, a top analytics consultant at the Boston Consulting Group (BCG), was tasked with solving this problem for the group's bank client, which wanted to develop its profile across Australia.

First, Artem analysed the bank's demographical data to show the number of its customers for each of Australia's residential districts. He realized that, as the bank did not have its branches spread evenly across Australia, it did not have data for all of the Australian districts. In order to make predictions for these areas, then, Artem had to carry out comparative data analyses between districts that were both 'known' and 'unknown' by the bank through census information that was publicly available. By applying such demographic data as average age, gender percentage, education levels and living costs, Artem was able to fill in these grey areas for the bank. This use of the data enabled him to utilize the potential success of establishing branches in new districts that showed similar data as districts that had already been proved beneficial.

To solve the bank's needs, Artem used the random forest algorithm:

> We took the whole customer base from the bank's data records and used a random forest statistical model to determine the correlation between the profitability of the customers and their demographics. The predictions were made for areas where the bank already had customers, so we only had to cross-check whether or not a district would be profitable by matching the demographic data.
>
> (SuperDataScience, 2016)

Having identified the areas that were significant for the bank, Artem then profiled the company's competitors and the number of their branches in that area, again using random forest to determine the percentage of market share that the bank held in relation to its competitors.

Through random forest, Artem did not need to explain precisely which demographics contributed to the final metrics, which was helpful in enabling him to bypass the issues of personal data protection and show the bank precisely which areas would be the most cost-effective for them.

Steps to random forest classification

1 Choose the number of trees you want to build For many programs, the default parameter is 10 trees. The number that you eventually select will depend on the context. Fewer trees may result in less precise predictions. Conversely, it is possible on most occasions to use as many trees as you wish, so there is no need to worry about the algorithm over-fitting to your data.

2 Fit the classifier to the training set Fitting our random forest classifier to the training set enables it to learn how to make future predictions for new data points. We can then compare these predictions against the actual results in our dataset in order to see how accurate the classifier is.

The random forest algorithm will randomly select N subsets from your dataset, where N is the number of trees you specified for the parameter in Step 1. These subsets can be overlapping; however, no two of them will be identical.

Once the subsets have been selected, each one will be used as an input dataset to build a unique classification tree. In this way, each classification tree only sees its own subset of the data and has no knowledge of the fact that the actual dataset is broader. This approach ensures variety in the generation of the trees – which is precisely where the 'power of the crowd' comes from in the random forest algorithm.

From this logic, to help the algorithm make more accurate predictions, we can simply add information to our dataset – the more data we have in our training set, the more accurate our algorithm's forecast will be.

Decision tree or random forest?

While the random forest algorithm might be considered an 'update' to decision trees, both have their benefits depending on the task at hand. For projects that use relatively little data, using a random forest algorithm will not give optimum results because it will unnecessarily subdivide your data. In these scenarios, you would use a decision tree, which will give you fast, straightforward interpretations of your data. But if you are working with a large dataset, random forest will give a more accurate, though less interpretable prediction.[5]

K-nearest neighbours (K-NN)

K-nearest neighbours uses patterns in the data to place new data points in the relevant categories. Let's say that a doctor based in San Francisco has read about a recent increase in the number of diabetes sufferers in the United States, and she wants to address this epidemic in her practice. The doctor knows that diabetes Type 2 is easier to prevent than it is to treat, and so she calls upon a data scientist to develop a model that assesses the likelihood of the practice's new patients suffering from the condition in the future, based on records from current patients who were either diagnosed as healthy, or who were diagnosed as having diabetes. By doing so, our doctor hopes that she will be able to apply this model to identify at-risk patients early on and help them towards leading a healthier life through consultations and prevention screenings. The practice has already identified two attributes as being pertinent to successful diagnoses: amount of exercise per week and weight. It is now up to the data scientist to create a reliable model for helping the practice to predict at-risk patients reliably.

What should I expect from K-NN?

K-NN analyses 'likeness'. It will work by calculating the distance between your new data point and the existing data points. And since the existing data points represent previously diagnosed patients, we can group them into two classes: (1) Diabetes Sufferer and (2) Healthy. The new data point (here, the new patient) will then be classified according to the surrounding patients. This is where we witness the underlying assumption of this algorithm: K-NN assumes that even *unknown* features of patients will be similar, provided that some known features are alike.

Steps to K-NN

1 Choose the number of neighbours *k* for your algorithm It is essential that we first establish how many of the data point neighbours in our training set we want to analyse for a new data point being successfully classified. K-NN functions by analysing the distance between our new data point and the existing points around it, and it will classify the new data point according to the category (here, either (1) Diabetes Sufferer or (2) Healthy) that is represented by the greatest number of neighbours. For example, if we want to classify our new data points by analysing the five closest data points, then we would identify our *k*-value as 5.[6]

2 Measure the (Euclidean) distance between the new data point and all existing points If we were to say that *k* was equal to 5, then we would need to identify the closest five neighbours to our data point. To do this, we must first measure the distance from our new data point to all of the points that we already have.

Measuring distance can be quite complex in data science, as there are many different ways to define it. What tends to be used is the most natural definition of distance – the one many of us studied at school: Euclidean distance. Put simply, Euclidean distance is the length of a straight line between two points. It is measured by finding the differences in coordinates between two points for each axis (eg X2 – X1), then squaring those differences, adding the resulting values, and finally extracting a square root.

For example, if P1 is our first data point and P2 is our second, as shown on this graph, then the Euclidean distance would be measured with the formula

$$\text{Euclidean distance} = \sqrt{(x_2 - x_1)^2 + (y_2 - y_1)^2}$$

6.4   Measuring Euclidean distance

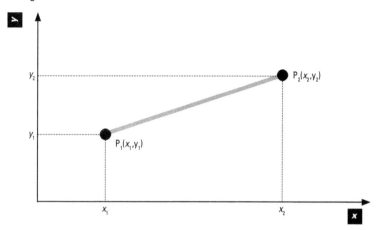

You will probably remember Pythagoras' theorem from school, and this is exactly the same principle. The two points given in this graph are two points on a right-angle triangle. You can find the hypotenuse by first determining its squared length: do this by adding together squares of the other two sides.

3 Count the number of data points in each category Once you have found the Euclidian distance between the new data point and each of the old data points, you must rank these distances in ascending order. At this stage, it will be easy to identify the K nearest neighbours – they are simply the top five points on your list. Visually, we might want to circle our nearest data points as follows:

6.5   The K-NN algorithm

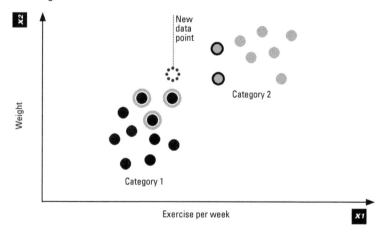

4 Assign the data point to the category with the most neighbours We can see that there are three closest neighbours for our new data point in (1) Diabetes Sufferer and there are only two closest neighbours in (2) Healthy. As there are more identified close neighbours in (1), we would now assign the new data point to that category, meaning that this particular patient, given their weight and amount of exercise they do, is at risk of developing Type 2 diabetes. Having classified this new point, the model is now ready.[7]

Multi-dimensional spaces

What happens when we have more than two variables to describe our data points? What if, in addition to weight and exercise, we also had information about our patients' age and their average daily calorie consumption? As we have a number of variables, we can no longer draw a two-dimensional scatter plot. Instead, we would need to have a four-dimensional diagram.

Imagining or visualizing a 4D scatter plot is near impossible, but the good news is that the K-NN will work regardless. This is because the K-NN algorithm is based on the concept of likeness which operates through distance – and the formula which we introduced for distance can be re-written for any number of dimensions. There will simply be more elements under the square root.

Testing

While K-NN is a good method for making accurate predictions, it is important to note that its results will not be correct every single time. This is perfectly normal – there will always be a few incorrect prognoses, and no algorithm will be able to get each and every prediction correct. The key to making a good model is to test it multiple times, tweaking its functions (here, the k value) until you find the best solution for your task.

Pros and cons to using the K-NN algorithm

The K-NN algorithm is often the right choice because it is intuitive to understand and, unlike the Naive Bayes as we will see below, it doesn't make assumptions about your data. The main disadvantage of K-NN, however, is that it takes a very long time to compute. Having to calculate the distance to every single point in the dataset takes its toll, and the more points you have the slower K-NN will run.

Naive Bayes

Naive Bayes is named after the Bayes theorem, which enables mathematicians to express probabilities of events in such a way that any newly uncovered evidence can be easily included in the algorithm to dynamically update the probability value. It is a fascinating algorithm because it enables us to see past the illusion that our minds can create, and instead casts light on the real state of affairs.

To best understand the Naive Bayes algorithm, we must first look at the Bayes theorem and its equation. Once we have grasped these concepts, the transition from the theorem to the classification algorithm will be seamless.

Police checks and the Bayes theorem

Have you ever been pulled over by a police officer for a breathalyser test? This is common in Australia on Friday and Saturday nights when people are returning home from an evening out – Australian police have been known to cordon off a major road at its busiest point. Anyone who drives down this road, regardless of their driving, must stop for a breathalyser. It's a quick process as you don't even have to exit your vehicle to do it, and it has the benefit of helping police officers to keep drunk drivers off the streets. We're going to use this example here to better understand the intuition behind Bayes theorem.

Let's talk about the breathalyser device they use. We're going to assume that this device is designed very well and if somebody is drunk it will pick them out every single time without failure. That's its primary purpose after all. But the breathalyser is not perfect and will pick up false drunkenness 5% of the time. Meaning that out of 100 people who are *not* drunk it will mistake five of them for being drunk. (Such results are called false positives. They come up as positives on the test but in reality these people are not drunk.)

Now imagine that a police officer has just breathalysed a random driver and the device says that the driver is drunk. What is the probability that he or she is actually drunk?

The impulsive response would be to say 95%. But the correct answer is actually around 2%. How so? This is where Bayes theorem comes in.

Let's assume that for every 1,000 drivers on the road there is only one person who is driving drunk. If the police test 1,000 drivers, they will have the following results:

- The 1 driver who is actually drunk will be detected without failure.
- Of the remaining 999 drivers, 5% will be detected as drunk. That is 5% × 999 = 49.95 drivers. (Don't worry about the decimal point in the number

of drivers – we can always scale this example up to 100,000 drivers to make the result a whole number.)

In this example, the breathalysers detected a total of 1 + 49.95 = 50.95 drunk drivers. So the probability that any one of these drivers is truly drunk is 1/50.95 = 0.0196% ≈ 2%. We can illustrate this in the following table:

	Actually drunk	Actually not drunk	Total	
Tested	1	999	1000	
Detected	× 100%	× 5%		
	= 1	= 49.95	50.95	P = 1/50.95
				= 1.96/100
				= 1.96%

Surprised? You're not alone. To this day, whenever I come across an example of Bayes theorem applied to a situation in real life, I am always intrigued. It's fascinating how we so often jump to conclusions about presented evidence instead of considering the bigger picture.[8]

Bayes formula

Now that we have a taste for Bayesian inference in practice, let's look at the equation for the Bayes theorem. Here are the notations that will be used in this example:

P(Drunk)
P(Drunk | Positive)
P(Positive | Drunk)
P(Positive)

where P stands for probability and the vertical bar signifies a conditional probability.

Each of the elements above has a mathematical name. P(Drunk) is the probability that a randomly selected driver is drunk. In Bayesian statistics, this probability is called the *prior probability*. If we recall our initial assumptions, we can calculate the prior probability as P(Drunk) = 1/1,000 = 0.001.

P(Drunk | Positive) is the conditional probability that a driver is actually drunk, given that the breathalyser test was positive (detected him or her as being drunk). This probability is called the *posterior probability* and this is what we are interested in calculating.

P(Positive I Drunk) is the conditional probability that the breathalyser will test positive, given that a driver is actually drunk. The name for this probability is *likelihood*. In our case, any truly drunk driver is detected by the device without failure, and therefore P(Positive I Drunk) = 1.

P(Positive) is the probability that any randomly selected driver will test positive on the breathalyser. This probability is called the *marginal likelihood* and in our example is calculated as P(Positive) = 50.95 / 1,000 = 0.05095.

Don't worry – you don't have to remember all these names, but one day you may come across them and you'll remember our breathalyser example. And now that we've completed all of the preparations, we can introduce the equation behind Bayes theorem:

$$P(\text{Drunk} \mid \text{Positive}) = \frac{P(\text{Positive} \mid \text{Drunk}) \times P(\text{Drunk})}{P(\text{Positive})}$$

Plugging in the numbers gives us the following:

$$1 \times 0.001 / 0.05095 = 0.0196 = 1.96\%$$

Although this equation may look complex, it is actually very intuitive. If you're unsure, just retrace your steps to when we calculated this type of probability for the first time using the table approach and you will see that we performed exactly the same calculations as suggested by the Bayes formula. The only difference is that our inputs were normalized to 1,000 drivers (instead of 0.001 we had 1, and instead of 0.05095 we had 50.95).

Additional evidence

We've been so carried away with the Bayes theorem that we have forgotten all about our police officers. They breathalyse a person, the device reads Positive, and yet there's only a 2% chance that the person is actually drunk. What are they meant to do?

At this stage they might resort to more precise methods of verification (eg a blood test for alcohol levels) or they could choose to go with a much simpler solution: Performing an additional breath test. Let's see how this could be helpful.

We know that out of the 1,000 drivers who were tested, 50.95 were detected as being drunk. We also know (for the purposes of this example) that only one of these drivers is *actually* drunk. By breathalysing each of the 50.95 'drunk' drivers a second time, we can apply the same logic as before – the breathalysers will detect:

- the 1 driver who is actually drunk
- 5% of the remaining 49.95 drivers as drunk. That is 5% × 49.95 = 2.4975 drivers

A total of 1 + 2.4975 = 3.4975 drivers will therefore be detected as drunk a second time.

As we can see, we're narrowing our results and now the probability of a driver actually being drunk, given that he or she has tested positive on the *second* breathalyser, is equal to: 1 / 3.4975 = 28.59%

Does that still seem low? Then why not breathalyse the remaining drivers again? Applying the same logic, we will get the following detection results on our third round:

- As always, the 1 driver who is actually drunk will be detected without failure
- Of the remaining 2.4975 drivers, 5% will be detected as drunk. That is 5% x 2.4975 = 0.124875 drivers

Now, only 1 + 0.124875 = 1.124875 drivers have been detected as drunk. So the probability of a driver actually being drunk, given that he or she has tested positive on the third breathalyser, is equal to: 1 / 1.124875 = 88.89%

That's much better. At this point the police officers might order the drivers who have tested positive to step out of their vehicles. A fourth test would be even more accurate, and would make the probability tip over 99%. Feel free to perform this calculation in your own time. To prevent you from getting lost in all the numbers, use this table as a guide:

	Actually drunk	Actually not drunk	Total	
Tested	1	999	1000	
Detected	× 100%	× 5%		
	= 1	= 49.95	50.95	P = 1/50.95
				= 1.96/100
				= 1.96%

(continued)

	Actually drunk	Actually not drunk	Total	
Test 2	× 100%	× 5%		
Detected	= 1	= 2.4975	3.4975	P = 1/3.4975 = 28.59%
Test 3	× 100%	× 5%		
Detected	= 1	= 0.12487	1.12487	P = 1/1.12487 = 88.89%

If you want to follow along with the Bayes formula (as opposed to the table approach), all you need to do is update your inputs (prior probability and marginal likelihood) with every step by incorporating the results of the preceding step. This is the mathematical way of saying that you have obtained new evidence and that you want to leverage it to revise your existing (prior) view of the world.

I like the breathalyser example so much because it illustrates two things:

1 We must take prior knowledge into account from the outset (in this example – that only 1 out of 1,000 drivers is actually drunk). Ignoring the bigger picture can lead to hasty and oftentimes incorrect conclusions.

2 We must update our inputs into the Bayes formula as new evidence comes in. Only in this way can we ensure that we have the most up-to-date picture of a problem. Sometimes we may need to actively seek new evidence to help devise more accurate conclusions.

With all this mind, it should no longer come as a surprise to readers that police officers will sometimes ask drivers to breathe into their detection devices more than once.

That was a brief excursion into the world of Bayesian statistics. Armed with the Bayes theorem, we are now ready to proceed to the Naive Bayes classification algorithm.

Why is it naive?

Naive Bayes relies on a strong, *naive* independence assumption: that the features of the dataset are independent of each other. Indeed it would be naive to think so, as for many datasets there can be a level of correlation between the independent variables contained within them. Despite this naive assumption, the Naive Bayes algorithm has proved to work very well in many complex applications such as e-mail spam detection.

Classification with Naive Bayes

After all that work on breathalysers, we've been approached by a wine-maker in California. The weather on the West Coast has been unpredictable this year and the winemaker is unsure about the quality of wine from the annual grape harvest. To help assess the risks, he has asked for our help in predicting the chances of him winning the regional top wines of the year prize with this year's harvest.

As you can tell, a lot is at stake for our winemaker. The good news is that he has some data for us!

The winemaker has found that, over the years, the two independent variables *hours of sunlight* and *millimetres of rainfall* are two of the variables that have a positive effect on the grapevines and thereby the taste and chances of success of his wines. Thanks to this knowledge, he has since been able to improve his process of grape growing and increase the number of successful wines.

Based on his previous wins and losses, the winemaker has divided his data into two categories: 'Winner' and 'Loser'. We can visualize them like this:

6.6   Success of wine harvests according to hours of sunlight and rainfall 1

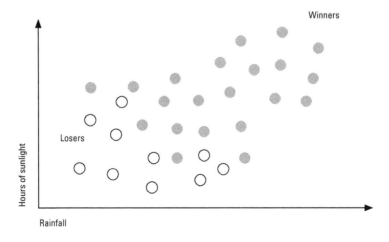

Here, the value on our x axis is millimetres of rainfall, and the value on our y axis is hours of sunlight. The white category is 'Loser' and the grey is 'Winner'.

We can now help the winemaker analyse the chances of success for this year's harvest, based on the amount of rainfall and sunlight it has experienced. Let's say that a specific harvest received 23.7 inches of rainfall and 3,543 hours of sunlight in the past year. Using this information, we can plot this year's harvest on the scatter plot and the Naive Bayes classification will help us identify into which category this year's harvest will fall:

6.7   Success of wine harvests according to hours of sunlight and rainfall 2

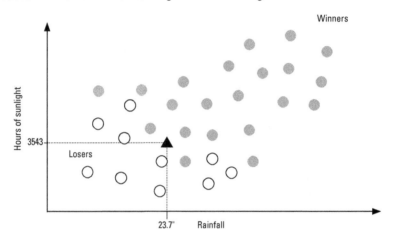

Steps to Naive Bayes

Naive Bayes uses our data point's variables to place it into the best suited class. Here's how it works:

Step 1: Work out the prior probability Here, we want to find out the likelihood of an individual data point as belonging to a category from our training set. Given our sample of wines and the number of them that lost versus those that won, what is the likelihood of a new wine belonging to the Winner category?

At this point, we need to assume that we do not know anything about our harvest – we don't know how long the grapes spent in the sun, nor do we know how much rain they got. So the best guess we can make is to take the number of winners from our previous data (hence the name, *prior* probability) and divide it by the total number of data points:

P(Winner) = Number of winners / Total observations = 20/30, or 0.667

Step 2: Calculate the marginal likelihood 'Marginal likelihood' refers to the probability of us observing a new data point in the vicinity of the area where the one in question actually fell. Is it usual or unusual for harvests to have a similar amount of sunlight and rainfall as ours had? This *similarity condition* represents an area around our data point which would look something like this on a scatter plot.[9]

6.8   Calculating marginal likelihood for Naive Bayes

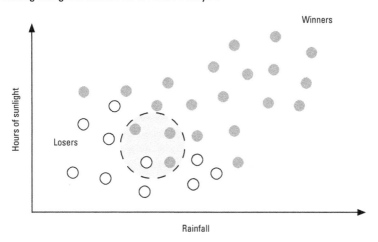

(Note that we are not actually placing our current harvest on the scatter plot – this is to avoid confusion when we start counting the data points in the circle. Instead, mentally visualize it as being in the middle of the circle.)

The radius that we choose for our circle is up to us; it is a parameter that we can adjust to affect the algorithm's performance.

Within our circle, then, the contained data points are deemed to be similar. These wines came from harvests with about the same amount of sun and water as our present harvest. Let's say that our circle encapsulates 4 data points. To find the probability of our new data point (X) as falling within the circle, we need the following formula:

P(X) = Similar observations / Total observations = 4/30, or 0.133

Note that this value will not change for the duration of our analysis and so need only be calculated once.

Step 3: Calculate the likelihood As we remember from the Bayes theorem, *likelihood* is a conditional probability. With that in mind, what is the probability that a data point in our dataset will fall within the circle we identified, *given that* it already belongs to the category of winners?

6.9   Calculating likelihood for Naive Bayes

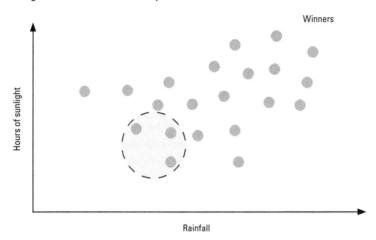

To find the likelihood, we simply need to divide the number of our similar observations within that category (in this case 3) by the total number of data points in the category:

$$P(X \mid \text{Winner}) = \frac{\text{Number of similar observations among winning wines}}{\text{Total number of winners}}$$

$$= 3/20 = 0.15$$

(In case you are finding the notation $P(X \mid \text{Winner})$ confusing, think of the letter 'X' as a way of us requiring that the harvest we are taking into consideration has features (sunlight, rainfall) very similar to the ones reported by the winemaker. So writing $P(X \mid \text{Winner})$ is equivalent to saying 'What is the probability of a wine having features like the winemaker observed, given that it's a winning wine?')

Step 4: Calculate the posterior probability (the one that interests us!) Now we need to find the probability that our harvest will yield a winning wine, given that it has the features (hours of sunlight and millimetres of rainfall) that the winemaker reported for this year. This step is carried out by simply following the Bayes formula:

$$P(\text{Winner} \mid X) = \frac{P(X \mid \text{Winner}) \times P(\text{Winner})}{P(X)}$$

Plugging in the numbers gives us the following:

$$0.15 \times 0.667 / 0.133 = 0.75 = 75\%$$

This tells us that *any* harvest which falls in the area defined by our circle has a 75% chance of turning into a winning wine. Therefore there is a 75% probability that *our* harvest will become a winning wine.

Step 5: Derive the posterior probability of the opposite scenario (that our harvest will result in a losing wine) We can now derive the probability of our future wine falling into the losing category with a similar formula: [10]

$$P(\text{Loser} \mid X) = \frac{P(X \mid \text{Loser}) \times P(\text{Loser})}{P(X)}$$

Note that steps 1 and 3 would have to be repeated with the losing category in mind. Plugging in the calculated probabilities will give the following result:

$$((1/10) \times (10/30)) / (4/30) = 0.1 \times 0.333 / 0.133 = 0.25 = 25\%$$

This tells us that *any* harvest which falls in the area defined by our circle has a 25% chance of turning into a losing wine. Therefore there is a 25% probability that *our* harvest will become a losing wine.

Step 6: Compare the two probabilities We know now that the probabilities of a new data point (with the features observed by the winemaker) belonging either to the Winner or Loser category are 75% and 25% respectively, meaning it is more likely that a data point with these features will be part of the Winner category. Thus, while there is still a 25% chance that a harvest will lose, the likelihood of it winning is greater, and so the data point that we are investigating (this year's harvest) will be placed into the Winner category.

Naive Bayes is good for:

- non-linear problems where the classes cannot be separated with a straight line on the scatter plot
- datasets containing outliers (unlike other algorithms, Naive Bayes cannot be biased by outliers)

The drawback to using Naive Bayes is that the naive assumptions it makes can create bias.

Probabilistic and deterministic classifiers

That was a long excursion into Naive Bayes, wasn't it? I'm glad we got through it, as it's an important algorithm. We ended by saying that there is a 75% chance that this year's grape harvest will yield a prizewinning wine and 25% chance that it should be classified as losing the competition. Did you notice that this conclusion is conceptually different to the K-NN algorithm?

Had we applied K-NN to this example, we would have been given a straightforward answer: the harvest must be either a winner or a loser. K-NN's black and white solution offers no probabilities because these two classification algorithms belong to two different families: deterministic and probabilistic.

Deterministic models like K-NN assign a new observation to a single class, while probabilistic models like Naive Bayes assign a probability distribution across all classes. This distribution can then be used to assign the observation to a class.

When you read the following section on the logistic regression algorithm, ask yourself: *Is the algorithm a deterministic or a probabilistic classifier?* I'll tell you if you're correct at the end of the section.

Logistic regression

Despite its name, logistic regression is actually not a regression algorithm; it is a type of classification method. It will use our data to predict our chances of success in, say, selling a product to a certain group of people, determining a key demographic opening your e-mails, or in many other non-business fields such as medicine (predicting, for example, if a patient has a coronary heart disease based on age, sex and blood test results).

But first, we should wind back. Logistic regression has its roots in linear regression, and it is essential that we understand the principles of this preliminary type. There are two types of linear regression that we need to know about:

1 **Simple linear regression.** This type of regression allows us to analyse the relationship between one dependent and one independent variable. This is especially useful for analysing how one variable reacts against another, for example when we look at the changes in a country's against its GDP crime rate.

2 Multiple linear regression. This type of regression allows us to analyse the relationship between one dependent and *two or more* independent variables. This is better suited for analysing more complex data sets, and might be used to learn, for example, what the best predictors are (eg age, personality traits or social involvement) for the levels of anxiety experienced on moving house.

How linear regression works

Below is an example of a linear regression model on a scatter diagram, which shows survey respondents' salaries and years of experience. Our dependent variable is on the *y* axis and our independent variable is on the *x* axis.

.10   Scatter diagram to show respondents' salaries based on experience

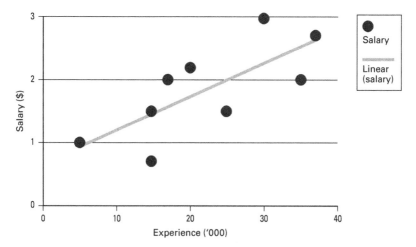

The simple linear regression that we see here puts a line through our data and so models our observations. That means that if we know a person's experience, then we will be able to predict their salary. While this works well for scatter diagrams where the *x* and *y* axes contain many values, it may be more difficult to see the benefits of linear regression for a *y* axis with only two possible values: 0 and 1. This is often the case when we are dealing with 'yes/no' data that has been gathered from questions requiring one of two answers. Questions like 'Did you buy this product?', 'Would you buy from us again?' and 'Do you have a pet?' all fall under this category because they require one of two answers.

> ## Yes/no responses
>
> 'Yes/no' responses are *categorical variables*, that is, variables with a fixed number of responses.

Working with categorical variables Is it possible to find a regression for categorical variables? Yes, it is. Let's use another example to illustrate this. Let's say that after an e-mail campaign to our customers we want to analyse open rates. In this graph I have plotted whether or not customers have opened our e-mail based on their age. The yes/no values have been translated into 1 and 0 respectively.

6.11   Scatter diagram to show whether or not respondents opened our e-mail, based on their age

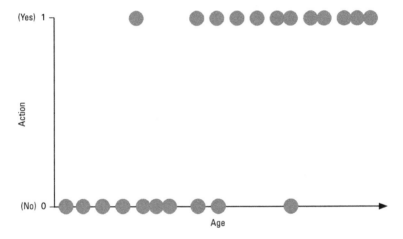

At this stage, we may start to wonder what we can do about all that space between our two *y* axis values. How could we draw a line of *regression* through a graph that shows no gradient of change?

Yet if we were to look more closely, we can see that there is some gradual change between the values. Observations on the *y* axis 0 value lean toward the left of the *x* axis, while observations on the *y* axis 1 value lean more toward the right of the *x* axis. This implies that our campaign resonated more with the older demographic. As the values on the *x* axis increase (ie as age increases), so does the incentive to open our e-mail. This is a powerful insight, and now we can begin to make some assumptions about the actions a person of a specific age might take.

Our graph's *y* axis contains values 0 and 1. We should also know that probabilities always have values between 0 and 1. So, it appears that a linear regression that runs through the gap between these values would give us information about the *likelihood* of a person opening our e-mail based on their age.

5.12   Straight linear regression to show the likelihood of respondents opening our e-mail, based on their age

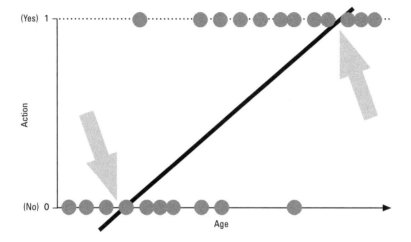

Smoothing the line of regression   You may have noticed that the regression line runs off the edges of our graph. This is not ideal for probabilities, since they can never be less than 0 or greater than 1 but can only be in between the two values.

So we must discount the parts of the line that cross over our two values of 0 and 1. Once our linear regression line hits 0 or 1, then, it should remain on the line and not continue below or above it. By ensuring this, we can continue to use the line to create assumptions, and be confident that our results will remain within the limits of probability. The first impulse is to clip the non-conforming parts of our line:

6.13   Adapted linear regression to show the likelihood of respondents opening our
e-mail, based on their age

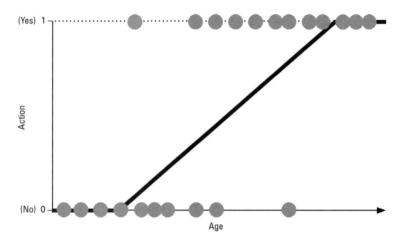

This is a good start, but there is a more scientific approach.

Working out logistic regression mathematically A linear regression line
can be described by a simple equation:

$$y = b_0 + b_1 x$$

We can then get a logistic regression formula if we combine the above
formula with what is known as a sigmoid function[11] (an equation that will
give us an S-shaped curve):

$$p = \frac{1}{1 + e^{-y}}$$

Solving the sigmoid function for y and reinserting our result from the into
the first formula gives us:

$$\ln\left(\frac{p}{1-p}\right) = y = b_0 + b_1 \times x$$

This formula will convert our graph from a straight regression line into a
logistic regression function:

6.14 Linear regression transposed to a logistic regression function

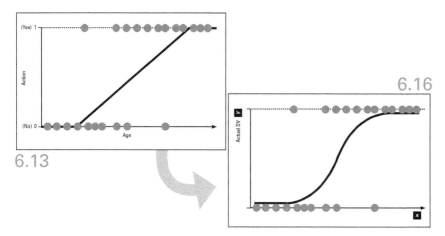

6.13

6.16

Step 1: Understand the elements of the graph Let us break our graph down to its most basic elements:

6.15 Graph containing categorical variables

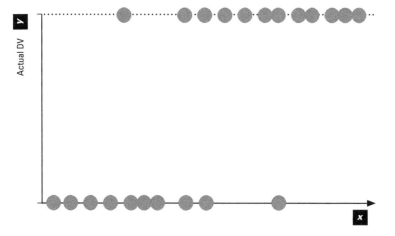

Here, the x axis contains our independent variable, and the y axis contains our dependent variable with the yes/no outcome. The points on the graph are the observations that have been taken from our dataset.

Step 2: Create a slope line for logistic regression We do so by plugging the dataset into the logistic regression formula and finding the best fitting coefficients b_0 and b_1:

$$\ln\left(\frac{p}{1-p}\right) = b_0 + b_1 \times x$$

This results in the following line curve:

6.16   Logistic regression line

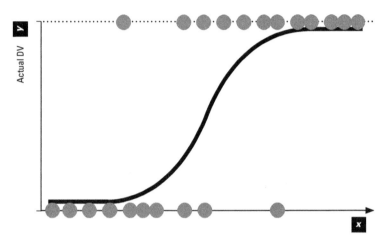

This curve has provided the best-fitting logistic regression line for our datasets. Once we have this line in place, we can erase the observations from our graph so that we can concentrate on the *line* itself.

6.17   Logistic regression line (without observations)

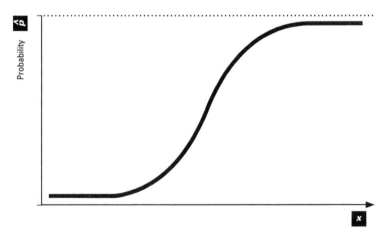

Notice how the label of the *y* axis has changed. This is because we can use the logistic regression to predict probabilities, or the *likelihood* that something will happen. (You will be seeing the symbol ^ in the following pages – for example p̂. It stands for predicted probabilities. It's said out loud as 'hat': p̂ is p-hat.)

Step 3: Use the line to make predictions for new data Let's return to our example and suppose we want to predict the likelihood of a 20-year-old, a 30-year-old, a 40-year-old and a 50-year-old opening our e-mail, given that we already have our logistic regression line. First, we would project our age values onto the curve. This means drawing a line parallel to the y axis from each relevant point on the x axis until it reaches the regression line. These become the fitted values.

We would then project these values to the left in order to determine our probability. This means drawing a line parallel to our x axis from the fitted value until it hits the y axis.

.18   Logistic regression including fitted values

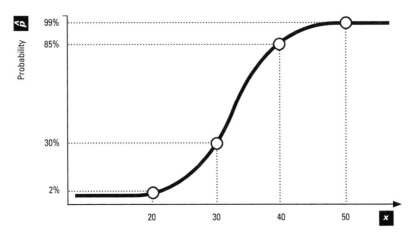

Step 4: Find the probability for each value Let's say (for argument's sake) that we get the following results:

- age 20 yields a probability of 2% (or p̂ = 2%);
- age 30 yields a probability of 30% (or p̂ = 30%);
- age 40 yields a probability of 85% (or p̂ = 85%);
- age 50 yields a probability of 99% (or p̂ = 99%).

Step 5 (optional): Set up restrictions So far, we know how to obtain a probability p̂ for any new data point. But how can we get a yes/no value?

Although we can never be absolutely certain what will happen, we can get a *prediction* for our y actual (this prediction is usually labelled ŷ) from our logistic regression.

It is very simple to work out ŷ: just select an arbitrary level on our *y* axis between 0 and 1. You can set this line higher or lower, depending on how much you know about the issue at hand. For example, if you are selling a niche product, fewer people might be likely to buy it, so you may want to set the line higher in order to discount more people. For this example, let's draw a line right through the middle at 0.5 (this is also the most common approach).

6.19   Logistic regression line (segmented)

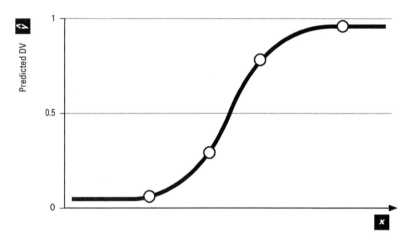

The part of the regression that falls below the line set at 0.5 (50 per cent probability) will be projected onto the 0 line, to become ŷ = 0. This means that if the predicted probability of opening our e-mail falls below 50 per cent, then we can assume that the customer in question will probably not open our e-mail. Anything above the horizontal 0.5 line will be projected onto the 1 line to become ŷ=1.

Logistic regression is good for:

1 analysing the likelihood of a customer's interest in your product;

2 evaluating the response of customers based on their demographic data;

3 specifying which variable is the most statistically significant, that is, which variable has the most impact on the dependent variable we want to predict. For example, logistic regression may help us determine that whether or not a customer has logged into their online banking account in the past six months is a stronger predictor of churn than the amount of savings they have.

Clustering

So far, we have talked about classification where we always know in advance the categories into which we want to group, or *classify*, new data points. Now we're moving onto clustering, which is an entirely different family of algorithms.

If you do not know what the groups resulting from an analysis might be, you should use a clustering technique. Clustering techniques are definitely trickier than classification techniques for the precise reason that we enter into the task unsure as to what groups we will find.

None of that should worry you. This is why we looked at classification techniques first. And what we are now getting to is something potentially much more exciting, because clustering algorithms allows us to use data in order to discover new possibilities and patterns, to highlight new areas that we may not even have considered, rather than to merely respond to our initial question.

In this section, we will cover two algorithms: K-means and hierarchical clustering. These two are similar in many ways, as they help us to segment our data into statistically relevant groups.

K-means clustering

K-means clustering is one of my favourite data science models. ('Model' and 'algorithm' mean the same thing. I am going to use the terms interchangeably.) Although it is able to solve complex challenges, K-means is also easy to understand and has a graceful intuition behind it.

K-means discovers statistically significant categories or groups in our dataset. It's perfect in situations where we have two or more independent variables in a dataset and we want to cluster our data points into groups of similar attributes. For example, K-means could help us to identify subscription levels for a cinema's membership dataset, or it could show combinations of interest groups for an e-commerce website.

Steps to K-means

Let's illustrate K-means with a theoretical example of an e-commerce company, similar to Amazon or Alibaba, that sells a wide range of low- to high-end products. Some account holders pay for a monthly subscription to enjoy 'premium' services, from free shipping to early access to new products. This company has gathered a good deal of data (gender, age, annual income, purchase history, number of unique visits to the website per week and annual spend) from its premium account holders and has derived a 'spending score' for each of these customers, computed from a combination of numerical data variables.

The company now wants to learn what kind of customer segment can be identified among its existing account holders. Such insights would significantly improve the targeting of their offers and marketing and, ultimately, help deliver a much more tailored consumer experience. They do not yet have any idea as to what groups they might find, making this a problem for a clustering algorithm.

To solve this example, we have made a decision to analyse the customers' annual income against their spending scores.

Why not use your common sense?

We might be tempted to identify clusters simply by plotting our data points onto a scatter plot and *seeing*, visually, where the most significant groups appear to be. But using the K-means clustering algorithm shows us groups that the human eye cannot see and helps us to draw a line (literally) between groups that may be hard for us to identify manually.

This is especially the case with multidimensional datasets. For simplicity's sake, we have boiled down the problem in our example to two variables: annual income on the x axis and spend score on the y axis. It is very often the case that we will want to perform clustering on more dimensions – three, four, five, ten, sometimes even more. While it's impossible to visualize an N-dimensional scatter plot, just as we saw in the section about K-NN, the K-means algorithm will gracefully tackle the task of N-dimensions by using principles similar to those that we discuss below.

1 Select a number K of clusters Here is our dataset:

20   Dataset for e-commerce company customers

Index	Customer ID	Gender	Age	Annual income (k$)	Spending score (1–100)
0	1	male	19	15	39
1	2	male	21	15	81
2	3	female	20	16	6
3	4	female	23	16	77
4	5	female	31	17	40
5	6	female	22	17	76
6	7	female	35	18	6
7	8	female	23	18	94
8	9	male	64	19	3
9	10	female	30	19	72
10	11	male	67	19	14
11	12	female	35	19	99

To help us understand the intuition of K-means, let's say that our dataset looks like this on a scatter plot (a real-world version would be much busier):

.21   Scatter plot for two independent variables

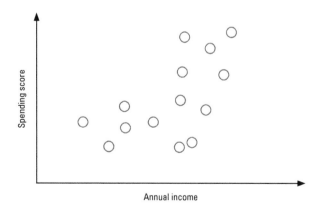

Our first step is to select the number of clusters ('K') with which we will work. Although one of our goals in K-means is to find the optimal number of clusters, we will get to this later (see 'The elbow method and WCSS'

below). For now, we need to understand how the core of the algorithm works. To do so, we will select a random number of clusters and choose two clusters as our starting point.

2 Select the centroids at random K points Since we are looking for K = 2 clusters, we will input two data points (we call these our centroids) into the algorithm at random.[12] These selected data points are where our algorithm will begin its journey. It is important to note here that these data points will not affect our dataset – they are simply imaginary points that the algorithm uses in its process of classification.

6.22   K-means assigning random centroids

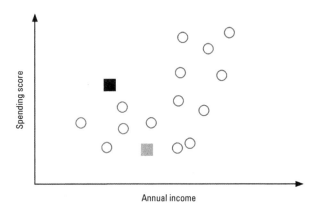

3 Assign each data point to their closest centroid The centroids now engage in a struggle for territory. Data points that are closest to centroid A on the diagram below will be assigned to it, and data points closest to centroid B will be assigned to B.

6.23   Assigning data points to closest centroid

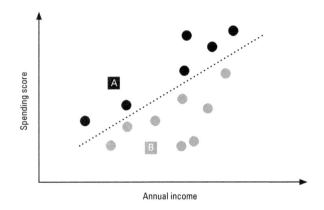

The dotted line in the diagram, equidistant from both centroids, is there to help us see which points are closer to centroid A and which are closer to centroid B.

4 Determine and place the new centroid of each new cluster The algorithm will now compute the 'centre of mass' for both of the clusters that we have formed. It will then move each centroid to the centre of mass in the corresponding cluster.

6.24 Re-computing centroids

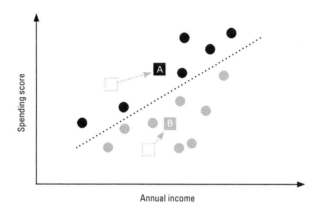

5 Reassign each data point to the new closest centroid The power struggle continues – now that the centroids have moved to new locations, the distances between the centroids and the data points have changed. At this point, the algorithm will reassess which points belong to A and which belong to B.

Drawing an equidistant line between our A and B centroids will once again help us to visualize the process.

6.25 Reassigning data points to closest centroid

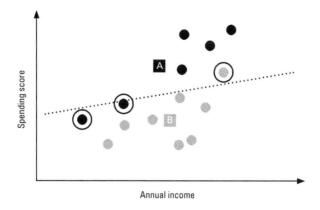

As we can see in the diagram, the three data points that have been ringed are in the wrong territories. The algorithm will therefore reassign these points so that we get the following result.

6.26   Centroids are displaced

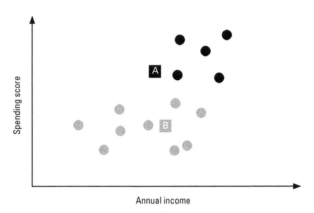

It is clear from Figure 6.26 that the centroids are now once again displaced – they are not at the centre of mass for each cluster. Therefore, the algorithm will repeat Step 4, placing the centroids in their correct locations.

6.27   Repeat re-computation of centroids

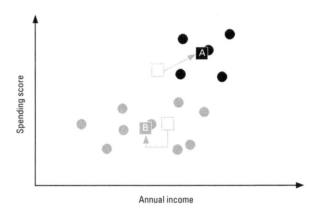

Once the centroids have been moved, Step 5 will be repeated and the data points will be reassigned again to the correct centroids. The algorithm will keep repeating steps 4 and 5 until it converges.

When does it converge? When no data points are reassigned to a different centroid in Step 5 and there is therefore no reason to repeat the steps, as nothing will change.

This is how our final result will look:

.28   K-Means, visualized

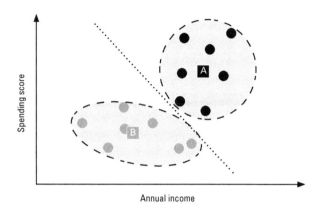

As we can see, the centroids have travelled a long way from their starting points. We have also ended up with two clusters of data points that may not have been obvious groupings at the beginning of our exercise (compare Figure 6.21).

The elbow method and WCSS

Now that we know how the K-means clustering algorithm works, the only question that remains is: how can we find the optimal number of clusters (K) to use? This is a job for the elbow method.

The elbow method helps us to identify our optimal number of clusters. As a hypothetical example let's look at a different dataset to which we have applied K-means with K = 3:

.29   Three clusters, identified by K-means

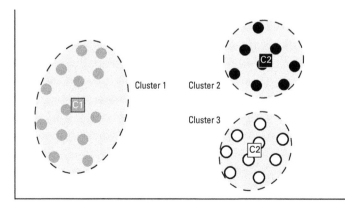

This may look neat, but it does not *necessarily* show us the optimal groups for this problem. The customers in Clusters 2 and 3, for example, may not be different enough to warrant them being split into two groups. Conversely, it may be more desirable to split the data in Cluster 1 into two or more groups.

To get our optimal number, we must evaluate how different numbers of clusters perform by using the Within Cluster Sum of Squares (WCSS). For three clusters as above, we would use the following WCSS formula:

$$WCSS = \sum_{P_i \, in \, Cluster1} distance(P_i, C_1)^2 +$$
$$\sum_{P_i \, in \, Cluster2} distance(P_i, C_2)^2 +$$
$$\sum_{P_i \, in \, Cluster3} distance(P_i, C_3)^2$$

Looks complex? Don't worry – it's actually a very simple equation to execute. The three elements $\sum_{P_i \, in \, ClusterX} distance(P_i, C_1)^2 +$ are simply calculated for each cluster, and these values are then added together in order to find the WCSS. In the second element of the equation above, for example, we are looking only at Cluster 2. First, we find the distance between each point and the centre of the cluster (marked by its centroid), and then we square these distances and, finally, sum up the resulting values.

Let's now find the WCSS if we run the algorithm with just one cluster (K = 1):

6.30   Finding the distance between data points in one cluster

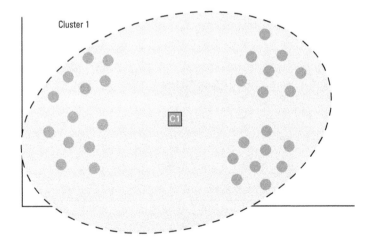

Cluster 1

C1

Here, our WCSS would demand that we add the squares of all of the distances between the data points and the centroid. We will end up with a large WCSS value because, as you can see, the centroid is quite a distance from the other points.

If we increase the number of clusters to two:

6.31   Finding the distance between data points in two clusters

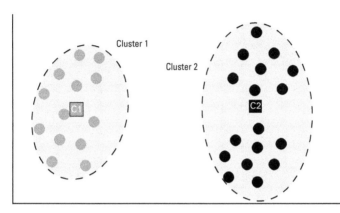

We can see that the total WCSS value will be less than the calculation for one cluster, as the distance between the data points and their respective clusters' centroids is not as great. Therefore, as the number of clusters increases, the WCSS value will decrease.

What, then, is the limit to the number of clusters that we can have? We can have as many clusters as we have points in our dataset. For example, 50 data points in a dataset will allow us up to 50 clusters. If we have the same number of clusters as we have data points, our WCSS will equate to 0 because the centroid of each cluster will be precisely where the data point is.

Now that we know the WCSS value is inversely proportional to the number of clusters, we can examine the rate of change and derive our optimal number. If we were to plot these WCSS values on a graph, we would get the following line:

6.32

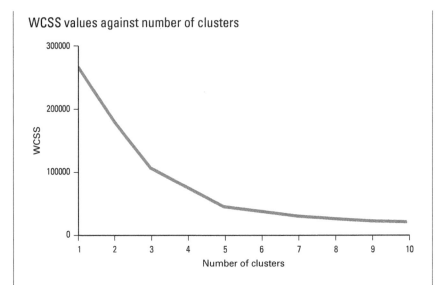

WCSS values against number of clusters

Here, we can see that after three and five clusters, the WCSS curve has a kink. To find the optimal number of clusters, all we need to do is look for the biggest kink on the graph; this point is known as the 'elbow'. In the case above, it would be at three clusters. Therefore the optimal number of clusters would indeed be K = 3.

The biggest advantage of K-means is that it can be applied to datasets of any size. Execution time grows in a linear way with the number of data points. This is not the case with other algorithms such as hierarchical clustering (see below), where execution time is proportionate to the number of data points squared. The difference wouldn't be noticeable at ten or even one hundred records, but imagine clustering ten million points. Perhaps one of the biggest drawbacks of K-means is that, even using the elbow method, it may be hard to find the optimal number of clusters.

Hierarchical clustering

Just as with K-means, we would use hierarchical clustering when we want to segment customers but don't know how many groups we should have or how our data can be partitioned. At the same time, even though the two algorithms share the same goal of identifying clusters in the data, hierarchical clustering and K-means have fundamentally different concepts behind them, and so the resulting clusters are likely to be different. That's yet another reason to know about both methods.

There are two types of hierarchical clustering – agglomerative and divisive – and they are essentially two sides of the same coin. Agglomerative hierarchical clustering uses a bottom-up approach, working from a single data point and grouping it with the nearest data points in incremental steps until all of the points have been absorbed into a single cluster.

Divisive hierarchical clustering works in the opposite way to agglomerative clustering. It begins from the top, where a single cluster encompasses *all* our data points, and works its way down, splitting the single cluster apart in order of distance between data points. The process for both types of hierarchical clustering is recorded in something called a dendrogram.

We will focus here on the agglomerative hierarchical clustering, as it is the most frequently used.

Steps to agglomerative hierarchical clustering

Step 1: Make each data point a separate cluster First, we must consider our individual units of data as 'clusters'.

Step 2: Combine the two closest clusters Take the two clusters that are closest to each other and combine them. In Figure 6.33, that single step has reduced our initial six clusters to five. Now we will repeat this step but with these five clusters in mind.

Keep repeating this step until only one cluster remains.

Defining distance

Even if we stick to Euclidean distance (see 'Steps to K-NN'), then – unlike with individual points – the distance between clusters is still unclear and needs to be defined precisely. Here are a few possible options for the distance between two clusters:

A   Distance between their 'centres of mass'

B   Distance between their two closest points

C   Distance between their two furthest points

D   The average of B and C

Distance between 'centres of mass' of two clusters is usually the default option. However, your selection here can significantly affect the end results – use your intrinsic knowledge of the problem at hand to make an educated choice.

6.33   Steps to agglomerative hierarchical clustering

1 Treat each data point as a single-point cluster
→ *You have 6 clusters*

2 Take the two closest elements and make them one cluster
→ *You have 5 clusters*

3 Again, take the two closest elements and make them one cluster
→ *You have 4 clusters*

4 Repeat
→ *You have 3 clusters*

5 Repeat
→ *You have 2 clusters*

6 Repeat until you have a single cluster

Why is agglomerative clustering useful?

This type of clustering maintains a record of each step in the process. It records both the order in which the data points were absorbed and the distance between them in a tree diagram known as a dendrogram.

What are dendrograms?

A dendrogram will plot the points of your data (P1, P2, P3, P4) on the *x* axis of a graph. The distances between data points are represented on the *y* axis.

The process of agglomerative clustering, as shown in a dendrogram

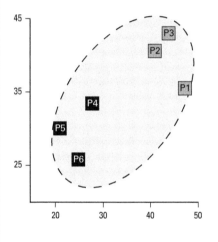 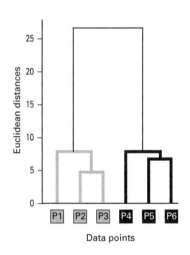

As we can see, the height of the vertical lines depends on the distance between each data point, and the horizontal lines show the order in which the clustering occurred. The lowest horizontal lines represent the first clusters that were combined; working our way up shows us the grouping process. In this example, we can see that the first two clustered points were P2 and P3, followed by P5 and P6. P1 was then clustered with P2 and P3, and P4 was clustered with P5 and P6. Finally, these two groups (P1, P2, P3 and P4, P5, P6) were clustered.

Step 3: Set a threshold With a dendrogram, we can set a threshold, which will allow us to find out how many clusters are optimal for our project. If we drew a threshold on our dendrogram at a certain point:

6.35 Splitting into four clusters

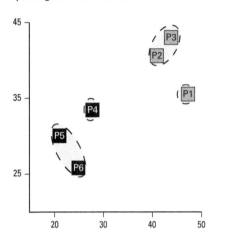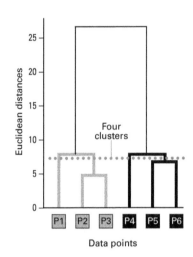

Those vertical cluster lines that hit or fall below this threshold line will be included in our analysis, and anything above the line will be excluded. In the example above, P1, P4 and the clusters of P2/3 and P5/6 will be included. That is how the dendrogram and the data points (or clusters) are linked. But a question remains: how can we find the optimal number of clusters? Can the dendrogram, as with the elbow method, help us to select an optimal number of clusters?

The standard method searches the dendrogram's vertical lines. It looks for the longest vertical segment that is in between the *levels* on which the horizontal segments reside (this is important – the segment we are looking for must not only be uninterrupted by horizontal lines but also by their imaginary extensions). In our case, the largest uninterrupted vertical distance is shown here:

.36   Identifying the largest vertical segment

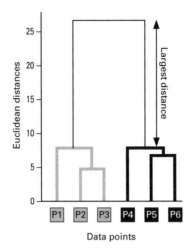

Once you have found the longest vertical line, set the threshold line at a point so that it crosses the segment. The resulting number of clusters is optimal for your problem. In our case, this is two clusters. I'm sure you would agree that, from the scatter plot, this feels intuitive:

.37   Splitting into two clusters

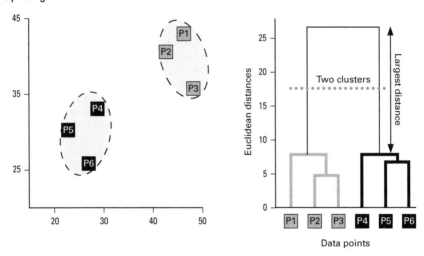

The biggest advantage of using the hierarchical clustering algorithm is its dendrogram. The dendrogram is a practical visual tool which allows you to easily see all potential cluster configurations.

There are many more algorithms for both classification and clustering – those I have shown you above only scratch the surface. If you want to learn more, and if you want to learn how you can work with them in a data science program, just head over to SuperDataScience to find a number of resources, tutorials and courses.

In the following chapter, we will continue our investigation of algorithms by looking at one of my very favourite types of data analytics: reinforcement learning.

References

SuperDataScience (2016a) Data Science A-Z: Real-Life Data Science Exercises Included [Online Course] Available from: www.udemy.com/datascience/ [Last accessed: 05.06.2017]

SuperDataScience (2016b) SDS 007: Advanced Analytics, Dynamic Simulations, and Consulting Round The Globe with Artem Vladimirov [Podcast] 21 October. Available from: www.superdatascience.com/39 [Last accessed 05.06.17]

SuperDataScience (2017) Machine Learning A-Z: Hands-On Python & R In Data Science [Online Course] Available from: www.udemy.com/machinelearning/ [Last accessed: 05.06.2017]

Notes

1 The reason I have opted for these groups is because they represent, to me, the most exciting families of algorithms. These handpicked algorithms are neither the easiest of the bunch (such as regression algorithms) nor the hardest (such as neural networks and deep learning). To my mind, they are the most useful examples of data analysis which you can take away and apply as you read this book.

2 Although we will be using two variables here, your algorithm doesn't have to be limited to only two.

3 To avoid making silly mistakes, I find it best to keep my approach clear with consistent labelling. As you can see in the flowchart, all 'Yes' branches are on the left, while all 'No' branches are on the right. This may all sound obvious, but you'd be surprised by the number of people who neglect to do this.

4 The rules of the game vary. Sometimes you have to guess the exact number of sweets, sometimes you only need to be the closest to the actual number. The strategy provided here works best for the latter case.

5 Due to the averaging of 'votes' of the trees it can be extremely complex to trace the logic in predictions.

6 The commonly used value for k in K-NN is 5, and it is the default number for many data analysis tools.

7 This demonstrates why common practice is to pick $k = 5$: testing an odd number of neighbours helps to avoid situations where categories become tied, with an equal number of 'nearest neighbours' (eg 2 and 2 nearest neighbours if $k = 4$).

8 See Julia Galef's YouTube video 'A visual guide to Bayesian thinking' for some unexpected real-life applications of Bayes theorem. www.youtube.com/watch?v=BrK7X_XlGB8

9 Note that we are not actually placing our current harvest on the scatter plot – this is to avoid confusion when we start counting the data points in the circle. Instead, mentally visualize it as being in the middle of the circle.

10 If there are only two categories in the dataset then it is possible to derive the probability of the second result from the first, as these probabilities must after all add up to 1 (or 100%). However, running the equation for all categories to double check that they add up to 1 is a good exercise for verifying your results.

11 We will avoid going into too much detail here, and will instead focus on intuition. For this reason, some equations will be given without proof.

12 We say 'at random' for simplicity's sake. Although certain pitfalls do need to be avoided when selecting the starting locations for the centroids, this topic is more advanced and is usually taken care of by the algorithm.

Data analysis   07
Part 2

For decades, the media has been enthralled by the potential of robotics, whether in the shape of innocent toy dogs or the more threatening substitutes for labourers and shop workers. We have moved on a great deal from the rudimentary automatons created in the last century, and much of this development has to do with the advancements made in reinforcement learning. That is why this second part to our consideration of data analysis is entirely devoted to algorithms within this domain.

Reinforcement learning

Reinforcement learning is ultimately a form of machine learning, and it leans on the concepts of behaviourism to train AI and operate robots. Rather than simply telling a robot what to do, reinforcement learning will teach it the best methods for completing a task through the robot's exploration of its environment. Let's take a robotic toy dog as an example. It would of course be possible to provide the dog with a set of step-by-step instructions that tell it what to do for it to walk (front right paw forward, left back paw forward, left front paw forward, right back paw forward). This method was used in earlier tests on robots by inputting the sequence of actions needed for it to accomplish a given task. Thus, however, we restrict the robot to this particular sequence of movements, making it, well, only robotic. But by applying an algorithm from reinforcement learning, we can get the robot dog to teach itself how to walk.

Using reinforcement learning in the case of robotic toy dogs only scratches the surface of how this method can be applied. There have been some truly fascinating discoveries in the field. Most recently, scientists at the artificial intelligence lab OpenAI (founded by leading tech entrepreneurs Elon Musk and Sam Altman) taught AI bots to begin building a shared language system, so that they may learn from each other about how to complete tasks (Recode, 2017). Once the reinforcement learning algorithm had been installed, the bots began testing different communication methods to see whether they would be successful in completing a given task. Through this process the bots develop a shared language that worked by associating actions, locations, objects and even one another with abstract characters. The results suggest that AI is not all that dissimilar to us: OpenAI's researchers found that their bots sought to perform the tasks more efficiently by evolving their shared language in such a way as to suit the given problem.

The way reinforcement learning works is through trialling all the variations available to the machine and then working out the optimal actions from those individual experiences. Returning to our simpler example of robot dogs – where the goal is for the dog to step forward and not fall over in the process – scientists would implement reinforcement learning by associating successful progression with a reward, and an unsuccessful progression (eg falling over) with a punishment. Unlike real dogs, you don't have to give it a real treat – you just record a successful result as a '1' in its algorithm, while an unsuccessful result is a '0' or '–1'.

The intricacies of robotics require far more attention than the scope of this book can provide. However, now that I have whetted your appetite with just what reinforcement learning is and how it can be applied, we can move on to some specific problems that it can solve, and the algorithms that can help the process along.

Reinforcement learning and human behaviour

Machine reinforcement learning is surprisingly similar to our human processes of knowledge retention. One of the clearest examples of this is a baby learning to walk. At this stage of development, the child acts instinctively. Therefore, we know that any behaviour is driven by a system that is stored deep inside the brain, something that's unconscious, something that comes pre-coded in our DNA. Let's see how it works.

When a baby starts learning to walk, it will often fall over. When it does, it usually hurts itself – and its nervous system sends pain signals to the brain. Pain, then, is nothing more than an electrical signal that is sent to the brain – it doesn't exist separately to us. It's a feeling that your nervous system creates to *train* you. And since the brain is part of our nervous system, we have a very interesting set-up: when a baby falls over, one part of the nervous system gives another part of the nervous system negative feedback in the form of pain, in order for it to understand that the action was bad. As a result, the baby learns that the action which led to falling over is something it should not do again. Mind-blowing when you think about it.

On the other hand, if it manages to step forward – let's say to catch the cat by its tail or reach the candy on the side table – then its nervous system will send positive signals to the brain, and the baby will be rewarded. By repeating these actions, it will learn to walk.

It's staggering to think that we are creating reinforcement learning algorithms in AI and robotics, and all the while our very own nervous system is the most impressive reinforcement learning algorithm of all.

The multi-armed bandit problem

The multi-armed bandit might bring to mind the sort of character you would expect to find in *Game of Thrones*, but it is simply the name of a common problem associated with reinforcement learning. Popular solutions to the multi-armed bandit problem are the upper confidence bound algorithm and Thompson sampling, both of which we will cover here.

So why the grandiose name? The multi-armed bandit problem was first devised with reference to the earliest casino slot machines. Rather than the button-operated gambling machines with which we are familiar today, earlier models of these machines sported levers on their sides, which the player would pull in order to spin their (usually) three reels. This single lever – together with the fact that these machines were the quickest ways for gamblers to lose their money in a casino – led to them being called 'one-armed bandits'.

The first evolution of the slot machine offered an almost 50 per cent chance that players would win or lose. A short while later, casinos rigged their machines to reduce the players' chances significantly. Would it ever be possible to beat the system, when the odds are so heavily stacked against the gamblers? The multi-armed bandit problem arose to answer this question. There is normally more than one slot machine in a casino (thus, multi-arm rather than one-arm). Given that each of these machines has a different distribution of success, and we do not know which one has the best distribution, how can we play a selected number of slot machines in a particular order to maximize our return?

The multi-armed bandit problem can be applied with a much broader brush: it can be used to find the most effective advertising campaign (the algorithms we will explore rival the infamous A/B test, a randomized experiment where two variants – A and B – are tested against each other to identify the optimum variant), to allocate resources most efficiently across research projects, or to help robots improve their operational functions.

UCB vs A/B testing

What makes reinforcement learning so powerful is its ability to exploit the options available based on an approach that has been guided by the data. With other testing options, such as the A/B testing frequently used in marketing, a decision can only be made once all of the options have been explored an equal number of times, and when we have a large enough sample with which we can draw confident conclusions. Exploring each option in such a uniform way wastes a great deal of time and money, when other algorithms such as the upper confidence bound can organize an approach to finding our optimal result by running tests *dynamically*, that is, combining exploration (random selection) with exploitation (selection based on prior knowledge). We will explore exploration and exploitation in more detail later on in this chapter. This approach is designed not only to find the best option as quickly as possible but also to maximize your profit in the process. Basically, the UCB algorithm blows A/B testing out of the water.

Testing the problem

For now, let's turn our sights to the bright lights of Vegas. I'm not endorsing or encouraging gambling; this example is simply a great way of showing how the multi-armed bandit problem developed.

Suited and booted, we have entered Caesar's Palace and have five slot machines before us. In what order should we play them, and how many times, in order to maximize our return? We must first acknowledge an assumption here, that each machine has a set distribution of outcomes (losses and successes). Once we have pulled its lever (or pressed the button), our chosen slot machine will randomly select a result (win or lose) from its distribution (for simplicity's sake, if you insert 50 cents then you will either get back $0 (lose) or $1 (win)).

All we need to know is each slot machine's distribution of success to find and exclusively play the one that gives us the most favourable chances of winning.[1] Easy.

But that's precisely the problem: we *don't* know these distributions, and Caesar's Palace is very unlikely to hand that information over to a couple of optimistic data analysts!

The stakes for solving this real problem in the casino are high. We must spend our money to carry out these experiments, and the longer we take to find the solution, the more money we will have spent. For that reason, we must figure out our solution as quickly as possible in order to contain our losses.

To maintain efficiency, we must take two factors into account: exploration and exploitation. These factors must be applied in tandem – exploration refers to searching for the best machine, and exploitation means applying the knowledge that we *already* have about each of the machines to make our bets. The fact is that without exploration, we will have no data to drive exploitation, and without exploitation we will be making less money than we could be, based on the information that we have gathered.

Before we get started with the nuts and bolts of the upper confidence bound and Thompson sampling algorithms, let's begin by exploring the set-up of the multi-armed bandit problem. First, we will assume that we are dealing with five slot machines. If we were to illustrate an imagined set of distributions for them, the chart might look something like this:

7.1

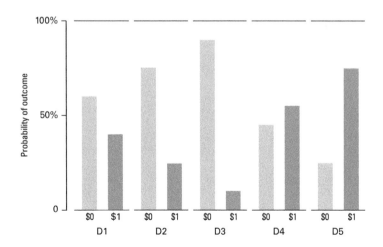

This figure illustrates the probabilities of getting a loss ($0) and a win ($1) from each of the five slot machines. For example, if you insert 50 cents into machine D3, there is a 90 per cent chance that you will get $0 back, and a 10 per cent chance that you will get $1 back.[2]

By looking at these graphs, it is apparent that slot machine D5 is going to give us the best number of outcomes overall, because it has the highest probability (75 per cent) of generating a win.

To simplify, we can calculate and plot the expected return for each of the machines. The formula for this is:

$$E(X) = (p \times Return1) + (q \times Return2)$$

where $E(X)$ is the expected return, p is the probability of winning, q is the probability of losing, and Return1 and Return2 are the returns generated in the event of a win and loss respectively.

For example, for machine D2 the expected return will be calculated as:

$$(25\% \times \$1) + (75\% \times \$0) = \$0.25$$

The most intuitive way to think about expected return is: if you play machine D2 for a long time and then average out your results over the number of games played, then in theory the average you calculate should be equal to $0.25. In essence, expected return is your theoretical average return.

Thereby, the more favourable a machine is, the higher its expected return will be, and vice versa. The expected returns for all five machines are denoted by the tags in the following chart. As a quick exercise, feel free to verify that the calculations are correct as a quick exercise.

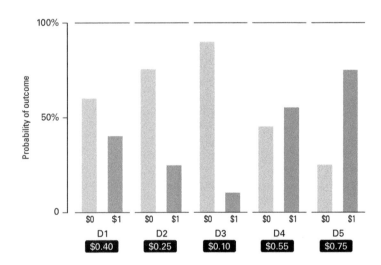

Again, I am only giving you these distributions and expected returns as an example. If we knew the expected returns in advance, we would go directly to the fifth machine and bet on it constantly, as we would on average get the best results. The reality is that we will only come to know these expected returns (or come closer to finding them) when we literally play the game.

This is one of the joys of data science, and it is why the multi-armed bandit problem is one of my favourites. Working out the best solutions and building a dataset for them through trial and error, through exploration and exploitation, reminds me of the techniques that Alan Turing and the Bletchley Park crew used to solve the enigma code. In the world of business, these methods are frequently used in online advertising and marketing to test consumer responses to different variations of posters created for a single product.

Machines have regrets too

Our goal in the multi-armed bandit problem is to find and exploit the best slot machine but also to spend the least amount of time (and money) in exploring all of our options. As we don't know in advance which of the bandits is best, we get what is known in mathematics as 'regret'. Essentially, regret is what happens in an experiment when we use non-optimal methods. In the case of our Vegas slot machines, playing on the non-optimal machines will give us regret, which is quantified as the difference between the optimal outcome and the non-optimal outcome. In practical terms, regret is the opportunity cost of exploring the slot machines that a magical crystal ball algorithm would have rejected. The longer you continue to explore non-optimal options, the higher the regret will be.

Regret stops accumulating once we find the optimal machine. However, there is a risk that if we don't explore the five bandits for long enough, then a sub-optimal machine might appear as an optimal one – and in our haste to find the 'best' machine, our regret will continue to accrue. It is therefore important that we take the time to explore before we jump to any conclusions. Taking the example of our five distributions above, we can see that D4 is also a reasonably good slot machine for profit gains. However, it is not the optimal one. If we were unaware of these distributions and had to explore the machines first and did not fully explore our five options, D4's expected return could be potentially dangerous in its masquerading as the optimal machine.

Of course, we may still be earning money, certainly more than we might have earned from machines 1, 2 and 3, but it would not be the best possible outcome.

Now that we have learned what the multi-armed bandit problem is and how it can be used in our work, what algorithms can we apply to our projects that require such processes? Two of the most common, at least in the world of business, are upper confidence bound (UCB) and Thompson sampling. Both of these algorithms test variants incrementally, and they keep a record of the process so that they can update their logs of the best- and worst-performing distributions. In what follows, we will learn the facets of each algorithm, and the benefits and pitfalls of using them.

Upper confidence bound

An urgent warning here: we are going to continue with our example of the slot machines, but this should only be taken as a hypothetical example. Carrying out the following experiment in Vegas is, at best, not going to make you very popular and, in the worst case, could get you thrown in jail.

Applying the upper confidence bound algorithm (UCB) to our problem will determine which machine will give us the best revenue, leading us to the key difference between the algorithms covered in the previous chapter on classification and clustering, and those that appear here. In our earlier examples, we tended to use datasets with independent variables and dependent variables already collected. For reinforcement learning, however, things are different. We begin with no data at all. We have to experiment, observe and change our strategy based on our previous actions.

When you play one of the slot machines and win, the upper confidence bound algorithm will record it in its dataset as a 1. A loss, on the other hand, will be recorded as a 0. For every game that is played, the UCB will add the result to its dataset. This is how the algorithm learns through exploration, thereby developing a strategy that avoids picking its machines at random.[3] The path that the algorithm will take from machine to machine will depend on the outcomes from each previous round. It is a dynamic strategy that increases in accuracy as additional information is collected. For example, the machine that is chosen by the algorithm in round 281 of our test will have been picked on the basis of all the data gathered in the past 280 rounds.

Steps to the upper confidence bound algorithm

First, the preliminaries: we begin with a specified number of 'arms' – in our case, these refer to the five Vegas slot machines. Choosing one of the five slot machines constitutes a 'round' or a 'game' (I will use these terms interchangeably). Each time we put our money into the machine and pull the lever, we have completed a round. Once the round is complete, we will either be rewarded with a win, or we will have lost our money. This information will be recorded by the upper confidence bound algorithm as 1 for a win, or 0 for a loss.

As we discussed, our goal is to find the machine with the highest expected return. Let's plot the returns we are looking for on a chart.[4]

7.3

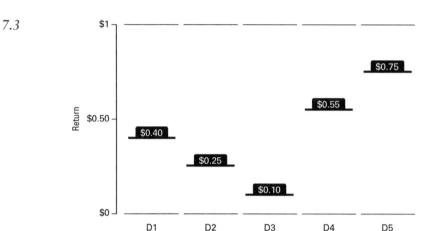

1 Assume a starting point

The upper confidence bound will place a universal starting point across all arms, and it is based on the assumption that all arms will produce the same returns. In the case of our slot machines, the algorithm will set as its starting value the midpoint between a win and a loss: 0.5 (the dotted line). This line will then move for each machine as successive games are played.

7.4

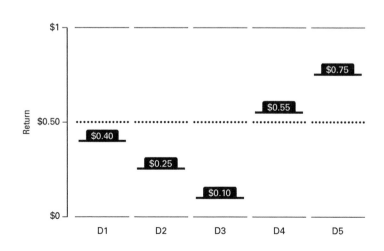

2 Establish the initial confidence bound

The algorithm will establish upper and lower confidence bounds that cover all of the possibilities for expected returns. In our example, this would mean the upper confidence bound will sit at 1 (a win), and the lower confidence bound will sit at 0 (a loss). We can be certain that the upper confidence bound must end here, because our games cannot result in anything greater than a win. The same logic applies to the fact that our games cannot result in anything less than a loss.

7.5

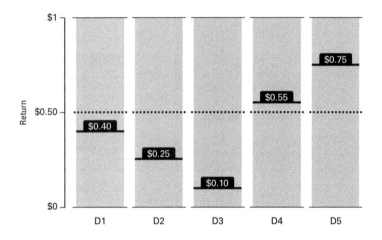

It is important to understand the purpose of the confidence bound. In a real-life situation, we wouldn't know exactly where the expected returns are. At the beginning of the first game, we wouldn't know anything about them at all. What the algorithm 'sees' at the beginning of the initial round actually looks something like this:

7.6

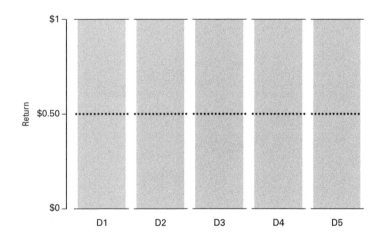

What the confidence bounds do is ensure that the expected returns are captured within them. For example, machine D2's expected return could be less than $0.5, or it could be more. We can't know for certain. However, the grey box of the confidence bound is constructed in such a way that we know the expected return of D2 *must* fall somewhere within it. At this stage it's obvious, as the return logically cannot be less than $0 or more than $1. However, as you will see in later steps when games are played on the five machines, the algorithm will continue to move and resize these confidence bounds so that they capture the expected returns. This is key to the UCB algorithm.[5]

3 Conduct trial rounds

The first few rounds played will be trial runs. They will gather for us our first data that will then be used to inform the decision making of later rounds. In this step, each of the machines will have to be played several times so that we can reconfigure the confidence bounds for each of our distributions.

Let's say that we played machine D3 ten times, which generated the following sequence of wins and losses: 1, 0, 0, 0, 0, 0, 1, 0, 1, 0. This makes the *observed* average return equal to:

$$\$(1 + 0 + 0 + 0 + 0 + 0 + 1 + 0 + 1 + 0) / 10 = \$0.30$$

True vs observed returns

By *true* expected return (or simply 'expected return') we mean the *theoretical* expected return which results from the distributions programmed into each machine as shown in Figure 7.2. This should not be confused with the *observed* average returns which we will calculate based on the data generated from interaction with the machines. The first is theoretical; the second is empirical.

Now that these games have been played, the algorithm will shift the dotted line of D3 down to $0.30.

7.7

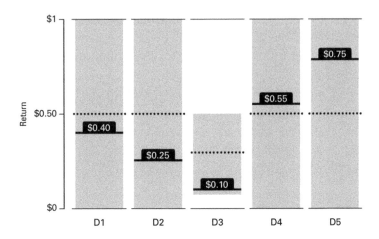

But what happens to the grey box that represents our upper and lower confidence bounds? It will *shrink* every time we play a round. This is because the more rounds we play, the more accurate our observed average will become and, therefore, the narrower our confidence bounds will be. The size of this box, then, will be inversely proportional to the number of rounds we have played on that machine. The smaller this box is, the more confident we can be that we are getting closer to the machine's true expected return. This is a direct consequence of the law of large numbers.

Law of large numbers intuition

The law of large numbers (LLN) is by far my favourite law in mathematics. This is because it's so intuitive and applicable to real life. We're not going to go into all the details here but will instead illustrate the underlying concepts of LLN intuitively.

Let's say that you're tossing a fair coin. The probability of getting heads or tails is 50/50, but this is no guarantee that you will always get an even split in your games' results. Sometimes you will get more heads, and sometimes you will get more tails. For example, if you were to toss the coin 10 times, it would not be uncommon to get seven heads and three tails. The resulting split of heads/tails in this outcome is 70%/30%.

But if you toss the coin 100 times, what is the chance of getting 70 heads and 30 tails? It is much lower. Just think about it – if you were to get 70 heads out of 100 coin tosses, wouldn't you think that the coin is rigged? It would be much more plausible if you got 59 heads and 41 tails, for a split of 59%/41%.

Further, what might happen if you tossed the coin 1,000 times? The likelihood of getting 700 heads and 300 tails with a fair coin would be almost zero. Again, without going into the maths – how would you *feel* if you got 700 heads out of 1,000 coin tosses? On the other hand, it would feel like a much more realistic outcome if you got (say) 485 heads and 515 tails, for a split of 48.5%/51.5%.

Therefore, we can see that with a fair coin, as the number of coin tosses increases, the *observed* split gets closer to the *true* expected split of 50/50. This is the law of large numbers: as the sample size grows, the observed average will always converge to the true expected return.

Let's assume that we have played 10 games on each of our slot machines. The results may look something like this:

7.8

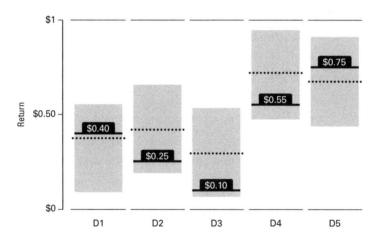

4 Isolate and exploit the optimal arm

Once it has enough data across all the arms, the upper confidence bound algorithm will then start to whittle down its analysis to the arms that have the highest upper confidence bound while discounting the non-optimal arms. It is intuitive: as a machine's true expected return could be anywhere within that machine's confidence bounds, the algorithm assumes that the optimal machine is the one that has the highest upper confidence bound (hence the name). In this example, the optimal machine appears to be D4.

However, when looking at the true expected returns, you will see that D4 is clearly not optimal. Don't worry – the bounds will protect us from choosing a non-optimal machine in the long run. If we play with a non-optimal machine for long enough, its observed average will get closer to the expected return and the box will eventually narrow to a point where the algorithm will consider another machine optimal. This is because another machine that has not been played as often will have much wider confidence bounds. In our case once the D4 observed average comes closer to the expected return for this machine and its confidence bounds narrow sufficiently the algorithm will switch to machine D5.

7.9

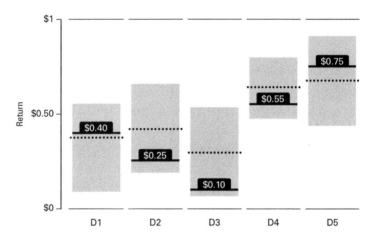

While we exploit machine D5 its confidence bounds will also narrow, and the algorithm might even switch back to D4 for some time. However, this is only until the D4 confidence bounds narrow sufficiently again. In the long run, the optimal machine's upper confidence bounds will end up staying above the upper confidence bounds of all other machines (arms).

The upper confidence bound algorithm is good for:

1 finding the most effective advertising campaigns;

2 managing multiple project finances.

The UCB is not the only algorithm that can solve the multi-armed bandit problem. The following section will consider how Thompson sampling can also be applied, and consider when we might want to use this algorithm over UCB.

Thompson sampling

Before you continue, understanding the UCB algorithm will help us to grasp the methods that we apply here, so if you have been cherry-picking the sections that you read, I recommend that you go through the section on reinforcement learning in full, paying careful attention to the problems outlined in the multi-armed bandit problem, in order to get the most out of Thompson sampling[6]. (A word of caution: Thompson sampling is harder to grasp than upper confidence bound. If you prefer, you'll be fine to skip this algorithm for now and return to it later.)

Remember that the goal of solving the multi-armed bandit problem is to find out how to explore and exploit our variants in the most efficient way possible so that we can maximize our return. In the example here, we will scale back the problem to three 'bandits' (our slot machines), as Thompson sampling is a slightly more complex algorithm when compared to the upper confidence bound.

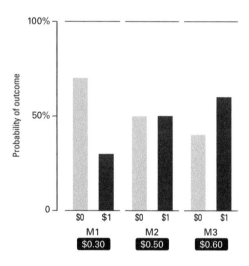

This chart is similar to Figure 7.2 in the section on the upper confidence bound. Here, the expected return for machine M1 is calculated as (0.7 × $0) + (0.3 × $1) = $0.30. Expected returns for machines M2 and M3 are calculated using the same approach.

Steps to Thompson sampling

As we did with the UCB algorithm, let's start by plotting our expected results from each of our three machines onto a graph.

7.11

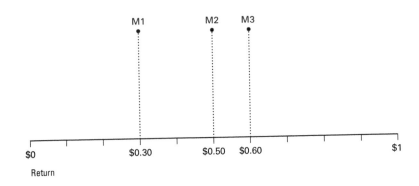

On this graph, the x axis shows the expected return, and the vertical dotted lines represent our machines M1, M2 and M3.[7] As with the upper confidence bound algorithm, these lines show the *true* expected returns of the machines.

Although the distributions of success for each of the machines are plotted in the graph, we will not know what they are (unless we happen to be related to the casino owner). Therefore, in a real-life situation we would not know these true expected returns; our goal would be to find them. We are visualizing them here to reveal the intuition behind the Thompson sampling algorithm.

1 Conduct trial rounds

Before we can test our data, we must first gather it. This means playing a few rounds to start assessing our machines. Let's say we have played these three machines 12 times each, and that machine M3 has returned the following sequence of wins and losses: 1, 0, 0, 1, 1, 1, 1, 0, 1, 1, 0, 1. This makes our average return $0.67. But the Thompson sampling algorithm is smart – it knows that this is merely the *observed* average return and that the true expected return isn't necessarily $0.67. For now, our sample size is small and we can only say that the true expected return is somewhere in the vicinity of this amount. To address this issue the Thompson sampling algorithm will construct a probability distribution curve to estimate where the true expected return might be.

7.12

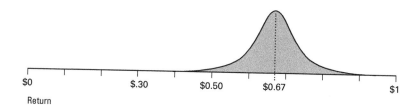

We can see that the distribution is centred around $0.67. This means that based on the data the algorithm has, it estimates that the true expected return could be exactly or close to $0.67. The further away from $0.67 we get, the lower the chances that this amount is our true expected return. This is a reasonable estimate to make because if the true expected return was, for example, $0.1, then it would have been very unlikely that in our trial run we got the series that we did (with eight wins and only four losses); we would instead have had a much lower number of wins.

If we now overlay the true expected returns (which the algorithm doesn't know), we can see that the true expected return for machine M3 is quite close to the centre of the distribution curve.

7.13

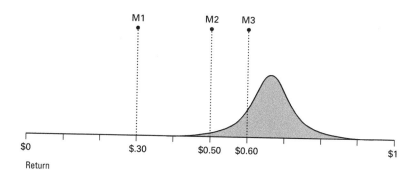

Note that what we have done so far is very similar to the steps we took for the UCB algorithm. For that, instead of distributions we had confidence bounds (boxes) within which the true expected return must fall. Now, let's plot the other two distribution curves after the initial twelve trials.

7.14

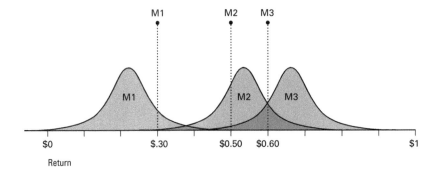

2 Take random values from the distributions to synthesize a multi-armed bandit problem

This is where the fun starts. At the beginning of a new round, Thompson sampling will first draw a random value from each of the machines' constructed distributions and use those values to create its own hypothetical 'view of the world'. This step is very important, as we don't know where the true expected returns are. However, the constructed distributions tell us where these returns might be. That's why we draw a value from each distribution and, for the duration of the round, pretend that these are the true expected returns of the machines. In a sense, we have created an imaginary universe and we now need to solve the problem within it.

Given the nature of a distribution curve, it is likely that the algorithm will take a data point from an area where the curve is the highest.[8] Yet it is also possible that points are taken from the tail ends of the curve, as we can see here:

7.15

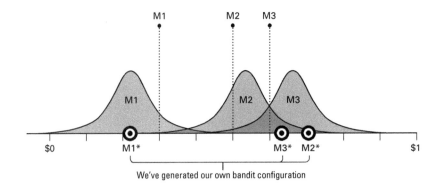

We've generated our own bandit configuration

The above three data points (M1*, M2* and M3*) represent the algorithm's hypothetical configuration of the expected returns for each machine. Since we're pretending that this is the correct view of the world (ie that M1*, M2* and M3* are the true expected returns), it now becomes trivial to solve the multi-armed bandit problem: the M2* data point is the furthest along the x axis, so machine M2 will give us the best return in this round.

Probabilistic and deterministic reinforcement learning

We encountered probabilistic and deterministic approaches in Chapter 6. These two philosophies of approach come up quite often in analytics and it's good to remember the conceptual differences between them.

Thompson sampling is probabilistic while the upper confidence bound is deterministic – and it's easy to see why. Both approaches are similar in that through playing rounds they approximate the value of the true expected return. UCB does this through confidence bounds, while Thompson sampling constructs distributions. However, the UCB operates under rigid rules; when we need to pick a machine to exploit, we simply choose the machine that has the highest upper confidence bound. In Thompson sampling, instead of (deterministically) picking a machine to play, at the start of each round we draw values from our probability distributions and base our choice of machine on those values.

If we were to apply the upper confidence bound algorithm to the same problem twice, for both exercises we would get exactly the same result after the same sequence of iterations. If, however, we were to apply Thompson sampling to the same problem twice, then for both exercises it is likely that we would get the same result (ie pick the optimal machine) but the way the rounds would have been played would have been entirely different because we are randomly generating hypothetical bandits each time. This is the key difference between deterministic and probabilistic approaches.

---

3 Play the 'optimal' machine

Based on our hypothetical configuration (M1*, M2* and M3*) we can now play the 'optimal' slot machine for that round. This will then produce data (either a success or a failure) that will update the distribution curve. Let's say that when we played machine M2, it returned a failure (a zero). This zero will be added to the series of outcomes we have from this machine and update M2's distribution.

7.16

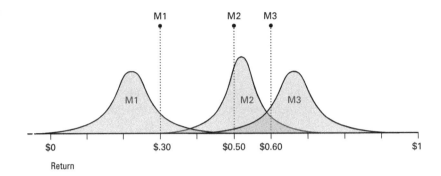

The zero outcome for this round reduces the observed average return for machine M2, so the distribution curve moves to the left.[9] We can also see that the curve has become narrower – it is more focused around the centre. This is because playing the additional round increased the sample size for this machine, and as we now know from the law of large numbers, a larger sample size means we can be more confident that we are close to finding the true expected return.

It's worth noticing that, with this new distribution curve, it is less likely that machine M2 will have the highest imaginary expected return M2* when we synthesize a multi-armed bandit problem for the next round. This is because its distribution curve is now further to the left *and* narrower, so chances are that the value picked from M3's curve will be greater than the value picked from M2's curve. This relative positioning of the M2 and M3 distribution curves aligns with the true state of things – M3's true expected return is greater than M2's.

4 Continue to play rounds in order to refine the constructed distribution curves

Now we can play additional rounds. Each time we play, the algorithm will yet again pick out three data points for an imagined configuration, and will pick the best of these (the one furthest to the right along the *x* axis) to play the round. The result will then change the constructed distribution curve of that machine.

Naturally, the more rounds we play, the more accurate our distribution curves will become and the better they will estimate our true expected returns. After a certain number of rounds have been played, our distribution curves will have become much more refined, so that our graph will look something like this:

7.17

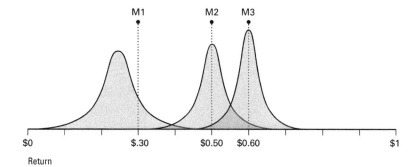

M1   M2 M3

$0 $.30 $0.50 $0.60 $1

Return

As with the upper confidence bound algorithm, the machines with higher true expected returns have more refined distribution curves. This is because the algorithm works in such a way that it will naturally exploit the better machine to a greater degree.

Nevertheless, there is still room for exploration. Occasionally, even machine M1 can synthesize the highest imaginary true expected return. However, this will only be in rare cases.

The Thompson sampling algorithm is good for:

1 finding the most effective sales funnels;

2 processing large amounts of customer data to ascertain the best-performing advert.

Upper confidence bound vs Thompson sampling: which is preferable?

There is no 'better' and 'worse' algorithm for solving the multi-armed bandit problem. However, UCB and Thompson sampling have their individual benefits depending on the task.

The main differences between the two algorithms is the way in which each selects the variant to test. The upper confidence bound is deterministic. This makes the algorithm very straightforward – once we have played a single round, we use that data to alter the bounds of one of our variants. We then continue to test the variant that has been deemed optimal, until the data has reduced its upper bound to a point below another variant.

Thompson sampling, however, is probabilistic. By randomly selecting the imaginary expected returns from its distributions in every round, it makes assumptions about where the actual return for each machine might be and plays the optimal machine according to that speculation. Thus, in every round, we could end up playing any one of the machines; there is no way to tell which one it will be until the imaginary expected returns are drawn.

Both of these types have individual implications. The first is that the upper confidence bound is updated after each round has been played. This means the data that you get has to be incorporated into the bound values before you can proceed to the next round. If you do not adjust your values based on the gathered data, the algorithm will not work: no new data means that the following round will be identical to the one preceding it, and therefore the algorithm will not learn. With Thompson sampling, however, the algorithm can accommodate delayed feedback – even if you don't update your distribution curves with the gathered data frequently. Due to its probabilistic nature, the algorithm will continue to generate hypothetical expected returns, test the machines and learn from rounds.

This is one of the features that gives Thompson sampling the edge: we don't have to update the algorithm with our data every time we play a round. This might not matter in the case of slot machines because, if we're pulling levers, we are bound to playing a small number of rounds and will be gathering a small amount of data. If, however, we are using this algorithm for websites and advertisements – where we might be getting thousands of clicks per day and where all that data might become computationally difficult to manage – not needing to update our algorithm after every round is a major advantage. Thompson sampling, then, allows us to deal with the data in batches rather than processing it each time a new unit of data is provided. In the case of websites, this means we can wait until a time after we have received a certain number of clicks, and only then update the algorithm with this new information. This is called batch sampling.

The end of the A/B test

At the beginning of this chapter, we touched on the infamous A/B test. Now that you know about the upper confidence bound and Thompson sampling algorithms, I hope you can see that there are much more powerful (yet simple) tools available to you for making the same investigations.

A/B tests are focused on exploration and have a minimal capacity for exploitation. All variants are tested equally, and therefore exploitation of the optimal variant is very limited. UCB and Thompson sampling, however, focus on exploitation. The way they are designed means they will conduct only the absolutely necessary exploration and rather spend the bulk of their efforts taking advantage of the optimal variant.

My view is that for minor ad-hoc investigations you could still use A/B testing, if that is what you are comfortable doing. But for serious business projects, especially where significant funding is involved, UCB and Thompson sampling are far better solutions.

The future for data analysis

Well done for reaching the end of this section; the hardest part is now over. If you have read these two parts to data analysis, you should now be well prepared to know *intuitively* which type of algorithm, from classification and clustering to reinforcement learning, you should use to best resolve a problem.

Take a breather here before you move on to the final part; you deserve it. Data preparation and analysis are by far the most technical stages of the Data Science Process, but if you take your time to complete them, you will head into the final two stages of the process with everything you need.

Reference

Recode (2017) These AI bots created their own language to talk to each other [Online] www.recode.net/2017/3/23/14962182/ai-learning-language-open-ai-research [accessed 20.11.2017]

Notes

1 We are going to assume for this example that there is at least one slot machine that in the long run lets the player win more than it lets the player lose. This doesn't contradict what we have said before: collectively, the slot machines could still be set up in a way where, more than 50 per cent of the time, the casino will win overall.

2 Such probability distributions – that describe 'yes/no' outcomes – are called Bernoulli distributions.

3 Naturally, there will be some level of randomness at the start as we won't have any data at that point, but we all have to start somewhere, after all!

4 Remember: this exercise is only to help us understand how the algorithm works. In a real-life scenario, we would not know about the expected returns.

5 To be entirely correct – we can never be 100% certain even about the range where the expected return lies. It could be anywhere! And that's why the bounds are calculated in such a way that the expected return falls within them with a certain level of confidence (eg 95%). This also explains why they are called the *confidence* bounds.

6 Named after its creator, William R Thompson.

7 This is a little different from the chart for the UCB algorithm, where the expected return was on the *y* axis.

8 Think of the area under the distribution curve as a space from which a data point may be drawn. Logically, you should be able to see that there are more opportunities for a data point to be taken from the point where the curve is the highest, because it takes up more space on the graph than the tails of the distribution.

9 This is reinforcement learning in action! The algorithm has made a bad choice and is being punished for it with a failure (a zero). The distribution moves to the left so that the algorithm remembers that this is a potentially bad choice and must try to avoid it in the future.

PART THREE
'How can I present it?' Communicating data

We're now into the final stretch, which, as I mentioned in the conclusion of the last chapter, should be easy to manage if you took your time to appropriately prepare and analyse your data. Even so, we must be careful here – while data preparation and analysis are very technical, it is not entirely true to say that the final stages of the Data Science Process will always be plain sailing – they simply require a very different toolset. The previous section gave you the technicalities for the process; in this part, you will be required to exercise your creative thinking.

For the two final stages of the Data Science Process, we must look to our stakeholders in order to ensure that the message which emerged from the previous steps is succinctly and clearly displayed. In this part, I will tell you about the many ways in which data scientists can communicate a project's results, and will give you my best tips for visualization, presentation, and for carving out your own niche in the field.

Looking good

Data visualization is not just about making pretty pictures. There are reliable guidelines that we can follow in ensuring that our visuals are compelling and make an impact on the people who matter. In Chapter 8, then, I will outline the techniques that are sure to persuade your stakeholders.

As certain aspects of visualization hinge on analytics, I have also incorporated visual analytics in this chapter. This isn't just because they have a similar name – visual analytics are often considered the intermediary stage between data analytics and data visualization. This type of analytics can be used to inform both stages, either before Step 3 (data analytics), in order to start navigating a reasonable route for our algorithms, or before Step 4 (visualization), to add further weight to our results.

You're not finished yet!

Some people make the mistake of thinking that, once they've got the results in front of them, they're done. These people fail to understand the importance of learning how to present your data. This is why there are five, not four, stages in the Data Science Process. And this is the subject of Chapter 9.

Everyone is different. You might be more interested in the technical side (the algorithms and software), or you might enjoy mulling over the insights that you've found. Either way, it is a mistake to neglect your training in presentation skills. This might sound harsh, but if you aren't a good communicator, then you haven't fulfilled the criteria needed for being a top data scientist. You might be a skilled number cruncher, but there are plenty of those people around, and relatively few of them can present well. In Chapter 9, I will give you the best tricks that I have learned when making presentations, and how you can apply them to your own talks.

The career shaper

This final chapter will return to the concepts I proposed in Part I. The first section explores the areas available for readers looking to have a career in data science, and highlights the current options in the field. I also give some guidance for readers who have to prepare for an interview, giving suggestions as to the kind of questions they might be asked, and how to impress the interviewers.

Finally, we will also consider how to develop a persuasive strategy for including data science within a company. You might be an employee of an institution that has been using data for some time, but only in a limited way, or you might be an entrepreneur keen to develop a plan for implementing gathered data. This section will tell you how to establish data science as a necessity rather than a luxury, thus ensuring for yourself a long and fulfilling career.

Data visualization

There are two branches to visuals in data science: visual analytics and visualization. The difference between the two is important in this chapter. Think of *visual analytics* as an additional tool for stages 1 to 3 in the Data Science Process (identifying the question, preparing the data and analysing the data). *Visualization* is what lies at the core of stage 4, data visualization.

In this chapter, we will learn to understand the differences between these two branches and the multiple ways in which they can enhance our projects. Essentially, visual analytics are back-facing – they are strictly for us and our team to take stock of our results – while visualization is front-facing – a powerful way to show our findings to the project's stakeholders.

In what follows, we will learn about the best visualization and visual analytics tools on the market, why data scientists need to learn these techniques, and the basic strategies for ensuring that you are always using the most effective visuals in your presentations.

What is visual analytics?

Visual analytics technically bridges the divide between analytics and visualization as it borrows principles from both areas, and it can be carried out either before, during, or after our data processing. Put simply, visual analytics helps us to 'see' the data – to give us a bird's-eye view of the trends and anomalies within its records. With visual analytics, we are putting the data we have prepared into interactive objects, charts and graphs that allow *us* to see where trends and anomalies fall. A huge benefit is that we can apply it at any point in our process to take stock of how our data is responding to our questions.

While visual analytics may end up oversimplifying a problem – particularly to the untrained eye – it can also help us to either formulate a starting point to, or round up the results of, a more detailed study. When we are working with large amounts of data, the reality is that it is difficult for a human to understand it through numbers and tables alone. Once we put this data into shapes, and add colours, vectors and movement to it, the data becomes much easier to grasp.

Once we have understood how important visual analytics is to us as data scientists, making the case for visualizing our data for our stakeholders will be simple. So, before we move into visualization 'proper', let's spend a little longer in the cradle of analytics.

Topping and tailing our analysis with visual analytics

To illustrate how visual analytics can contribute to the Data Science Process, I like to apply the Pareto principle. This states that 80 per cent of the effects result from 20 per cent of the causes – a concept frequently applied in business to describe how, for example, 80 per cent of sales can come from 20 per cent of clients. Visualizing our data, then, should clarify where our most relevant data records are and, if we are pressed for time, show us effortlessly where in the dataset we should focus our energy.

This approach can greatly help us before a project begins, when we can isolate correlations early in the process. Visual analytics can additionally help us to revise what we have already found out, and to add a little more context to our results after we have carried out our analyses. This is exceptionally useful for people who work with the same datasets on a long-term basis – by frequently running visual analyses on our records, we can quickly identify changes and emerging trends without relying on detailed algorithms.

The question remains: should I visualize before or after my analysis? I recommend that new data scientists seriously consider visualizing their data both before *and* after they carry out their analytics 'proper'. After all, when we are knee-deep in a project, we get so close to it that it can be difficult to recognize trends. And this is precisely what Megan Putney, Category Development Manager at Mike's Hard Lemonade Co (a US-based beverage manufacturer), does to keep track of her company's product sales.

CASE STUDY   Mike's Hard Lemonade Co

Megan visualizes her company's large datasets of over two million units on a weekly basis to show store and product performances both across the United States *and* within each state. Her visualizations on the program Tableau (see section on using Tableau) provide an informative start to Megan's week, not only helping her to report company performance to stakeholders but also highlighting whenever a state falls behind, thereby ensuring that her team is working on areas of improvement.

In regularly visualizing the company's data, Megan also found out where it would be beneficial to collect further information. Oftentimes, visualization software will have features for filtering and isolating key trends in our data. Filtering in such a way enables data scientists to look at individual categories and how they operate in relation to other variables in the data, moving from a top-level view to one that is very specific – all at the touch of a button.

In her weekly effort to generate visual reports of her data, Megan one day stumbled upon a gap in the information. She had already gathered the data from Walmart stores, but found that she had not geocoded Sam's Club stores – shops that are owned by Walmart and where Mike's Hard Lemonade Co also sold products. She spent time gathering the data and pulled it into the dataset with Walmart. From there, she was able to find out how close stores were in relation to each other:

> First, I geocoded all the stores to figure out which of them shared parking lots. Then I took the sales data to understand our lift for those stores. This showed us that selling demos in a Sam's Club also improved our sales in the Walmart next to it. From that we were able to work out that selling in Sam's Clubs that were close to Walmarts could benefit our sales – and we learned that all through data visualization.
>
> (SuperDataScience, 2016)

Sam's Club, a chain of membership-only retail clubs, offered yet another area of interest for Megan and her team – and she could only have learned this through the use of her visualization software. Megan knew that Sam's Club and Walmart are often near each other, sometimes even sharing a car park. Through her visualizations, Megan started to see a pattern emerging between sales made in stores that were close to each other. And this enabled her to synchronize product sales between Walmart and Sam's Club franchises that shared car park spaces.

Using Tableau

Tableau is a business intelligence and analytics software that allows people to drag data directly from a database to instantly create beautiful visualizations of the information – with the added benefit of the resulting visuals being easy to share online. The full version of Tableau is not freeware (at time of writing, it was $999 for a personal-use licence), but it is likely you will come across it in your work at some point as it has a widespread, global application in the field of data analytics.

There is also a free trial option, Tableau Public.[1] In this version of the program some of its functions are limited (such as the ability to save files directly onto your computer), which does not make it ideal for corporate use. Nevertheless, this option is a great way to begin learning how to use the software – just make sure that you're not working with any company-sensitive data.

If you want to play around with Tableau, remember that you can use any of the public datasets listed in the introduction to Part II of this book. When you upload a dataset to the program, Tableau gives you the option to drag and drop a variety of visual tools (eg geographical maps, pie charts, scatter plots) to help you segment your information. Charts and graphs can be further embellished by defining colours, which Tableau will identify intuitively, and a wide range of formatting options are also available to highlight segment labels. The best way to learn is through practice, and Tableau offers enough help to let you arrange your own training: carve out some time for yourself on a weekend, upload a dataset to the program and get visualizing.

Using visual analytics to begin our analysis

Let us imagine that we have been called in as data scientists to a nationwide German bank that has already identified its problem: it wants to review and ultimately change the way it markets and sells insurance products to its customers, and to segment them according to interest areas.

We might first consider if there are any obvious categories into which we can group people, based on the data that the bank has prepared for us.

As we have seen in Chapters 6 and 7, we could take many different approaches to solve this problem. With visual analytics, to add further colour (literally and figuratively) to our findings we can *also* grab any demographic data that the bank has collected from its customers – age, postcode, tenancy, customer loyalty, average spending, family size – and explore the inferences and relationships between these demographic details. By throwing the data into Tableau, Power BI, or any other visualization software, we can come across some great insights that might otherwise have been harder to see. Running data through a visualization tool will enable us to isolate demographics and gain an understanding of how the data functions in combination with a variety of demographical pairings.

My first approach, given the context of banking, would be to identify customers by their age. I can make the logical assumption that the age divide is often exploited in the banking industry because bank loans (for students, for first-time house owners, for families) are primarily relevant to age range. What a data visualization tool would do is show us the key trends for age across the other demographic information the bank has given to us.

Using dashboards

What a visual analytics program will do is investigate the relationship of our age variable across other variables. If we are using Tableau or Power BI, this relationship can even be visualized in an interactive segmentation dashboard, which groups our customers in terms of behaviours and demographics.

Let us say that our visuals tell us that the bank's customers living in Saxony are largely between the ages of 45 and 55, and the majority have low incomes. The bank's customers who live in the neighbouring federal state of Bavaria, however, tend to be between the ages of 25 and 35 and are high earners. What this means is that our visuals have drawn attention to two relevant demographics in addition to age: location and income.

Even if we are marketing the same product, then, we might want to position our marketing differently in these areas. In Bavaria we could highlight loans beneficial to younger customers – first-time homes, marriages, and families. In Saxony we could target protection beneficial to older customers – life insurance, estate planning and low-risk investments.

We can of course continue to cross-section our data as we see fit, but these subcategories have already added value to our project, and this is all thanks to our visual analysis of the data. This is far more elementary than the analytics tools we covered in earlier chapters: all it took was a piece of software to transform our structured information into visually appealing shapes of apparent areas of interest. Not only can the bank now send out brochures that are relevant to their consumers' age range, but we can also advise the bank's marketers to tailor those brochures using the additional subcategories we have identified: low income, high income and so on.

We have now seen an example of how visual analytics can help to support and drive the third stage of our project, as well as how we can continue to use it to keep tabs on emerging trends, divergences and gaps in our data. In our next step, we can move on to visualizing our data so that it can be appreciated by those most important to our project: the stakeholders.

What is data visualization?

By now it should be clear just how useful visualizing our data can be in helping us to investigate it. So, just imagine how powerful visuals can be for presenting our information to stakeholders.

Data visualization is the process of creating visual aids to help people see and understand information. It couches our data in a context. We already know that without context data is meaningless. We need to apply a question to our data. We need to prepare our data in a standardized format and then analyse it. All of these steps contribute to adding the necessary context required for understanding the information that we have been given. But while that context helps us to recognize the trends and results of our data, we must continue adding to it for our stakeholders to appreciate all our hard work. After all, we cannot present our project's stakeholders with merely our analyses – it is unlikely that they will know the principles of data science. All the blood, sweat and tears that you have put into your data preparation and analysis will very likely be meaningless to them. Don't take it personally.

All we need to do now is ensure that we can translate our results into something that is easy for our stakeholders to digest. This is where we can learn something from our friends in the business world. Business intelligence is primarily concerned with developing and presenting reports that help to improve and change the way that businesses operate. Carrying out BI might seem unsophisticated, given our previous chapter on data analysis, but dismiss it at your peril; I don't know a single executive who would genuinely prefer to read a 50-page report over a visual representation of the problem and its solution. If visualized well, BI dashboards will engage and persuade your audience to make the changes that you suggest.

But this is also where we must take care to understand how visuals work – they have a language of their own, and if we don't learn their specific rules, our representations may confuse rather than persuade our stakeholders.

The importance of visuals

Here's a thought that I know will get many data scientists upset: in a way, your project is neither about data, nor is it about visuals. Ultimately, it is about *people*. We have been brought in to solve a business question that will impact our *stakeholders*, whether they be customers or executives. And if our information is not presented in a way that is accessible to the decision makers for implementing the changes that our data recommends, all the hard work we put into the project will have been wasted.

Simply put, we cannot see insights as easily on a spreadsheet as we can in a chart. But that doesn't mean we have to crack open the paint set – even adding something as basic as a fill colour to an Excel spreadsheet can go a long way to highlighting results.

I would argue that this is part of the reason why many data science projects sadly *don't* go anywhere once they have been undertaken – because after the analysis has been done, too many practitioners feel that the data will speak for itself. Unfortunately, this isn't the case. We must learn to persuade our audience of what is at stake, and visualization is the conduit through which your data must pass, or you risk damning your insights to company limbo forevermore.

Do we always need to visualize?

Some people ask me if data scientists must always use visuals in their projects. The simple answer to this is no, not *always*. We only need to visualize data when insights *cannot be effectively conveyed without* visuals. But for the reasons we have established, visuals will in almost all cases be beneficial to projects that require examination of datasets. You will rarely find yourself on a project that only gives one direct answer about just one aspect of the data – in those cases, though, no visualization is strictly necessary.

Speaking a visual language

Visuals have a real power to transmit information in a way that text cannot. While with words our argument can be restricted by many things – among others the speed of the reader and their ability to comprehend the case and variety of recommendations we have put forward in a linear fashion – a single image can illustrate patterns, highlight anomalies, and define distinct groups of data, effectively churning through hundreds of rows in our dataset to inform our audience of our argument – and all this quite literally at a glance.

A further benefit to using images to convey our data-driven message is that we are living in a very visual culture. From image-focused social media networks to internet memes, our appetite for communicating through the medium of the image has increased. Even in the world of business, infographics and other visual representations of information are becoming the go-to method for institutions that want to show their audience at a glance what they do. So, images are no longer a decorative addition to a PowerPoint presentation; people now *expect* to process information in this way. Therefore, by using images to represent your data, you are simply fulfilling these expectations.[2]

This change in our society has also familiarized us with a visual language. Most of us will have picked up an innate knowledge of how different colours and shapes can be interpreted simply by being responsive to our society and culture. You might be surprised by how much you know of what follows. And while we must consider that visual language is not always international, we can frequently use it to good effect.

Self-serve analytics

Thankfully, developers have responded to the increasing demand for powerful visuals by creating software and add-ons to build *interactive* visualizations. With programs such as Tableau and PowerBI we can design visuals that show both the broad picture and, through careful use of filters, will allow the audience to drill down into the details, picking out the category they want to highlight at the touch of a button. Being dynamic, these programs reduce the workload for data scientists as visuals can be manipulated on the go by end users to present the data in exactly the way they need to see it.

There are also add-ons available for the most popular data analytics programs, R and Python, which means that you can create visuals while you are analysing, without ever having to leave the program. Seaborn is a free data visualizer package for Python, which allows users to draw statistical graphics from their data, while Plotly will allow you to create interactive visualizations for self-serve analytics. In R, the same can be achieved with ggplot2 and Shiny.

With the rise of data science as a discipline and the data-driven approach to business, the trend for self-serve analytics has experienced a recent upswing. Getting others to find answers *to their own questions* benefits everyone, and I have made it one of the driving forces of my career. I think all data scientists should.

Steps to creating compelling visuals

Good visuals inform our audience. They will help people to see our data. While I truly believe that visual language is very much intuitive, particularly in the Computer Age, there are a few tricks that you can learn to ensure that you are optimizing your visuals for your audience.

1 Go back to the beginning

Return to the first step of the Data Science Process: Identify the questions. Ask yourself which questions you identified, and keep them in mind when you come to make your visuals. What does your audience want to know? Are you presenting the visuals to more than one stakeholder, and if so, will the stakeholders have diverging interests? At what points do their interests intersect? What can they learn from your data?

If you have run your analyses on the data, you should have these insights already. If you have found more than one result that is of interest to your stakeholders, rank them in order of importance and ensure that the most important gets the highest priority (most page space) and/or place it in the top left-hand corner, so that it is the first thing that they see.

2 Limit the amount of text

My preference is to use as little text as possible, letting the visuals do most of the work for you, so that you only have to add the embellishing touches during your presentation. Having said that, there are two purposes that your visualization could serve; you simply need to identify which of the two it is.

If you are going to be physically present and can guide your audience through your visualization, then the less text the better. You will still need labels and titles for your diagrams, but your goal should be to keep the audience's attention on you. The visuals are there to aid *you*, not the other way around.

If, on the other hand, you are sending a report or a self-serve analytics dashboard to your audience to browse at their leisure, then you may need additional text to help explain what's going on and to guide your readers. A good way to check if you have conveyed your message well is to ask a member of your team to review your deliverable and see if they can understand it without any interjections.

3 Keep objects distinct

If you have more than one object in your visuals, make sure that the boundaries between the objects are clear. You don't want your audience to be interpreting relationships where there are none, otherwise you would be manipulating the data inadvertently. When your visuals contain a legend (an explanation added to a chart to describe categories) make sure that it is placed within a distinct box.

4 Guide your audience

All visuals should be answering a specific business question, which will often require a step-by-step explanation that shows the interlocking relationships between insights. For that reason, it is beneficial to lead your audience through the visual.

Thankfully, we are predictable creatures, so using a simple top-to-bottom-and-left-to-right approach for each of your objects will ensure that your audience is reading your visuals in the order that you wish them to. While you might be shaking your head at how rudimentary this point is, I am sure you can think of a few circumstances when a well-intentioned text or poster turns into a meme on the internet.

5 Tame the creative beast

Sometimes, creating visuals can bring your inner graphic designer charging into the office, ready to change the world, with one heat map at a time. This can be tempting, especially when we've spent so much time absorbed in our analyses. However, do not give in to this urge; leave your artistic predilections at home.

Don't think that playing with font sizes is going to help your audience discriminate between the most and least important information. Actually, the opposite will happen: most of your audience will be striving to read the smallest text, giving the most attention to those areas you thought you'd simply add as footnotes. So, stick to two sizes, one for titles and the other for object content, and if you are tempted to reduce the font size for any information, ask yourself whether you should simply throw it out altogether.

6 Keep everything simple

If you have more than one object, make sure that they sit well together. Be consistent and avoid using more than one colour scheme if you can, unless you are deliberately using a clashing colour to make a statement about that particular piece of information. Likewise, try not to use similar colours for objects that are not associated in your diagrams, because the eyes of your audience will inevitably associate them.

There is a deeper look at how you can use the science of colour in the insets on pages 190–193.

Just remember that less is more, and that's never been truer than for presentations. Don't crowd your objects, and don't go crazy with colours. Make sure your text is visible over the colours that you use. Stick to a colour scheme and embrace the white space – if something is not necessary to your argument, drop it like a hot potato.

7 Consider the visually impaired

When using colours in visuals, remember to be considerate of people with sight impairments. You could research special palettes of colours designed for this purpose. Some programs like Tableau already come pre-packaged with them.

8 Don't be afraid to boil down

When you visualize, be aware that visualizations may lose information. Often, visualizations require certain reductions in order for the message to be most effective, aggregating the information in order to produce an optimum image. What visuals will never do is *add* information (if they do, you are manipulating your data, which goes against everything in the field). For example, there is no need to include all the numbers from your dataset – the relative differences on the charts you use should represent some of those numbers for you. Sometimes column names can also be removed, depending on the message you want to get across.

In essence, reducing the visuals to their absolute bare essentials can create a much more powerful and compelling picture; just make sure that *you* know the mechanics behind it when questions are asked. This is the job of the data scientist – to find the right balance of information and visuals.

Continues on page 194

Colour schemes

A lot of people underestimate the importance of colours. I was the same, until I delved into the world of colour theory and saw how much I could improve my visualizations by simply combining the right colours.

The best part is that there is a science behind it. You don't have to guess or pick colours at random. Certain colours work better together. Some combinations work well as contrasts, while others are best for showing gradual progression. Colour theory is a secret weapon in my data science toolkit. Why secret? Because it isn't common for data scientists to think that colours are important.

The principles of using colours are not difficult. The best method, to my mind, uses the colour wheel. The full spectrum of colours runs (as in a rainbow) from red through to violet. If those two ends of the spectrum are connected to form a circle, the traditional colour wheel is created.

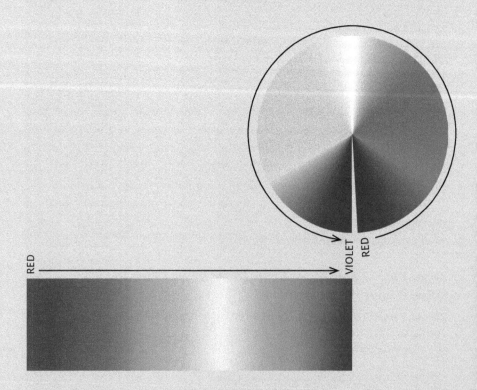

The exact spot where a colour appears on the 360° wheel is called its hue. Hues shade into one another imperceptibly. There are an infinite number of them. To keep things simple, I have divided the wheel on this page in to six main hues: yellow, orange, red, violet, blue and green. I have then sub-divided the six to get twelve segments in all, so that for instance the hue half-way between yellow and green is set off as yellow-green.

There are six colour rules explained on the following pages using the same wheel. All you need to take from each one is where the basic elements of the colour wheel fit together, and from there you can simply choose the best colour palette for your project. As the colour wheel is basically a logical representation of the entire colour spectrum, displaying it in black and white can (counterintuitively) help with thinking rationally about colour theory by avoiding subjective responses to the colours themselves.

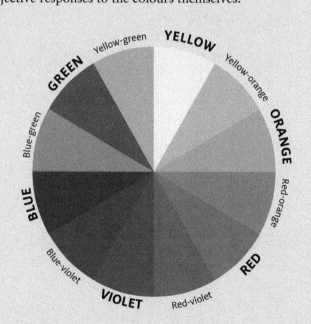

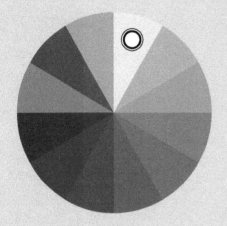

Monochrome

This is the simplest of the schemes as it works with just one colour. Once you have chosen a single colour, differentiate between your categories by selecting a lighter or darker shade. The benefit of using a monochromatic scheme is that there is little limit to the number of shades you can use.

When to use it
Great if you want to ensure that the colour-impaired will see it.

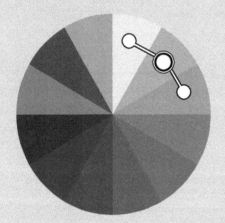

Analogous

Choose one colour and select two colours that fall on either side of it. An analogous colour scheme can be difficult for some people to see, as there is no great discrepancy between the colours.

When to use it
Excellent for heat maps, as well as for illustrating gradual differences between data.

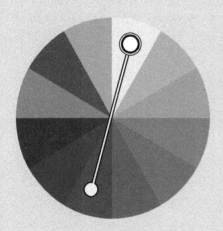

Complementary

Choose two colours that are diametrically opposite to each other on the wheel – maybe yellow and purple, or green and red, or blue and orange.

When to use it
Contrasting colours like this provide striking ways to depict comparisons between two values, and are commonly used when highlighting distinct categories.

Split complementary

As the name suggests, this uses similar principles to the complementary scheme, but with one additional colour. Rather than using the colour that is diametrically opposite, use the two colours either side of the opposite colour.

When to use it
Perfect when you have three categories but want your audience to focus on one in particular, in order to highlight trends or features.

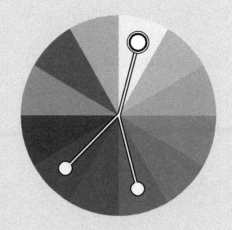

Triadic

Choose three colours positioned on an equilateral triangle. This is where the primary colour scheme of red, blue and yellow sits.

When to use it
Perfect for portraying three categories of equivalent importance, without the bias that you would exploit with the split complementary scheme. This is a much more democratic choice if you do not want to direct attention to a particular category.

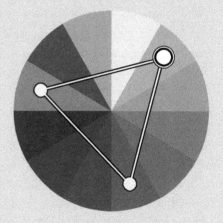

Tetradic

Similar to triadic, with the difference that it uses four colours rather than three.

When to use it
If you have multiple categories that should be given equivalent importance, use the triadic scheme for an odd number of categories and the tetradic scheme for an even number.

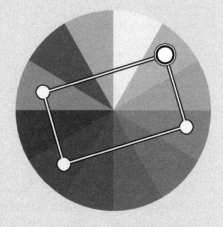

Continued from page 189

9 Add context

Without context, data is meaningless. Visuals pull data together, sometimes from disparate sources, and this may result in surprising contextual revelations even for seasoned practitioners. When we see things visually, we can better understand the relationship between otherwise scattered information. Visualization gives context to numbers. For most people, visuals provide a breathing space from the text in lengthy reports. They can help to form initial impressions, and can give you the opportunity to highlight anomalies and gaps in information (in the following chapter, I will show you how to make the most of anomalies in your presentations).

Adding relative values will help your audience to understand *why* something is important. Showing how much a company has spent over a period of time on a graph might turn a few heads, but setting that information in context (for example, setting the size of expenses of that company against those of its competitors) can really help to bring it home that the company is spending too much year on year.

The news is a good example of how information can be visualized in various ways. As a hypothetical example, let's say we were looking at how the pollution index of a country is handled by two separate news organizations, one within the country and another outside. A national news site might choose to report that their country has taken great steps to reduce pollution since the last climate summit, and that their pollution index is far lower than it had been in the previous year. This would make for a positive report on their country's measures to improve air quality. However, an outside news network could just as easily show that the index does not compare favourably with that of other countries when its relative size is taken into consideration.

Visualization, then, needs to be given a context.

Layers of meaning

The fashion for visualizing information can be traced back to the 19th century. Look at the chart on the next page. Created in 1869 by the civil engineer Charles Joseph Minard, it shows Napoleon's march towards – and retreat from – Moscow in 1812–13. It demonstrates one of the most important ways of representing information: through layers. It overlays a Sankey diagram (which we will discuss later) on a geographical map.

The chart takes the form of a map following the journey of the *Grande Armée* from Kowno (located in what is now Lithuania) to Moscow and back again. The grey line traces their march towards Russia and the black line their retreat. At any given point the width of the line shows the number of men. At a glance, we can see the devastating effects of the campaign on the French troops. Minard tells us how many soldiers started out: 422,000, the number at the far left above Kowno. By the time the army returned, the width of the black line tells us, the number of surviving soldiers had dwindled to 10,000. We can also see where the army split up, which cities they passed through as well as their geographic locations, which rivers they forded, and the temperature of the cities they passed.

In just one picture, we have been told a huge amount. Minard has told us the story of the French campaign to Russia by using layers of information:

1 number of troops (given by the width of the lines and the numbers along the route to show the decimation of soldiers)

2 distance and routes travelled (distance given in a legend, routes visualized by the branching of the lines)

3 temperature (shown directly below the map in numerical format)

4 latitude and longitude (represented by a line graph directly below the map)

5 direction of travel (the grey line is read left to right, the black line is read right to left)

This map shows us the tenets of telling a story through layers of information.

10 Maintain a balance

When we're compressing our data into visual bites, we will inevitably lose a little information. Therefore, it is important to ensure that we are not actually tampering with the truth when we finally come to develop our visuals. This can be difficult, particularly considering the preferences and biases that we can have over individual colours and shapes. A result given in green, for example, might be associated with profit, or intellect, when that may not be the case at all. We should be mindful of how these biases might misrepresent our data.

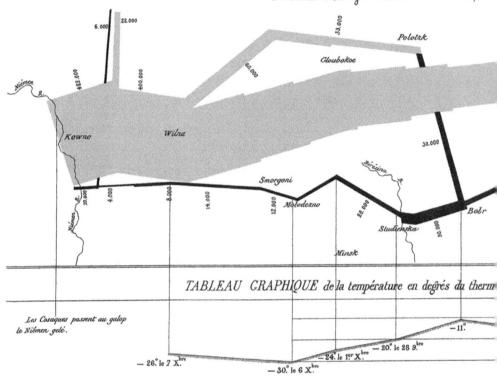

Carte Figurative des pertes successives en hommes de l'Armée Française
Dressée par M. Minard, Inspecteur Général des Pont

Les nombres d'hommes présents sont représentés par les largeurs des zônes colorées à raison d'un
des zônes. Le rouge désigne les hommes qui entrent en Russie, le noir ceux qui en sortent.
dans les ouvrages de M.M. Thiers, de Ségur, de Fezensac, de Chambray et le journal i
Pour mieux faire juger à l'oeil la diminution de l'armée, j'ai supposé que les corps du Prince Jérôm
et Mobilow et ont rejoint vers Orscha et Witebsk, avaie

TABLEAU GRAPHIQUE de la température en degrés du therm

Les Cosaques passent au galop
le Niémen gelé.

— 11.°

— 26.° le 7 X.bre

— 24.° le 1er X.bre   — 20.° le 28 9.bre

— 30.° le 6 X.bre

Autog. par Regnier, 8. Pas. St Marie St Gain à Paris.

Number of troops   **Distance and routes**

5
layers of
information

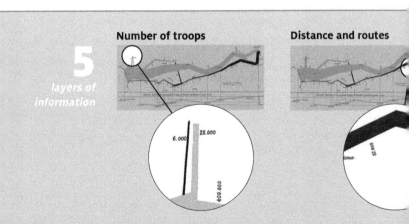

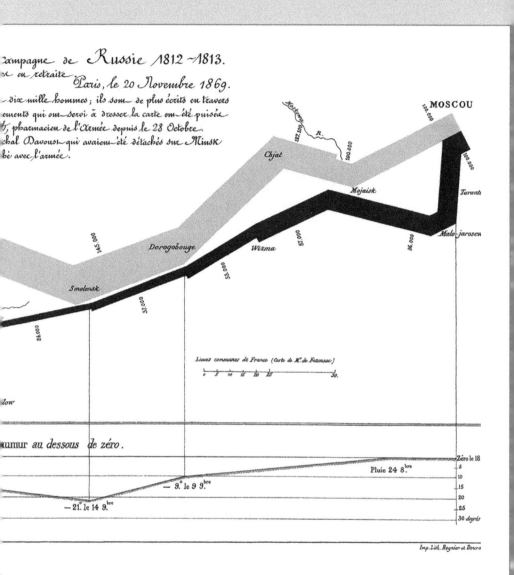

campagne de *Russie* 1812 ~1813.
en retraite   Paris, le 20 Novembre 1869.

— six mille hommes; ils sont de plus écrits en travers
— ements qui ont servi à dresser la carte ont été puisés
— , pharmacien de l'Armée depuis le 28 Octobre.
— chal Davoust qui avaient été détachés sur Minsk
— bé avec l'armée.

MOSCOU
180.000

Chjat

Mojaïsk   Taranti

Dorogobouge   Wizma   Malo-jaroseu
145.000   55.000   96.000

Smolensk
24.000   37.000

Lieues communes de France (Carte de M.ʳ de Fetensac)
0   5   10   15   20   25   50.

low

Réaumur au dessous de zéro.

Zéro le 18
Pluie 24 8.ᵇʳᵉ   5
                      10
— 9.° le 9 9.ᵇʳᵉ   15
                      20
— 21.° le 14 9.ᵇʳᵉ   25
                      30 degrés

Imp. Lith. Regnier et Dourd

Temperature   **Latitude and longitude**   **Direction of travel**

nature en degrés du thermomètre   Molodezno   MOSCOU
                                        25.000   180.000

— 11.°

20.° le 28 9.ᵇʳᵉ   Minsk   100.000

This is largely applicable to visuals that require benchmarking (comparing two or more ideas, institutions, products or services). As purveyors of the data, we should not push one claim above another due to our own preference; we must show how each aspect compares. Stakeholders will quickly see if a benchmarking visual is lop-sided – and they will ask why you haven't included relative information across all your categories. Don't bury the data that you don't like.

11 Know your options for telling a story

The hard truth is that data is boring for most people. There are many visual options for presenting your data, and each has benefits and pitfalls in terms of telling the story of your data. When used in the wrong context, a simple bar chart can be just as boring as a dataset.

Visualizing qualitative data

I've gone through some of my favourite visuals, from the simple to the most complex, in the section that starts on page 200. You will notice that almost all of them require quantitative, not qualitative data to be effective. It can be more difficult to visualize data that is non-numerical, although there are options. One of the best examples for showing the many ways in which qualitative data might be visualized is Sentiment Viz, a content generator that gives you the option to input one or more keywords and see how Twitter users feel about them from tweets submitted in the last 20 minutes.[3] The other option of course is Word Clouds, which were discussed in Chapter 3.

Final thoughts

For me, the visualization step straddles the stages on either side of it (data analytics and presentation) in the Data Science Process. Visualization can contribute significantly to and even help to guide our analytics both before and during our analytics stage, *and* it fundamentally supports our final presentations to our stakeholders. Visualizing information can therefore be an extremely rewarding process, not only in its power to persuade others of data's power but also in its potential to surprise ourselves with new insights.

We're now moving to the final furlong – presentation of our data. Visualization really is the last opportunity we have to make changes, to rerun analyses, and to filter our data. Thus, we must ensure that we are ready to present our results, before proceeding to this final stage of the process.

Reference

SuperDataScience (2016) SDS 012: Online learning, tableau insights and ad hoc analytics with Megan Putney [Podcast] 22 November [Online] www.superdatascience.com/12 [accessed 05.06.2017]

Notes

1 Another completely free alternative to Tableau is Microsoft PowerBI, a tool which offers similar functions, but my personal preference is for the former program.

2 For inspirational ideas for visualizing projects, look at data journalist David McCandless' website, informationisbeautiful.net, which takes visual storytelling to the next level.

3 It's a very interesting tool and I recommend checking it out. You can find it by typing 'Sentiment Viz' into Google.

Types of chart

Heat map

Heat maps represent our data in a matrix by using colours – typically conforming to those associated with heat, such as blue, orange and red. They most commonly help to highlight and compare the significance of key areas in physical regions, but they can also be used to emphasize patterns in tables.

The colour original of this heatmap shows the most crime-heavy days of the week for each month in Philadelphia in 2006–2015. The colours of the cells range from deep blue for the Sunday in February (least crime) to dark red for the Tuesday in July (most).

Data source: www.opendataphilly.org

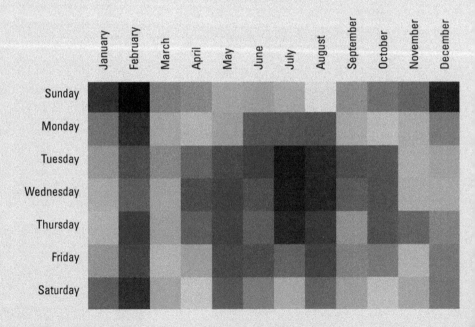

Bar chart

A bar chart will group data into proportional bars of information, which can be displayed either horizontally or vertically. This is a good visual aid to use when we are comparing and ranking quantitative data, because the x- and y-axes quantify our values by length.

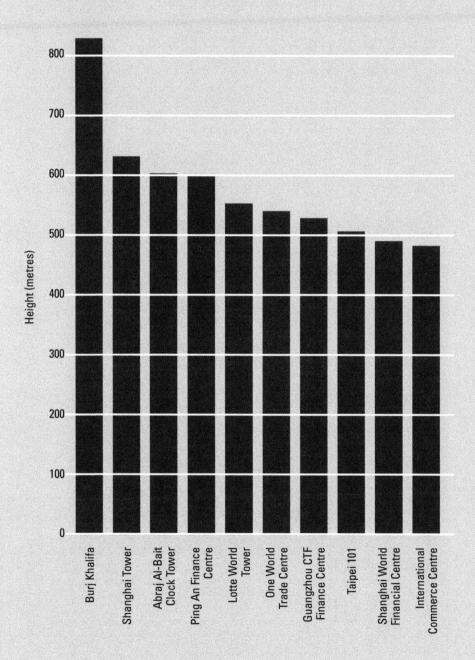

Histograms and probability distributions

Both options show how quantitative data is distributed. They are excellent for highlighting peaks and troughs in our data, which may happen when we are working with likelihoods or census information such as age.

In this histogram we can see the distribution of NBA players' height in the 2016–17 season.

Data source: www.scholarshipstats.com

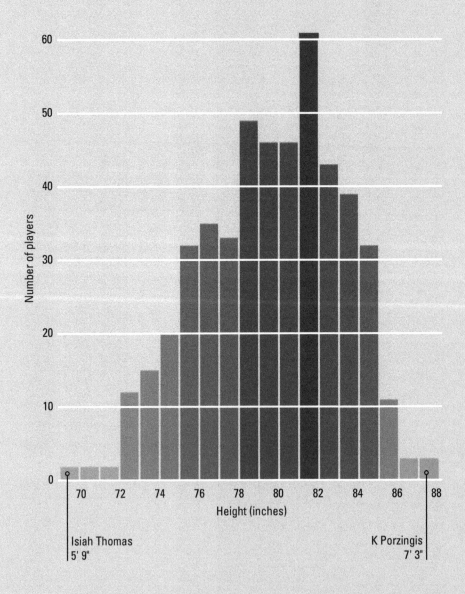

Line chart

A line chart links data points with a single line. It is most often used to show trends in a time series, such as frequency of product use in the course of a year.

In this chart we can see the growth of Apple's stock price over the past five years.

Data source: www.data.worldbank.org

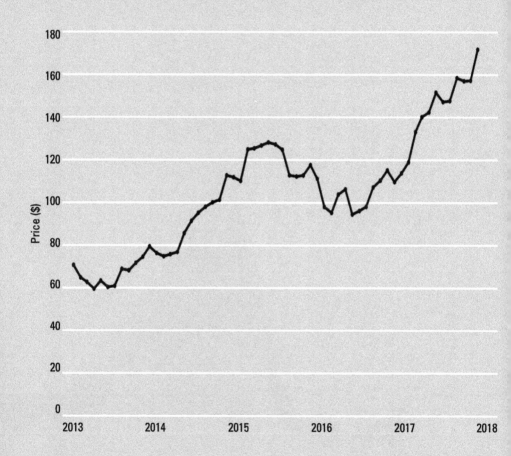

Area chart

An area chart is a line chart with the area underneath filled with colour. It is possible to stack area charts on top of each other to contrast categories. This type of chart is useful when we are working with segmented data, such as customers divided by age group or location.

This figure shows an area chart portraying long-term unemployment (27 weeks and over) for the period January 2005 to August 2017 for people in the US, split by gender. Note that stacked area charts add up to an area chart too, so adding the categories together must make sense.

Data souce: www.bls.gov

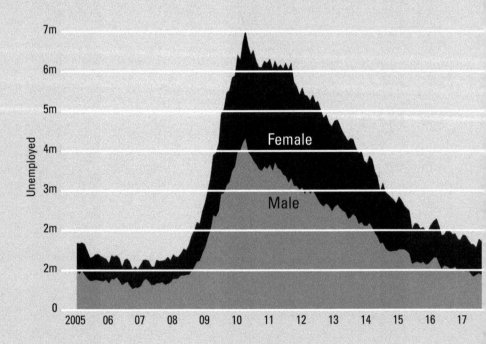

Scatter plot

This type of diagram will place our data on to a graph based on two variables of information on the horizontal and vertical axes. The location of our data points on the diagram will depend on their relationship to the variables.

This scatterplot allows us to explore the correlation between birth rate (how many children are born every year for every 1,000 existing citizens) and the percentage of people with access to the internet. Each point represents a country and shows its income group:

▲ high income

✳ middle income

● lower middle income

▼ low income

Data souce: www.data.worldbank.org

Note
This is a good example of when correlation doesn't necessarily imply causation. Or does it?

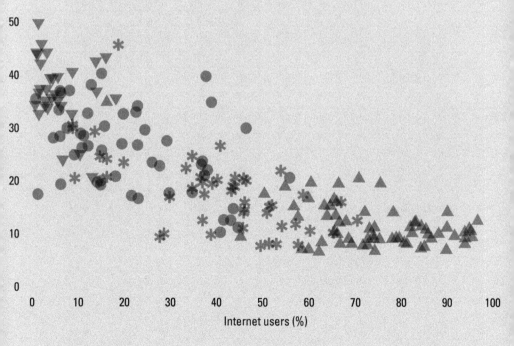

Internet users (%)

Bubble chart

Bubble charts can be of two types. The first kind is created by introducing an extra layer of information to a scatter plot ñ by adding sizes to the points (and thus, turning them into bubbles). For instance, in our previous example we could have assigned sizes to points to represent the population of each country.

The second type of bubble chart is much less sophisticated. The relative sizes of the bubbles still encode data, however there are no coordinates and the bubbles are arranged randomly.

Here are the average movie budgets in Hollywood by genre during 2007–2011.

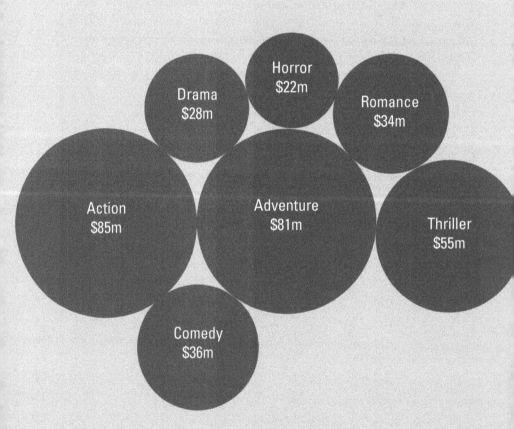

Pie chart

A lot of people hate pie charts because, unlike bar charts, it can be relatively difficult to see the difference between categories. Having said that, I think that they can be very effective if a) you have similarly proportionate data and you want to show it out or b) if you have extremely disproportionate data. As a rule of thumb, avoid using more than three or four categories with pie charts. Above three they become unreliable, because decisions have to be made about the sequence in which the data is presented, which in turn makes comparing slices difficult if they end up positioned awkwardly.

This pie chart shows how the New Generation gaming consoles compare in terms of total global sales for the years 2014–15 combined. The platforms in this dataset are PS4, One and Wii.

Data source: www.vgchartz.com

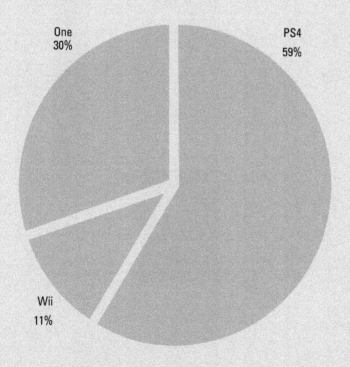

Tree map

Tree maps don't look *anything* like trees. Arranging data into different sized boxes, they are more akin to bubble charts – except that tree maps are a bit more organized.

This map shows the countries with the top 10 military budgets (2017 estimates in billions of dollars).

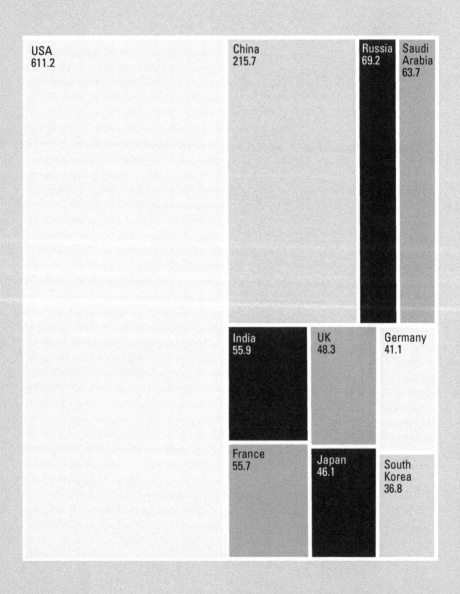

USA
611.2

China
215.7

Russia
69.2

Saudi
Arabia
63.7

India
55.9

UK
48.3

Germany
41.1

France
55.7

Japan
46.1

South
Korea
36.8

Waterfall chart

Waterfall charts visualize the cumulative effect of data in positive and negative values on a graph. They are good for breaking down components of an aggregate value such as profit.

This chart shows overall Star Wars *franchise revenue from movies and how much each film contributed to it.*

Data source: www.statisticbrain.com

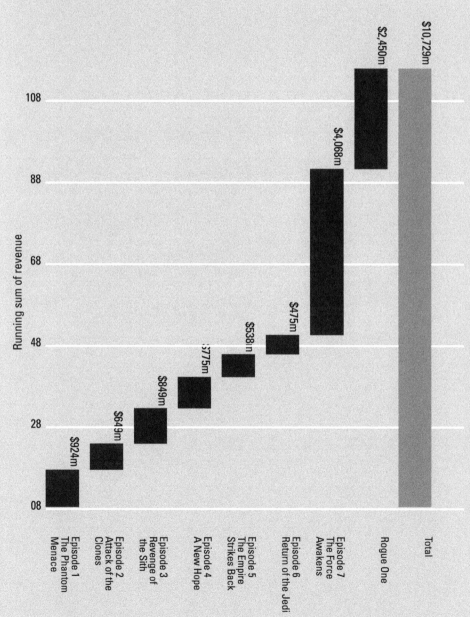

Sankey diagram

A Sankey diagram will show the movement of data through the size and direction of its arrows. This approach is perfect for visualizing any kind data flow – whether it is users going through a sales funnel or immigration patterns.

The example below demonstrates the migration trends between countries of the UK.

Data source: theinformationlab.co.uk

Likert scale

These are psychometric scales of information that represent the sum of responses to survey questions. Likert scales can only be used in instances where a Likert or similar system has been applied (typically, this requires a single response to a question on a sliding scale of five items).

This scale depicts what citizens think of the economic outlook in their countries for the next three to five years.

Datasource: www.arabbarometer.org

Q. What do you think the economic situation in your country will be during the next few years (3–5 years) compared to the current situation?

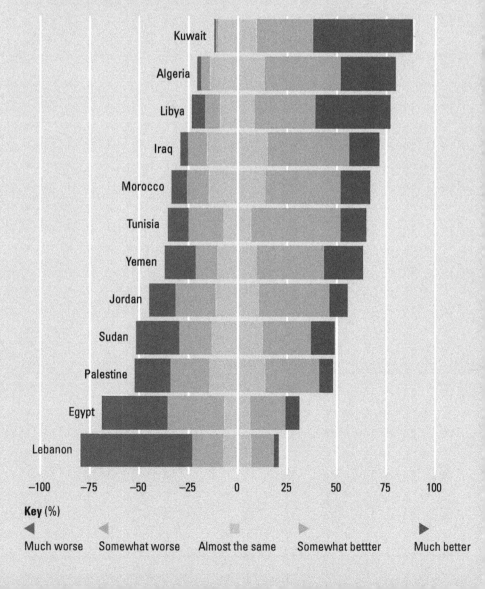

Key (%)

◄ Much worse ◄ Somewhat worse ▪ Almost the same ▷ Somewhat bettter ► Much better

Data presentation 09

This final stage of the Data Science Process takes our end users – the people who initiated the project – into consideration. If you have taken the advice of the previous chapters in this book, you will have at each stage kept an eye on our stakeholders and on what results they need. Now is the time for us to pass our insights on in a format that non-data scientists can handle and understand.

This chapter is essentially about communicating with people. It explains how the information you have gathered and processed can be refined and transmitted as a single, coherent message to your stakeholders. When people misunderstand your message, they will either take no action at all, or they will take the wrong actions – a disaster for any project.

That's precisely why, whenever I am asked what separates a good data scientist from a rockstar data scientist, my answer always is: the ability to communicate insights. And this chapter will provide pointers on how to hone your presentation and communication skills to set yourself up for success.

The importance of storytelling

Thinking back to our starting point in Part I, storytelling is a key part of the Data Science Process,[1] and it is up to *us* to make sure that our audience is engaged. Don't assume that, because you're speaking to the people who initiated the project, the onus is on them to make sense of your ideas and results. Remember they brought you in because they needed an expert to inform them about what their data is saying. Now is your chance to make an impact! Revisit each step of the process and ask yourself: what did I need to do at each stage? What questions needed to be answered? How did I resolve problems? What do the results show me? Has anything been left unanswered? Asking yourself these questions will help to set the narrative for your project in motion and will make the story specific to your experience – you are, after all, telling *your* story of how you communicated with the data.

Being able to convey our insights is exactly what is needed in workplaces with people who may not be particularly tech-savvy. Another benefit to taking care of how we communicate our data is that it can also give us an edge over number crunchers who might be able to write models and code but are less capable of conveying just how the results are relevant to the company.

CASE STUDY   Veros Credit – presenting to the end user

Anyone who has taken out a loan will know what a difficult process it can be. But the loan companies have complex processes of their own. After all, loan companies are not charities: they must assess whether taking on a new customer will pay off for them or not. To make a reasonable assessment, they must consider a variety of customer attributes, from credit score to employment history, and they must build a model from those attributes to drive down the risks for the company.

Greg Poppe is Senior Vice President of Risk Management at Veros Credit, a US-based financial services company that provides loans to people who want to purchase vehicles from car dealerships. His team oversees the company's data science and financial engineering projects, and one of their central tasks is to create a credit-scoring model to predict risk for each individual. Gathering the necessary data for potential customers determines a credit score, based on which Veros Credit will either approve or decline customer requests for a loan. That information is then returned to the car dealership, where a decision is made about whether or not to accept the terms laid out by Veros Credit.

The idea is to ensure that the interest rate of the approved loans and the fee charged for them will cover any of the risks that are associated with that loan and its operating costs. In order to maintain the model's intuitive nature, the risk assessment model is monitored on a monthly basis. During these observations, the parameters are adjusted in accordance with the additional data. That intuitiveness helps Veros Credit to isolate individual attributes for poor loan results, and enables them to decline customers as soon as they start to deviate from the established norm.

Talking to your audience

That's all complex work, but for Greg, the hardest part of his job is getting sign-off from the managerial and executive levels. To achieve this, he has to argue for his project – and as is the case with so many corporate positions, this means outlining it in a presentation. Relating data-driven models to a project's stakeholders is often tricky. While there are obviously exceptions, a CEO with no knowledge of the discipline or even statistics may well consider an outlier to mark the failure of a project. For this reason, when Greg creates a presentation he deliberately focuses on the end user, making sure that he strikes a tone that is understandable to those without a background in data science.

> When I was in college, I was a statistics tutor, which really helped me explain complex problems to people who were not invested in the subject, and in a way that they could understand. Once they understood, they got better grades – and they were happy. That experience helped me in my role as a data scientist, and I take the same approach when explaining my models to management. If you can't communicate what you're doing and why, then it'll always be an uphill struggle.
>
> (SuperDataScience, 2016b)

I truly believe that presentational skills are absolutely essential for a data scientist. Not everyone will come to data science with professional teaching experience, but you can learn valuable lessons from communicating the principles that you have learned in this book to friends and family. Doing so will have multiple benefits: the person to whom you're imparting this information will get to learn about the wonderful world of data science *and* you will get that valuable first-hand experience of, as the SuperDataScience mission encourages, 'making the complex simple'.

Creating data advocacy

Data science is a relatively new discipline, and as a result we cannot expect people to know what the subject entails or how useful it is for business. Some might think it is a fad (remember, our audience won't have read this book!) or they might think that its methodologies cannot be applied to their own line of work. We can and should see within our roles an opportunity to advocate using data for future company projects and for proving that all business people today have to be data-literate.

If we get buy-in from the stakeholders who listened to our presentation, we can make data science advocates of them as well. Prove to them data's value, and they will tell others, who will in turn become open to applying it to their own work.

CASE STUDY Processing communications

Presenting your findings can go much further than you think, if you only put in a little effort. It's not always the case that project leaders will require you to make a presentation, but I would always recommend that you take the initiative anyway – the advocates you create from highlighting how the data-driven work can help them will pay back in dividends.

When I worked at Sunsuper, an Australian superannuation fund, I was once called upon to optimize their efficiency in processing customer service communications about an annual campaign called the 'supermatch'. There was a significant backlog of messages, and consumers had to wait a long time before their request would be addressed. Quite simply, the company didn't have the capacity to process the number of customer requests that resulted from this campaign.

Through data science, I reduced the company's backlog of requests from 40 days to three.

This meant a lot for the customers, the business, and the company's revenue. I was also careful to ensure that my work didn't end with these results. I went back to the operations department and offered to present my findings, results and the approach I had taken. I didn't technically *have* to do this, but had I forgone this step, the department would not have understood what had actually happened – and may not have considered how beneficial data science could prove for their company. In effect, they were so happy with how the data had changed the course of their work that they continued to come back to me with questions about how much further we could increase company efficiency together.

That's how to create advocates: don't guard your secrets like a jealous magician. Go out of your way to show your clients the approach you have taken and how data science can vastly improve their business.

How to create a killer presentation

There are many, many books out there on how to design an effective presentation. In terms of methodology, there is not a lot to differentiate a presentation on data science from one on any other subject. The following section, then, details the best techniques that I have gathered from *my own experience* in devising presentations on data science. There is no single approach to writing and delivering a good presentation. I have developed my own style, one that I feel fits my voice and makes me feel comfortable. What follows are the techniques that I feel could be of use to rookie presenters of data science.[2]

Don't save these tricks only for when you are giving formal presentations – I also frequently use them when I'm speaking with new colleagues (and even friends and family) about my work, and some readers will also be familiar with these techniques from my online courses. If you have an opportunity to talk to someone about what data science is or any of its aspects, take it, and consider it as practice for presenting in more formal settings.

1 Prepare your structure

I begin every presentation by brainstorming what my project was about. For me, this means writing down the start (A) and end (B) points of my project opposite each other on a piece of paper (often I just imagine it in my mind). The blank space in between represents my journey, and I want to show my audience how I got from A to B. In this space, I simply write down the stages of the Data Science Process, filling it with these milestones and highlighting any areas that I found particularly surprising or revealing.

This one brainstorming session will give me a robust structure for my presentation, without me having to do any extra legwork at all. A focus on form is essential, as it gives my audience as many cues as possible with regard to what is coming next. Don't keep people at arm's length from your work, thinking that they simply won't be interested in what you have to say (or, worse, that *if* they don't understand they won't ask too many questions) – root them in your approach. The Data Science Process already has a logical, easy-to-follow structure, so why not explain the stages and then take them through it, step by step? When people feel comfortable that they know where the talk is going, they will retain more information and they will not only hear what you are saying but actually *listen* to you.

Writing when you're tired

This may sound counterproductive, but my favourite time to start writing presentations is at the very close of the day, when I'm exhausted and want to go to bed. The reason for this is threefold: 1) being tired limits my focus, meaning I am less likely to fill the page with technical detail; 2) if I know I only have a couple of hours, I'll be more likely to get something, anything, on the page, than if I know I have a full day ahead; and 3) I think people can get more creative when they are tired. It won't work for everyone, but this approach has definitely helped me make some major breakthroughs in my career. I don't know exactly why – maybe certain parts of your brain which inhibit creativity switch off and let the creative juices flow.

Of course, I can only recommend this for a first draft; don't expect to wake up the next morning with a pristine speech. However, if you struggle with the dreaded empty page, I wholeheartedly suggest trying it. Even if you can only use 10 per cent of what you write, you're still some way into your presentation the following morning. I find it so much easier to edit a text that has been written than to write something completely new.

2 Gather your materials

When I fill in the blank space on my brainstorming paper with milestones, I also consider the types of media that I could use to best illustrate my journey. From the previous step in the Data Science Process (visualization), I should already have a handful of graphics upon which I can draw. Depending on the nature of my project, I sometimes make use of additional images: company logos, software dashboards and product range, among others. Keeping in mind my audience's knowledge relevant to the project, I might also want to include some diagrams or flowcharts that will help people to understand the concepts I discuss more easily.

Remember that you don't need to restrict yourself to images. There might be videos or audio clips that you can use to support your arguments. You can even add a little humour – light-hearted memes can work wonders for a presentation about a particularly dry subject – just make sure that you can tie it to your topic and that you don't overdo it.

3 Know your audience

While I don't advocate deliberately 'dumbing down' or 'smartening up' a presentation for your audience, it is important to know who is in the room so that we can ensure that we hit their pain points. No matter to whom we speak – even people well versed in data science – our presentation must always be clear and well structured. Our arguments and results must be organized logically, and we must never assume anything of our listeners.

Nevertheless, if we want to place our stakeholders into different groups, this may have to do more with our own psychology – specifically with how we *perceive* our audience. For me, the most exciting of all audiences are those who hold the reins of the company: the executive team. This is why we will pay special attention to them in this section.

Most people are not exactly filled with joy at the prospect of presenting their findings to a company's suits. Imagine walking into a boardroom and seeing the CEO and four other executives staring you down. You *have* to say something of value to them – they're waiting for it. What's worse is that you know they have heard countless presentations before, which means you will have to work twice as hard here as you would for any other audience.

The best thing that we can do with this seasoned group of listeners is to remind ourselves that they're only people. True, they're very busy people, but that merely places greater weight on the importance of clear, coherent presentational skills.

There are a few other tricks that you can use to deal with executives that are worth mentioning here, which have always served me well.

1 Zero in on dollar amounts

Executives are largely concerned with the bottom line. If you haven't already done so, figure out how much your project will save, earn or cost the company, and try to quantify it in monetary values. Instead of an increase in revenue, your project's output may for example have been a recommendation for a different organizational or strategic approach, or a suggested improvement to customer experience, but don't think that this will get you off the hook. Changes will *always carry a cost* for a company, and you should consider it a part of your job to work out what that amount is.

Be specific with these values. If you've been looking at user experience, for example, consider how the alterations you have put forward will retain 'X' number of customers who will be paying 'Y' amount in a 'Z' time frame. Ask the relevant departments to help you with the numbers, both in terms of costs and expected gains. In short, think like an investor from *Dragon's Den* or *Shark Tank* and keep an eye on the bottom line.

II Be prepared for hard questions

Although it's a quickly growing field, we are lucky to be working as data scientists. It's still rare to find a key 'data guy' in a company, even in commercial industries, and it's even rarer that we will find ourselves facing someone with truly developed technical know-how at board level.

Many practitioners feel that this lack of knowledge will make us immune to questioning, and that is often true for a certain type of audience. But for executives, the information gap only adds another layer of complication for us – as they are responsible for the company, the executives will be especially cautious (and inquisitive) of new approaches. To prepare yourself, don't go on the defensive. Focus only on the facts – this is what benefits us. Data does not lie. It can be evidence for successful campaigns, or it can tell some hard truths. Either way, there should be no doubt that gaining better insight into data will only help a company. Convey as much detail as they need, show them the benefits, and try to keep your language jargon-free.

III Pave the way for a stress-free Q&A

You should prepare yourself for a detailed question and answer (Q&A) session – planning ahead and brainstorming the sorts of questions that you might be asked will make this a much less gruelling experience. This could be applied to all presentations, but CEOs are especially on the hunt for problems and issues that could leave the company short-changed. If you found gaps or anomalies in the results of your data analysis, it is reasonable that you will want to explain them in your presentation. But in my view the better method is to entice the audience with the perceived problems instead.

Why is that the case? Because these obvious 'issues' are almost guaranteed to be asked during the Q&A anyway. So this is both a good approach for getting the Q&A going (usually a difficult thing in any presentation) and a way to set up a question for which you can adequately prepare.

4 *State the problem upfront...*

In order to get the message across, we must make sure to remind our audience of the problem that we were brought in to solve – for this, we can simply return to our first stage: Identify the question. Try to keep it as succinct as possible. If it is possible to explain it in one sentence, then so much the better.

To train yourself to keep your statement brief, imagine that you've been asked to explain what you do to a group of six-year-olds. Throw out any information that points to your method or results, because all that is required of you at this stage is to clarify the *problem*. Once you have done so, you can expand on the steps you took to solve it.

5 ... then show them the benefits

One of the first rules in business marketing is that you should show your audience the benefits of what you are selling as early as you can. To keep an audience engaged in our presentation, we should highlight why their attention to what we are saying will be valuable to *them*. Once we have stated the problem, then we should tell them that what we have discovered will help improve sales, customer engagement, or whatever else our project revealed, and through that we can assure them that using data will improve their business. Once we've convinced them with this prospect, we must *make sure to deliver*.

Getting them engaged

Getting audience buy-in is not always easy. Many studies show that people have shorter attention spans in this Digital Age. While we can prepare our speeches as well as possible, there are some independent variables over which we have no control. Sometimes, we'll be speaking to our listeners at the end of the day, when they're tired and ready to go home, and at other times we might even get audiences who are hostile to our ideas. This means, on many occasions, we will have to work harder to get people on our side. One of the best techniques to achieve this is to interact with them.

In my experience, this has either meant making the audience laugh or asking them a question. For the former, when people hear those around them laughing, they will also feel a desire to engage. If you can, make a joke, but there is no need to force something if it doesn't come naturally to you. After all, humour can come across in different ways, so tread carefully. A safe joke to make is one that's at your own expense. I'm happy to admit that I will usually say something about how invigorating I find data science, a claim which is almost guaranteed a laugh. Cash in on the geeky charm, and when you show them that you can *also* directly help their business you'll have them eating from the palm of your hand.

If you're not a natural comic, or if you feel uncomfortable about breaking the ice in this way, try asking a question that calls for a show of hands instead. As an example, you might want to ask how many people in the room use a product or service relevant to your topic, or how many people know about a particular concept that you plan to discuss in more detail. Make sure that the question you ask is relevant to your talk.

Which of these is a preferable icebreaker? It depends on both your personality and your audience. Personally, I like to use the joke approach with larger audiences. It's easier to make 100 people laugh than five. Statistically (I'm using data science here!) the larger the group, the more people will relate to your humour and laugh. And once a few people are laughing, it's easier for the rest to pick up as well.

On the flip side, I find asking a question works especially well in the boardroom, because you can address people individually. It creates silence and they might start feeling uncomfortable. I embrace that silence. If I can get them to respond, I reward their engagement by thanking them – a method that encourages others in the audience to engage as well.

6 *Use clear, jargon-free language*

In my experience, the majority of data science presentations are unclear. Bad delivery aside, they are all too often unstructured, even rambling, and do not fulfil their aims. There are many motivations for this, and they range from a lack of interest in communicating one's results to a deliberate desire to keep things unclear to avoid questions. But a lack of clarity will kill future negotiations for us, both in terms of the achievements of the project and in terms of our career in the company.

First, make sure that everyone in the audience is on the same page. People will come to our presentation with different levels of understanding about our subject matter, and this is especially the case for a new discipline like data science. Appeal to the person with the least knowledge (if you're in any doubt, aim low). As we did when explaining the project's scope, try to make clear the details in sentences that are as short and snappy as possible. Don't only detail what was done; show *why* these methods were important for getting relevant results. Don't throw out data science terminology and software names without a brief explanation of what they are or what they do.

7 Tell them our story

If we promote data science only for its theoretical underpinnings, our presentation is bound to be a non-starter. We must show our audience that data science has practical applications. Do a little groundwork to learn about the departments from which our audience have come, and tell them about how the methods we use can be applied to their own work. This will get them thinking about data science and its implementation.

Offering mini 'walkthroughs' of how we went about our work can also help to ground our audience in the accessibility of data science. Even though I love the subject, I'm under no illusions: communicating certain aspects, especially data analysis, can be difficult when speaking to a group of people who are simply not interested in the subject. This gap between 'us' and 'them' gets even wider when we're rattling off a list of facts and figures. Walkthroughs gently introduce listeners to the subject by putting them *in our shoes* – any audience is much more likely to be receptive to a personal, human story than a shopping list of data details.

I believe that it was due to this approach to my presentation which I gave at the Conference of Major Super Funds (CMSF) that *Investment Magazine* ran an article about me entitled 'Sunsuper's Russian data scientist wows CMSF'. If I had only delivered a presentation on the results of the process, I am pretty sure that the title of the piece would have been different. There is no magic involved. Anybody can do this.

Techniques from motivational speakers

Many of the best public speakers I know will use this trick of adding a human element to the story they're about to tell. Popular motivational speaker Tony Robbins and scientist-turned-filmmaker Randy Olson frequently use relatable, personal stories to put forward their ideas.[3] Granted, Robbins' subject matter of life fulfilment makes it easier to draw upon his personal experiences, but it is also possible to do the same with our data science projects – all that's required is a change in mindset.

Rather than thinking about the cold, hard facts of your project, think about how you felt emotionally and what you experienced at each stage of the process. Did you have any interesting interactions with people? Was there anything that surprised you? Did you suffer any setbacks? How did your past experience help you in this project? What did the results mean for you? This will get the audience hooked with regard to *how* you achieved the breakthrough.

Also remember that, when you're building a narrative of your own experience, you shouldn't just focus on the positive elements. People love the underdog, because that's a position we can all relate to. No one wants to hear a riches-to-riches story. Tell them about the things that might have overwhelmed you and how you overcame these roadblocks. It's this emotional journey, so often used by motivational speakers, that our audience will remember.

8 Design your slides (optional)

Not all presentations will require supporting slides, but my personal preference is to use them. When executed correctly, slides can give the audience an extra layer of information and prevent their minds from wandering. The best two pieces of advice that I can give when writing slides are:

1 Don't go overboard – our audience needs time to digest the information we give them – try to keep the number of slides low, maybe no more than one every three minutes.

2 Limit the amount of text on each slide. If we add too much, we'll force our audience to both read the slides *and* listen to us – and they will end up doing both things badly!

While I will always make sure that I have a PowerPoint presentation to support me, I must emphasize that these slides support *me*, not the other way around. Introverts may not like this idea, but our audience should be looking at *us*. *We* are the conveyors of information – the slides are only there to back us up.

PowerPoint and Keynote are both excellent tools for designing presentations. We don't need to master these programs to see the benefits – I am sure that I am only using 15 per cent of PowerPoint's full potential, and yet I can make extremely effective presentations and courses using the software. Most corporate organizations use PowerPoint, and some will train employees in using the program. Don't dismiss these sessions, even if you've worked with PowerPoint before – each course leader will bring something different to the table and will show you what works for them in helping to create excellent supplementary material.

9 Practice, practice, practice

Providing your presentation doesn't contain classified information, I highly recommend reading it out to an audience of individuals in one or more practice runs. Knowing how the speech has been received by another group of people will give you a little confidence boost when you come to present your findings 'proper'.

Presenting your first draft to a 'practice' audience of (preferably) people without a background in data science will help you hone your language to reduce jargon and maintain clarity. Some issues concerning language when you first start presenting are:

- **Using too many, um, filler words.** After your presentation, ask your audience how often you have used these words like *um* and *like*. Better yet, record yourself on your phone and listen to it. Try to become more conscious of filler words in future practice runs. People tend to use fillers when they are nervous and feel they need to keep talking – but embrace the silences. Pauses in narrative might feel incredibly long for you as the speaker, but they can be very beneficial and also provide a helpful break in information for the audience. Consider pauses as a way for your audience to process what they have learned, not as a sign that you are lagging behind.

- **Avoiding eye contact.** A lot of analysts have this problem! Although it is slowly changing, people with a technical background as a whole tend to be less used to speaking on a public platform. In my experience, people uncomfortable with public speaking will often look at the ground, which means that they will not connect with their audience in a crucial way. Push yourself to look at the people you are talking to. A common trick is to imagine them naked – I've never taken it that far myself, but what helps me is to pick out the people who I think look the most open and friendly, and focus on speaking directly to them. Bonus points for those of you who find a handful of friendly faces at different places in the room: moving your focus from one to the other will trick your audience into thinking that you're engaging with them all.

- **Over-earnestness.** Data science is a serious business, but don't let that take over your presentational style. There is a danger that you can come across as overly serious and judgmental, which will not make your audience warm to you. It's relatively simple psychology here; just try to smile, even be vulnerable. This will build a connection with your audience and help to establish a rapport that will keep them on your side. To reassure people that you are open to their comments and opinions, tell them how they can contact you and how they can access your findings.

- **A lack of expression.** Another side effect of nerves is a monotonous delivery. You don't need to be a great actor to make positive changes to the way you speak. Experiment with your intonation and speed, varying both at points that require extra emphasis. This is very important if you don't want to put your listeners to sleep.

The end of the process

Congratulations, we've reached the final stage of the Data Science Process! All that's left now is for you to gather your materials, take a deep breath and present your brilliant work to your stakeholders.

Before you move on to the next chapter, take a moment to think about all you have learned. Perhaps return to Part I to really see how far you've come. Have you developed the mindset of a data scientist? If you have been reading this book cover to cover, you should by now have some idea with regard to your strengths and weaknesses. Jot them down on a piece of paper – this list will help you in formulating an approach when reading the final chapter on finding a career for yourself in data science.

References

SuperDataScience (2016a) SDS 010: Model validation, data exhaust and organisational cultural change with Yaw Tan [Podcast] 10 November [Online] https://www.superdatascience.com/sds-010-model-validation-data-exhaust-and-organisational-cultural-change-with-yaw-tan [accessed 05.06.17]

SuperDataScience (2016b) SDS 014: Credit scoring models, the law of large numbers and model building with Greg Poppe [Podcast] 12 December [Online] https://www.superdatascience.com/sds-014-credit-scoring-models-the-law-of-large-numbers-and-model-building-with-greg-poppe [accessed 05.06.17]

Notes

1 My friend and mentor, Yaw Tan, Senior Vice President of Financial Crime
Analytics & Programme Management at DBS Bank (Singapore) half-jokingly
refers to the presentation stage of the Data Science Process as requiring an
additional 80 per cent of your time (on top of the 100 per cent you spent on
stages 1–4), because it is so crucial that we deliver at this stage. I call this the
'80-20-80 rule of Yaw' (SuperDataScience, 2016a).

2 While this perspective may be useful to you, don't let it constrain your creativity.
There is no single best approach to writing and delivering a presentation. The
style that's most comfortable for you may be different from what works for me.

3 In his seminal work, *Houston, We Have a Narrative?* Olson puts forward the
benefits of using narrative to convey complex scientific concepts.

Your career in data science 10

By 2020, there will be a projected increase of 364,000 new data and analytics job openings in the US alone (Burning Glass Technologies and IBM, 2017). I use this figure to introduce this chapter because I want to push the point that data science jobs currently are and will continue to be in extremely high demand. With companies such as Airbnb running their own internal universities for teaching data science (Mannes, 2017), and redundant American coal miners teaching themselves coding skills (Rosenblum, 2017), it is clear that a vast number of companies in the field of technology (and beyond) are struggling with a lack of suitable candidates on the market. And in an age where so many jobs are at risk of being made obsolete within 20 years, data science should be an area of interest for anyone looking for job security, let alone an interesting career path.[1]

In this chapter, we will discuss how you can put your best foot forward in order to find, prepare for, and maintain a great career in data science. We will outline the top ways in which you can increase your chances of getting noticed in the field, what it is that employers want to see on your job application, and how you can prepare for your interview. And if you already have the position of your dreams, we'll discuss how you can stay there and grow.

Breaking in

There are a number of career paths that we can take in the field of data science. In this book, we have covered the demands of many of these roles, as they will comprise either the whole or select parts of the Data Science Process. Position requirements will depend on the institution and whether or not it has an established data science department, as well as how much of its budget it is willing (or able) to put toward a team of people.

Which job?

What this book has done is prepare you, at a top level, for each of the following job roles.[2] Let's now go through the kinds of titles that you might expect to find in your job search, and indicate in squared brackets where each might fit in the Data Science Process:

- **Business analyst.** This is much more comfortable terrain for many companies, as business intelligence roles are (currently) more common. This position uses BI to translate the analysed data into visuals, insights and recommendations. Strong presentation skills will always be required for this role. [Steps 4–5]

- **Data analyst (data preparation).** Chapter 5 showed us that data preparation is one of the longest stages of the Data Science Process, so this role shouldn't come as a surprise. This is an entry-level position in data science and it is responsible for cleaning and structuring data in preparation for analysis. [Step 2]

- **Data analyst (modelling)/data modeller.** This person is responsible for developing the systems and models that can be applied to a company's databases. While data preparation may not always be part of the job description (sometimes that step will be handled by the data preparation analyst), it's still very important to have skills in this area. [Steps 2–3]

- **Data scientist/advanced analyst/machine learning (ML) practitioner/ senior data scientist.** This is, for me, the 'real data science' role. A professional who fits this category of job must know the Data Science Process like the back of their hand, must take initiative, must be data-oriented, creative, and must show skills in programming and analysis. Most roles may also require visualization and presentation skills. [Steps 1–5]

- **Data science manager/analytics manager.** This is a less technical role and therefore not everyone would consider this a natural progression in career development – some people will choose to remain data scientists. The analytics manager handles the client-facing function of the team and/ or heads the team, making sure that the right resources and people are allocated to projects. [Step 1, Step 5]

When you look at these role breakdowns and at the jobs currently on offer, try to be flexible. Especially if you are at the beginning of your career, don't discount some positions in favour of others – sometimes the role you want can be achieved by working in another position for a while and then 'working up' to your dream job. One trick I have learned is to consider moving through the roles as you would through the Data Science Process, that is, begin as a business analyst or data preparation analyst and work through to your desired position. The benefit of this technique is that you will gain valuable experience in earlier steps of the Data Science Process, which means you will be better equipped to identify and deal with problems you encounter in the later steps.

Hidden roles

Note that data science roles aren't restricted to those that I have listed above. I have noticed a number of positions popping up for 'functional analysts' which, after doing a little digging, I found are excellent roles for people who are fresh out of university (or other courses of study) and want to get their feet wet in the field before jumping in at the deep end. These roles are a little like paralegals in a law firm – be prepared to work *for* someone and perhaps do tasks that you might consider menial. But if you're in a big company, these jobs can give you great exposure and be a great stepping stone to a higher position (and as you will learn later on in this chapter, getting to know colleagues and networking are key to any data scientist's success).

Another route that readers who might be more confident of their skills may choose to take is consulting. Don't be fooled by the name – while consultants in many industries will only start after having developed an expertise in their field over many years, data science consultants can start right away (as I did), acting as an advisor for company executives who want to know *how* they should read their data. Consultants might even be brought in for critical decision and policy making with regard to data science in companies. As a consultant, you not only get to work in the end-to-end Data Science Process but if you play your cards right you *also* gain exposure to a variety of industries. This will put you ahead of the competition, as after a couple of years of work you will likely know the industries in which you would like to develop your career.

Another reason why I encourage people to start in consulting is that this type of job is less likely to pigeonhole them before they are ready to specialize. This is especially the case in smaller, boutique analytics consulting firms where the number of staff is small and therefore every employee is trained to become a sort of data science Swiss Army Knife

(SuperDataScience, 2017b). Such firms provide excellent opportunities for the new kids on the block.

Yes, consulting does mean long hours and hard work, and for that reason this type of role may not be ideal for those who have private responsibilities. However, if you are able and prepared to set your personal life aside for a few months as your project gets started, you will develop a lot of experience and a great understanding of the industry and how data science roles fit within it. In effect, working as a consultant gives you a top-level view of the roles so that you can identify where you will want to fit in the future.

Which field?

As data science is in such high demand, I am sure that readers will want to know how they can develop a strategy to focus on a particular field. While many industries are actively looking for data scientists, there are fields where there are *more* jobs available, and for readers who are not yet sure in which area they may wish to enter, it would be logical to go where the demand is expected to grow. Burning Glass Technologies/IBM's 2017 report breaks down demand for data science job roles by six key sectors (professional services, finance and insurance, manufacturing, information, healthcare and social assistance, retail trade). In their report, the professional services industry (which typically includes but is not limited to management consultancy, law and medicine) takes the lion's share of the roles, with the finance and insurance industry coming a close second.

What we can make of this is, if you want the greatest chance of getting at least to the interview stage, consider applying in the professional services or finance and insurance industries, where there are more jobs on offer.

Another great way to find data science jobs is simply to follow the news. Chapter 2 will have introduced the broad landscape of data science to you – data and AI are hot topics at the moment and their newsworthiness is only set to grow, so stay informed and keep a folder of article clippings about areas that most interest you.

Even those data scientists who are well into their careers should continue to stay on top of developments. Dan Shiebler, data scientist at True Motion, says:

this is the information age. When I get curious about how data science is moving in another field, it's pretty easy for me to look up, read some research papers, and dive into it as much as I can. I've been interested in the cutting edge

of convolutional neural network models for image understanding and their relationship to neuroscience. I found a professor at Brown University who's done a
lot of research on this, and so I'm doing research with him in my spare time. It's
been cool being part of a cutting-edge field that's totally orthogonal to the sort
of stuff I do at TrueMotion.

(SuperDataScience, 2017a)

Remember that, in order to keep your ideas fresh and excel in the field, the
responsibility is on you to read about and research your discipline. Do as
Shiebler did, and go on the hunt for projects that you will find fascinating
and fun.

What else?

You have already taken the first step in learning about data science by reading
this book. But it is vital to emphasize here that this can only be the *first* step.
One book is never enough – it never should be! Continuing to build your pros-
pects in the field is an absolute must, before you rush in and apply for jobs.

Here are a few things that you should do before you think about writing
that first job application.

1 Take (more) time to learn the craft

Universities have responded to the demand for data science by establishing
fully fledged degrees in the subject. Some are masked under sexed-up titles
such as 'Online Master of Science in Predictive Analytics' (Northwestern
University), 'Business Intelligence and Social Media' (Brunel University),
and 'Computational Statistics and Machine Learning' (University College
London), but these courses all offer data science as a significant component.

In my honest view, there is not much point in getting one of these degrees.
Expense aside, the problem with holding an established degree in data
science is that the discipline ages *very quickly*. Universities can be incredibly bureaucratic, and designing a new programme can take well over six
months to be approved. By the time the course has gone through all of the
university's red tape, the discipline will likely have moved on already.[4]

What's more, most (if not all) of the information that you need in order
to master data science can be procured online. There are a great many practitioners teaching online courses (myself included) from whom you can learn
not only the theory but also the application of the discipline. This, in my
view, is currently a more reasonable option. Having said that, it's important
to be selective when choosing an online course – in this democratic age of the

internet, anyone and everyone can set up a course – but find the right course leader and you will have open access to knowledge that will be updated as and when new methods become available and older practices become defunct.

2 It's not what you know, it's how you apply it

What do you think was the most powerful tool in getting my career started? Programming? Tableau? Relational databases? Thompson sampling?

You might be surprised to hear that it was PowerPoint, but this is the reality. This simple tool changed everything for me. Out of all of the complex software packages and algorithms I have used, PowerPoint had the greatest impact and was largely responsible for gaining me my most prominent role. As I said in Chapter 9, there are lots of talented number crunchers, but those data scientists who can effectively communicate insights to an audience are rare.

The point I want to make here is not that PowerPoint should be the fix-all for every data scientist, but that I didn't discount anything based on its simplicity. Instead, I figured out a way to make my strengths and my knowledge work for *me*. While at university, I knew that I had particularly strong presentation skills, and I knew that the slides I designed on PowerPoint were an essential part of my presentations.

This is an example of how I applied my knowledge to benefit my career movement. Your knowledge will likely be in something else – take a moment to find out what that is and write a few ideas down. In *The Future of the Mind*, Michio Kaku quotes neuroscientist Richard Davidson to illustrate how important it is to broaden your mindset about your skills and ability to succeed:

> Your grades in school, your scores on the SAT, mean less for life success than your capacity to co-operate, your ability to regulate your emotions, your capacity to delay your gratification, and your capacity to focus your attention. Those skills are far more important…
>
> (Richard Davidson, quoted in Kaku, 2014)

You are not the sum of your grades. Having a flair for analytics will stand you in good stead, but being sociable and having an interest in ethics are important additional areas that are in danger of being overlooked by any but the most astute data scientists. Then, when you have the time, consider how these skills or expertise can be applied to any one of the steps in the Data Science Process.

3 Share and share alike

Data science is an unusual discipline in that its practitioners are keen to share their research and developments amongst each other. Let's use that to our benefit. There is a good deal of open source content available online that you can play with when you come to practise what you have learned in data science. As I said in Chapter 3, working through mock assignments and applying new algorithms to real-life datasets are an essential part of keeping your ideas fresh and your mind responsive to the discipline. So 'join the conversation', and share your data, developments and progress with others.[5]

If you're not yet ready to contribute yourself, there are also a great many crowdsourcing projects that require people to get involved in handling large datasets, in order to advance their algorithms. A quick search on Google for 'data crowdsourcing projects' will help you find them, and the added benefit is that you can work on many of these projects from the comfort of your own living room.

Caroline McColl, Associate Partner at FutureYou (a boutique data science consultancy firm in Australia), makes special note of sharing within the community as being a good and, thanks to the internet, practically cost-free way of getting heard and respected. The most successful data scientists I know write blogs, record vlogs (video blogs), share code on Github (a source code hosting service) and similar platforms, answer questions on Q&A websites such as StackExchange and Quora, do freelance work on Upwork (the largest freelancing network) and present at conferences. If you are confident or want to focus on a particular niche, blogging is a great way to combine your research with your career. Don't worry about making mistakes if you're just starting out – you will quickly learn from the community. Just remain humble and be open to that criticism. If you're concerned about posting something erroneous, ask your mentor nicely (see below) if you can run it past them first.

CASE STUDY   Finding mentors

I have multiple mentors, and would go so far as to say that they were responsible for my successful development in the field. Mentors will give you the knowledge and advice needed for success, and they can act as a buffer to stop you from making the mistakes that they may have made themselves when they started out. I actively encourage anyone, at whatever their stage of career, to find a mentor. But this is not always easy, particularly if you don't know anyone who might be able to help. You cannot just contact someone you don't know by e-mail and ask them to be your mentor – you need to establish a connection first.

I have a story about one of my mentors, Vitaly Dolgov, an independent business turnaround consultant – one of the best in the world, in my opinion. We originally crossed paths in 2012, when his housemate asked me and Artem Vladimirov (whom we met in Chapter 6) to help move their furniture. It was completely unrelated to work, but even then, I could see that Vitaly was someone inspiring and who could help me grow. I made sure to catch up with him after that time, at least to ask him for a book recommendation. And that's how we connected. Life sometimes brings you unexpected opportunities and you need to grab them by the horns. You never know when or where you might meet your next mentor.

They say that luck is what happens when preparation meets opportunity. So how can you prepare for when you meet your future mentor? I asked Richard Hopkins, a director at PricewaterhouseCoopers and another of my mentors (he has several of his own!), for his thoughts. He said that prospective mentees should first and foremost be introspective, and consider what they can bring to the table rather than how they expect their mentors to help them. This might sound like an impossible task – if you're just starting out in the field then how can you be of any use to its experts? While you might not be of assistance in such a direct way, you may have other skills or experiences that will be useful. When you find a potential mentor, consider their credentials and how *you* might fill a knowledge gap for them – coming to them with an offer of your own will encourage your mentor to think of your relationship as a two-way street rather than as a drain on their resources and time.

Another risk-free way of getting yourself known in the industry is to become a content curator yourself. What this means is nothing more complicated than setting up a social media profile and linking to information that is of interest to you. This is an easy way to get started, but be aware that the actual path to being heard as a content curator will be more difficult than that of a content creator. Nevertheless, all of these options are verifiable ways to build your portfolio.

Competitions

As may be expected, in a field where everything is at stake, there are a number of governmental and private initiatives to get data science projects started. In my opinion, the predictive modelling and analytics competition website Kaggle is one of the best providers for advanced data scientists who are looking to gain visibility in the community by participating. Potentially winning millions in prize money should only be considered a bonus.

Even if you're not yet ready to compete, you can find lots of interesting practice datasets on the platform. I recommend at least visiting Kaggle or other competition sites – a quick browse of their webpages may begin to ignite a few ideas of your own.

4 Build a network

I spoke with Caroline McColl to discuss the potential for new graduates in data science. McColl helps place people in companies from start-ups to established corporations, and she says that, for a field that is so new to so many, building a solid network of contacts is essential.

FutureYou runs data storytelling workshops (called 'Tell me the story') throughout the year, where practitioners from a range of industries meet to discuss ideas about how to make an impact and influence decision making in companies, as well as how to build rapport and trust. These meetups and events for FutureYou filled a gap in the data science market – at the time of our conversation, no one was covering these business-related skills.

This is just *one* event series – there are many others out there (you may have heard of hackathons,[6] but there are also meetups and conferences to attend). Go ahead and get involved – there is nothing wrong with taking a back seat at the beginning and simply listening to other people. Again, the key idea here is that you establish yourself in the community. Even if you aren't an event speaker, there are almost always other opportunities to connect (for instance through lunches, dinners and coffee breaks). And even if you don't have the nerve to speak to anyone there either, you'll now have a reason to contact these people online: saying that you were intrigued by someone's ideas at a conference you both attended is a far easier way of connecting with people than simply approaching them 'cold'.

McColl's 10 tips for networking

Caroline McColl has seen and placed a great many hopeful candidates in the data science job of their dreams. She puts considerable emphasis on the importance of networking, and lists 10 techniques for networking in the industry (SuperDataScience, 2017b):

1 Choose the specialization or industry that you most enjoy (you will be more likely to do your homework and find a job that makes you happy).

2 Find three mentors to help guide and shape your career (mentors can give you advice as to where you should look for jobs, help you identify your strengths and weaknesses, and put you in touch with the right people).

3 Partner with others who complement your skills (the most successful data scientists are self-starters – begin your own projects with people who can fill your skills gaps).

4 Organize and run an event, even if it's only for five people (the fact that you have organized an event proves that you are dedicated to the discipline and want to learn from others as well as give something back).

5 Host or participate in a podcast on data science (podcasts are an easy way to get your voice heard and to disseminate your ideas to an international community).

6 Set up a complete LinkedIn profile and include the projects on which you worked (LinkedIn is a great way to showcase your services to companies looking for data scientists, and the more information they can see about the projects you've been involved in, the better).

7 Set weekly goals that are achievable (if you're in doubt, start small and list your networking goals in order of simplicity).

8 Attend meetups and conferences in your area of interest (keep yourself informed and keep active – data science has a thriving community).

9 Blog and produce white papers (these articles, if well-written and shared, can significantly help to establish you as an expert in your field).

10 Facilitate introductions for other people, even if it doesn't bring direct value to you (you have benefited from the advice and help of others, and you have a responsibility to contribute to this community of sharing).

Applying for jobs

It should be clear to you by now that, as data science has not reached its disciplinary maturity yet, many companies are still only just starting to develop stable policies for data-driven tasks. If you are a graduate, you will likely be familiar with the catch-22 of looking for jobs: most roles require years of experience, but you cannot get your first role unless you *have* that experience.

I would say here that, even if a job requirement states 5–10 years of experience, you should apply anyway. Data science roles are to date overwhelmingly undersubscribed, and analyst roles will stay open five days longer on average than other positions. I would read between the lines here, and consider this requirement of experience in light of how long you have studied data science (either self-didactically or at an institution) and *practised* it.[7]

Getting real-world experience is simple – just return to the datasets I listed in the introduction to Part II and work your way through the Data Science Process given in this book. Platforms like Kaggle and SuperDataScience also regularly publish analytics challenges and case studies that you can sink your teeth into. Don't be afraid to highlight this experience and take it as an opportunity to outline your results. Companies will appreciate that you have been proactive in working with data.

Essentially, companies want someone who 1) understands data, 2) can deliver their vision and 3) help them to remain competitive. Persuade them in your application that you can deliver on those promises – employers need to be assured that the bottom line of data science means improving *their* bottom line.

Doing good

If you've been applying for lots of positions and not making it past the first round, consider taking on volunteering work.[8] There are a number of organizations such as DataKind and DrivenData that run projects and competitions about data science. Either would be a great place to get started.

There are also a number of charities that require volunteers to help them use their data to generate supporting evidence for funding, to establish a more coordinated system of work, or simply to spread the word about what they do. Ask around, search online, and if you have a favourite or local charity that you want to help out, then perhaps you could even come to them with an idea of your own.

Preparing for an interview

You've passed the first round of screening, and now the company wants to interview you. How can you prepare? My best tip, rather than focusing on committing to memory the algorithms and software you have used, is to learn all you can about the industry in which you will be working. After all, it is likely that at the interview you will get an executive or manager who will only understand what you do at a general level, in addition to a data scientist quizzing you – so be prepared for both technical and non-technical questions. Many data scientists forget this crucial aspect, but developing this broader kind of domain knowledge is critical. Just as you should consider what you can bring to the table for your mentor, you must also consider how you will be able to *help* this company. How could data science shake up their industry? What are the pain points that it can soothe? What are the company's competitors doing, and how might you be able to improve on that with the help of data science? What kind of tasks might the business expect of you, given your knowledge about the Data Science Process?

When you get to the interview itself, make sure you show enthusiasm for both the data and for what the company does. Show that you can get things done (if you can bring examples of the work you mentioned in your application, then so much the better), and be prepared for questions.

Fermi questions

You should expect to get the run-of-the-mill questions that are asked of everyone (Where do you see yourself in 10 years? Can you give an example of how you work in a team? What do you consider to be your greatest success?) and sometimes you should expect role-specific technical questions. While I cannot help you prepare for those types of questions (preparation will vary case by case), what I can help you with is with making you aware of Fermi questions.[9]

These questions are designed to test your logic and are popular in interviews for analytical roles. The good news is that you can develop a technique for working through them. The first thing you should understand is that you are not expected to get these questions *right* – they are there to test your ability to logically come to a reasonable conclusion, and to show your thought process around it.

Let's say that we have been asked the question, 'How many red cars are currently being driven in Australia?' Have a think about how you would answer the question yourself, and then read my answer below. Remember: the interviewers want to see evidence of a logical mind. Here is my answer:

That's a very interesting question. Without any figures before me I cannot give a truly accurate answer, but I can give an estimate based on certain assumptions. First, we will focus only on private cars since commercial vehicles are rarely red. Now, there are approximately 24 million people in Australia, and let's say that there is an average of four people per family. This means there are around 6 million families living in Australia. Based on what I know from personal experience, families have between one to three cars, so let's average that to two cars per family. That would make 12 million cars in Australia, on average.

Now, colours. There are lots of different colours, but as a starting point let's take the seven colours of the rainbow. Add white and black, gives us nine colours. But we can also safely say that in Australia, white cars are more popular because it's hot and white cars absorb the least sunlight, so I would count white twice, in order to account for this colour preference. That gives us 10 colours. As red represents one of them, we can divide the number of cars in Australia by 10 in order to find out how many red cars there are. So, 12 million divided by 10 equals 1.2 million. Based on my estimations, then, there should be 1.2 million red cars currently being driven in Australia.

As you should see from my answer, the crucial thing was *not* whether I got the answer right – it was that I exhibited an ability to think on my feet and to work out the problem logically. I got this interview question when I was applying for my role at Sunsuper – my answer above is almost exactly what I said.

The interesting thing about that interview is that I did not have the years of experience they were looking for (they wanted six; I had only three) and that job was double my salary at the time. As you can imagine, the chances of me getting the job seemed slim. But I was confident. This question came at the very end, and after delivering that answer in one non-stop rant, I could see from the look on the hiring manager's face – I'd got the job.

Interviewing them

Remember the old adage: you are interviewing them as much as they are interviewing you. Do your research on the company before your interview, and make sure you ask them pertinent questions about what they do. There are two reasons for this.

First is that companies appreciate interviewees who have clearly taken the time to consider why they want to work for them. Showing that you've done your research demonstrates that you're serious about the role. And, of course, there's nothing worse than when an interviewee has nothing to respond with when at the very end the interviewer asks if they have any questions for the company. Always have at least two questions in mind.

However, the second argument is by far the more important. An interview is an opportunity to find out about your future role, the company culture, the team you will be working with, opportunities for growth and more. Too many people nowadays are stuck in roles that they hate, working for companies they don't respect. I'm here to tell you that you are better than that! You have one life and by joining a company you are giving them your most precious and valuable resource – your time. I implore you, choose wisely and choose with your heart to whom you will give your time. An interview is not just for the company to find out if you fit their needs, but also for you to find out if they truly fit yours.

Nurturing your career within a company

You've been selected for the position. First, congratulations! Now you can start to spread your wings in the company. To do that, I want to tell you a story of how I built a name for myself in data science.

I count myself as very lucky to have secured a job at Deloitte directly after graduating. But even though I was fresh out of university, I didn't let my lack of experience get in the way of my career development – I made sure that I became the go-to person for all things data related. People *wanted* me on their projects. And part of this success was due to me actively promoting how data can be utilized to work *for* the company.

Whatever level you're at, helping people to see the value that data can bring to a task, project or company system will create advocates for data (and thus for your role) across the organization (see Chapter 9 for more information on creating data advocates). Get into the data science mindset and *share your research* with others. Set up meetings with colleagues to show them your results, especially those who helped you in that particular project.

At Deloitte, one of the projects I was working on involved developing a management information system (MIS) dashboard for a retail medical facility. The process itself was simple, but the improvements that our team made ended up saving the company $19 million. This is an example of a project you may want to tell your colleagues about – to share your breakthrough and also to open up to suggestions about how you could have done things better. Getting the conversation going is the key to nurturing an analytics culture.

Another way that you can develop your career within a company is to be proactive in finding new ways to improve company operations. Data generates ideas. Quite often, companies won't know what to do with data scientists beyond the specific task that they have been given. This can lead to your contract not being renewed once the project is complete or, if you're a permanent employee, you will grow bored – and that is unhealthy for everyone. Fight for your position (you earned it!); make a case for what you hope to find out and ask your line manager if you can work on it during less busy periods. Your work ethic will very likely be rewarded.

Finally, I cannot state often enough how important it is to master the art of presentation as early as possible in your career. Had I not developed my unique presentation style, I'd just have been another good data analyst. And while these people are undoubtedly important, there are plenty of them around. Take this as a sign to really digest the main points given in Chapter 9. When you present your data, you become the connector between data science and the decision makers for your project. That will inevitably make you a more compelling and persuasive advocate for what you do.

What to do if your company is unresponsive

It doesn't always work out. If a company isn't responsive to your advocacy of data or your requests to carry out new projects, you might want to consider applying elsewhere. I'm not saying you should quit your job over a lack of interest in what you do, but it *is* important to be mindful of where you spend your time and in what area you want to continue growing. I assume that you are reading this book because you want an exciting career in data science, and if you continue in a company that doesn't see the benefits of using data, then you will only end up frustrated.

You have reached the end of this book. Well done for working through it; it's been such a pleasure taking this journey with you. For your next steps, I would recommend that you first give yourself enough time to digest all that you have learned. Think about what really interested you, the areas in which you feel you are particularly strong, and where you may have weaknesses. Use that information to consider whether taking an additional course would be helpful – there are plenty of resources available at superdatascience.com to help you continue your journey. Good luck with your next steps, and don't forget to check in every so often and let me know how you are doing. And until next time, happy analysing!

References

Baeck, P (2015) Data for Good: How big and open data can be used for the common good, *Nesta* [Online] www.nesta.org.uk/publications/data-good [accessed 05.07.2017]

Burning Glass Technologies and IBM (2017) The Quant Crunch: How the demand for data science skills is disrupting the job market [Online] www-01.ibm.com/common/ssi/cgi-bin/ssialias?htmlfid=IML14576USEN& [accessed 26.06.17]

Crowdflower (2017) The Data Scientist Report [Online] visit.crowdflower.com/WC-2017-Data-Science-Report_LP.html?src=Website&medium=Carousel&campaign=DSR2017&content=DSR2017 [accessed 01.07.17]

Kaku, M (2014) *The Future of the Mind: The scientific quest to understand, enhance, and empower the mind*, Doubleday

Mannes, J (2017) Airbnb is running its own internal university to teach data science, *Techcrunch*, 24 May [Online] www.techcrunch.com/2017/05/24/airbnb-is-running-its-own-internal-university-to-teach-data-science/ [accessed 26.06.17]

Rosenblum, C (2017) Hillbillies who code: the former miners out to put Kentucky on the tech map, *Guardian*, 21 April [Online] www.theguardian.com/us-news/2017/apr/21/tech-industry-coding-kentucky-hillbillies accessed 26.06.17]

SuperDataScience (2017a) SDS 059: Changing human behaviour through a driving app [podcast] 7 June [online] www.superdatascience.com/59 [accessed 26.06.17]

SuperDataScience (2017b) SDS 049: Great Tips On Building a Successful Analytics Culture [Podcast] 13 July. Available from: www.superdatascience.com/49 [Last accessed 10.10.17]

Symons, T (2016) Councils and the data revolution: 7 ways local authorities can get more value from their data, *Nesta*, 15 July [Online] www.nesta.org.uk/blog/councils-and-data-revolution-7-ways-local-authorities-can-get-more-value-their-data [accessed 26.06.17]

Notes

1 In CrowdFlower's 2017 Data Science Report, 88 per cent of the polled data scientists said that they were either happy or very happy in their position.

2 Please note that these roles are not set in stone, and the job descriptions will change for each institution. It is always necessary to read the descriptions thoroughly before you write your application. While the following descriptions aren't exactly the same from institution to institution, they can certainly be used as a guideline for your application.

3 I've heard that, unfortunately, this trend has even emerged in some of the big consulting firms in the United States. Company culture and work diversity are things that you need to research before applying to any position.

4 Notice how the proliferation of university degrees and courses in data science shows that the world is beginning to recognize data science as a discipline in its own right.

5 If you are looking for a place to network with data scientists, then I would like to invite you to have a look at SuperDataScience, a social platform entirely dedicated to data science.

6 Events where programmers and data scientists collaborate on technological projects.

7 Even Artem Vladimirov, whom we met in Chapter 6, broke into the field with relatively little background in the discipline. He joined Deloitte following an accounting degree without even knowing how to program. Artem now has an impressive career in data science where he solves major analytics cases and gives presentations all over the world.

8 The UK's National Endowment for Science, Technology and the Arts (NESTA, www.nesta.org.uk) is an excellent resource for those interested in learning more about charitable work within the field of data science. See especially Baeck (2015) and Symons (2016) for a head start in thinking about how value can be derived from data.

9 Named after Enrico Fermi who estimated the strength of the atomic bomb that detonated at the Trinity test. Based on the distance travelled by pieces of paper he dropped from his hand during the blast, he made a remarkably close estimate.

ACKNOWLEDGEMENTS

I would like to thank my father, Alexander Eremenko, whose love and care have shaped me into the person I am today, and who has shown me through his firm guidance how I can take hold of life's opportunities. Thank you to my giving, warm-hearted mother, Elena Eremenko, for always providing me with an ear to listen to my crazy ideas and for encouraging me and my brothers to take part in the wider world – through music, language, dance and so much more. Were it not for her wise counsel, I would never have gone to Australia.

Thanks to my brother, Mark Eremenko, for always believing in me, and for his unshakeable confidence. His fearlessness in taking on whatever life throws at him is what still fuels so many of the important decisions I make. Thank you to my brother, Ilya Eremenko, wise beyond his years, for his impressive business ideas and well-considered ventures. I am certain that fame and fortune will soon be knocking on his door.

Thank you to my grandmother Valentina, aunt Natasha and cousin Yura, for their endless love and care. And thank you to the entire Tanakovic and Svoren families including my brothers Adam and David for all the dearest moments we share.

Thank you to my students and to the thousands of people who listen to the SuperDataScience podcast. It inspires me to keep going!

There are several key people who helped to make this book a reality. I would like to thank my writing partner Zara Karschay for helping to capture my voice. Thank you to my commissioning editor Anna Moss and production editor Stefan Leszczuk, whose feedback and guidance were fundamental to the writing process, and more generally to Kogan Page's editorial team for their diligence and rigour. Thank you to my friend and business partner Hadelin de Ponteves for inspiring me and for being a great source of support in tackling some of the most challenging subject matters in the field of data science, as well as for his help in reviewing the technical aspects of this book. We've only known each other for a little over a year, but our mutually supportive friendship feels as though we have been acquainted for much longer.

Thank you to Katherina Andryskova – I feel both privileged and grateful that she was the very first person to read *Confident Data Skills*. My thanks also go to the talented team at SuperDataScience for taking on so many additional responsibilities so that I could write this book. Thank you to the hardworking team at Udemy including my tireless account managers Erin Adams and Lana Martinez.

Thank you to my friend and mentor Artem Vladimirov, whose admirable work ethic and knowledge lay the foundations upon which I have built everything I now know about data science. Many thanks to Vitaly Dolgov and Richard Hopkins for being excellent role models, for believing in me, for always being there when I needed help, and for guiding me through times both good and bad. Thank you to Patrycja Jeleniewicz for teaching me about colour theory and being a dear friend.

I give my express thanks to the people whose work contributed to the case studies in this book: Hadelin de Ponteves, Artem Vladimirov, Richard Hopkins, Ruben Kogel, Greg Poppe, Caroline McColl, Dan Shiebler, Megan Putney, and Ulf Morys.

The motivational teachers at Moscow School 54, the Moscow Institute of Physics and Technology and the University of Queensland have my thanks for giving me such beneficial education. To all my colleagues past and present at Deloitte and Sunsuper, thank you for giving me the professional development I needed for creating my data science toolkit.

Most of all, I want to thank you, the reader, for giving me your valuable time. It has been my foremost hope that this book will give positive encouragement to those who wish to understand and implement data science in their careers.

INDEX

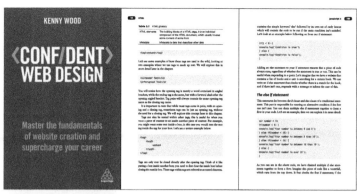
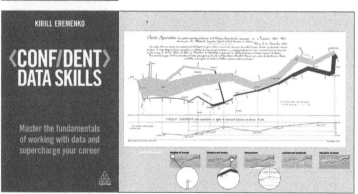
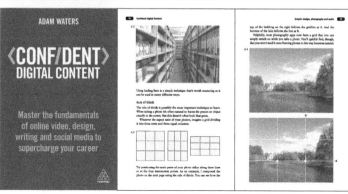